When the Odds Were Even

When the Odds Were Even

The Vosges Mountains Campaign, October 1944–January 1945

Keith E. Bonn

PRESIDIO

The opinions expressed in this book are those of the author alone, and do not reflect those of the Department of the Army or the Department of Defense.

Copyright © 1994 by Keith E. Bonn

Published by Presidio Press
505 B San Marin Dr., Suite 300
Novato, CA 94945-1340

Library of Congress Cataloging-in-Publication Data

Bonn, Keith E. (Keith Earle) , 1956–
    When the odds were even : the Vosges Mountains Campaign, October 1944–January 1945 / Keith E. Bonn.
        p.   cm.
    Originally presented as the author's thesis (doctoral)—University of Chicago, 1991.
    Includes bibliographical references (p.) and index.
    ISBN 0-89141-512-2 (hardcover)
    ISBN 0-89141-602-1 (paperback)
    1. World War, 1939–1945—Campaigns—France—Vosges Mountains.
    I. Title.
    D762.V67B66   1994
    940.54'21438—dc20   94-5062
                                                          CIP

All photos are courtesy U.S. Army Signal Corps.

Typography by ProImage
Printed in the United States of America

This book is dedicated to ACT, BCM, KJB, and all the other soldiers of the U.S. Seventh Army who made the history chronicled herein. It is dedicated especially to those who never came home, and who lie mutely beneath rank upon rank of white marble markers at Épinal and St. Avold and in other unmarked places forever known but to God.

CONTENTS

LIST OF ILLUSTRATIONS

ACKNOWLEDGMENTS

I wish to acknowledge the assistance of the following people or organizations for their significant contributions to the production of this book:

Dr. Robert Slonacker, director of research at the Military History Institute at Carlisle Barracks, Pennsylvania, for assistance and advice regarding German sources, particularly original German doctrinal source materials, and direction regarding U.S. unit histories.

Dr. Robert Wolfe and Messrs. Robin Cookson and Harry Rilley of the Captured German Documents Section of the National Archives, Washington, D.C., for their patient assistance in obtaining pertinent selections from the USAREUR Historical Series of German officer interviews, and also for their help researching the background of key German army officers.

Lieutenant Colonel Hugh Foster, U.S. Army (Retired), for his pivotal tip regarding the availability of company morning reports at the National Archives Records Annex in St. Louis, Missouri.

Oberst (im Generalstab) Roland Förster and Major Karl-Heinz Frieser of the Bundesmilitärgeschichtliches Forschungsamt (Federal Military Historical Research Bureau) in Freiburg im Breisgau, Germany, for their enthusiastic and professional assistance in providing various documents, especially the *Army Group G Kriegstagebücher. (Vielen Dank, meine Kameraden!)*

Colonel Robert A. Doughty, U.S. Army, for providing the exceptionally helpful Mary study of the Maginot line.

Lieutenant Colonel Daniel Lierville, Armée de la Republique Francais, for his enthusiastic and selfless assistance with my research trip to the Vosges in March 1988, which gave new meaning and life to this study.

Lieutenant Colonel Dave Gabbard, Military Intelligence, for his selfless assistance with the procurement of a suitable vehicle to conduct battlefield research in the Vosges, even if it did break down.

Lieutenant Colonel John C. Goertemiller, U.S. Army (Retired), for his support and critical feedback during this work's early stages.

Lieutenant Colonel Anton C. Kaiser, Jr., Infantry, for his support, encouragement, and critical feedback, especially with Chapters 3 and 4.

Frank Evans of Winchester, Massachusetts, for his devout friendship, tireless and invaluable research assistance in 1989 and 1990, and critical feedback in every stage of the study.

Lieutenant Colonel Mike Barbero, Infantry, for his timely research assistance in 1988 and moral support throughout.

Lieutenant Colonel Dan Bolger, Infantry, for his assistance and encouragement in developing the concept of the study.

Deborah DeMack, for her assistance with research and French translation, and her enthusiastic and patient support.

The expert artistry of Dennis Leatherman, who assisted with the creation of the basic features of most of the maps in this book.

The Association of Graduates, USMA, for the grant that helped fund my 1988 research trip to Freiburg and the Vosges.

F. Gregory Campbell, formerly of the University of Chicago and now president of Carthage College in Kenosha, Wisconsin, for his encouragement and guidance.

Professors Michael Geyer, Walter Kaegi, and William McNeill of the University of Chicago, the dissertation committee for this study, for their steadfast and patient encouragement, guidance, and critical review.

The late Professor Morris Janowitz of the University of Chicago, for his inspiration and assistance in developing the concept of this study, and especially his insights into the criticality of cohesion for success in combat.

The supremely professional understanding, assistance, and advice of Dr. Dale Wilson, executive editor at Presidio Press and onetime comrade-in-arms in the Department of History at West Point.

Patricia Douglass of Patricia Douglass Publication and Computer Training Services, San Francisco, for her research assistance, saintly patience, and particularly professional and talented production of the charts, parts of the drafts, and final version of the study.

Major Frederick Phillips, U.S. Army (Retired), who served as a captain in the 7th Infantry, for his assistance with procuring information about the 3d Infantry Division in the High Vosges.

The late Lt. Col. John Upchurch, U.S. Army (Retired), for his insights into the assault on Fort Schiesseck.

Henry Weronick of Queens, New York, a lieutenant in the 71st Infantry, for his insights into the battles near Gros Réderching.

Ray Denman, of New Providence, New Jersey, a rifleman in Company L, 397th Infantry, for his assistance with sources and for his warm support and encouragement.

William Alpern, of Greens Farms, Connecticut, a BAR man in Company I, 410th Infantry, for his advice on the latest sources, and for his resolute support, anecdotes, and constructive criticism during the latter phases of this work.

Colonel Robert Stegmaier, U.S. Army (Retired), G4 of the 100th Infantry Division throughout the Vosges campaign, for his incisive insights and guidance regarding the concept of this study.

Numerous members of the 100th Infantry Division Association (The Sons of Bitche), whose forthright comments and honest recollections first piqued my interest in the Vosges Mountains campaign. Especially inspirational were those of the late Brig. Gen. Andrew C. Tychsen, U.S. Army (Retired), whose insights on training and cohesion gained from fighting the forces of Pancho Villa, Kaiser Wilhelm II, Adolf Hitler, and Kim Il-Sung provided the original conceptual framework for this study. (General Tychsen commanded the 399th Infantry in the High Vosges and served as assistant division commander of the 100th Infantry Division during Nordwin.) Also exceptionally stirring were the recollections of the late 1st Sgt. Bennie C. Moree, U.S. Army (Retired) whose clear reminiscences of close combat with the Germans in two world wars provided colorful background and earthy insights into the balanced nature of this campaign. (First Sergeant Moree was first sergeant of two different rifle companies in the 1st Battalion, 397th Infantry, during the campaign in the Vosges.)

The skilled, sincere, and consummately professional teachers who propagated a love of history in general and a zeal for accuracy in particular throughout my secondary education, namely Ted Kelley, Robert von Klock, Edith Phelan, Louise Cone, and George Watson. Thank you for your patience and dedication, your devotion to the acquisition of knowledge, and the fun you made learning.

My parents, Mr. and Mrs. Keith J. Bonn, of Vero Beach, Florida, for their inspiration and absolutely unconditional support and encouragement throughout all academic and professional endeavors in general and this study in particular.

INTRODUCTION

Normandy . . . the dash across France . . . Arnhem . . . the Hürtgen . . . the Bulge . . . the Ruhr . . . what battles and campaigns have been the topics of more films, plays, books, and essays? What facets of the fighting in the European theater of operations (ETO) have not been studied, dissected, examined, and reexamined by countless authors in every manner from comic books to major works of scholarly research? Quite rightfully, at first glance, many would yawn at yet *another* book on battles in Europe in World War II. There often seems to be nothing more to say about this most recent chapter in the long history of major European wars.

History, of course, has many uses. If one accepts the modern historian's proud assertion that the study of history is the quest for truth, then one must also recall Kipling's warning about hearing the truth "twisted by knaves to make a trap for fools." The "selective" use of history, after all, plays a major part in many endeavors, from the political theorist's "science" to the propagandist's dark art. Since May 1945, the events of the war in the ETO have been used—and abused—to "prove" or illustrate myriad theories of politics, strategy, logistics, and tactics. One of the most recent and unquestionably most alarming trends in the historiography of World War II in the ETO is the use of the events of this era by certain military reformers to justify recommendations that the contemporary U.S. Army should discard its own uniquely evolved institutions and doctrines and instead simply imitate the Wehrmacht. Not only is such abuse of history invalid from an academic standpoint, it is also dangerous from a political and philosophical perspective.

The ammunition supplied to these reformers sometimes takes the form of perfectly valid historical work, used in an obtuse and biased manner, but more often consists of shoddy comparative historical efforts. These works either simply inaccurately represent the facts bearing on the respective combat accomplishments of the American and German armies or endeavor to superimpose analytical parameters on situations that occurred forty years before these parameters were formulated. Although it may sound redundant, it is implicit—and imperative—that when using a comparative approach to historical research, one must select situations allowing accurate comparison. Furthermore, one must compare historical entities in the light of contemporary, not modern, ideas and doctrines. Attempts to compare historical phenomena in any other light lead to obscuration and gross distortion.

The comparison of the combat proficiency of the American and German armies in the ETO would at first seem to be a fairly simple one to make. The armies *were* contemporary entities, and their records are well documented and reasonably available. The tactical and operational doctrines under which they fought are outlined clearly in still-existing manuals, and many of the participants are still alive and sufficiently lucid to fill in the historiographical holes or clarify the factual vagaries of the events of those critical months.[1] This simplicity, unfortunately, is dangerously deceptive.

The American and German armies in the ETO often operated under extraordinarily different tactical and operational circumstances. These differences went far beyond the fact that, by and large, one army was attacking and the other defending. The differences are more significant, strategically speaking, than the fact that one army was part of an allied effort whereas the other operated alone. The differences even transcend the important implications of one army being the armed force of a democratic government, whereas the other was the product of a totalitarian regime. The bottom-line, critical differences in the tactical circumstances under which the United States and German armies fought each other are primarily as follows:

1. The Americans almost always enjoyed tactical air superiority, if not air supremacy.
2. The American logistical situation gradually improved from June 1944 onward, whereas the Germans' deteriorated.
3. The American manpower situation did not deteriorate as rapidly as did the Wehrmacht's during the period.

Given these critical differences, it is difficult to construct any accurate and fair comparative appraisal of the combat effectiveness of the two opponents! The Americans' advantage colored the outcome of every campaign, every battle, and every engagement in which they participated. Indeed, it is the gist of much postwar literature on the subject. For example, it is not easy to count the number of ex–German army and Waffen SS officers' memoirs that are filled with exclamations of bitter resentment and frustration with *"die verdammte Jabos"* (the damned fighter-bombers). From some accounts, indeed, one would believe that the American logistical situation was so extravagant that U.S. Army Air Forces Thunderbolts routinely buried German positions under refrigerators and cartons of razor blades. It is often difficult to find American accounts of German prisoner hauls that do not include descriptions of fuzzy-cheeked teenagers and toothless grandfathers.

Although some of the material in which one finds such accounts is sometimes influenced, in the former case, by the need of defeated officers to justify failures of the "world's greatest army" in the face of a rabble of gum-chewing cowboys and, in the latter case, by the exigencies of wartime propaganda, the discrepancies nevertheless often mitigated the results of combat between the two very different foes.

For a truly fair and accurate comparison, then, it is necessary to find a campaign in which these differences were obviated, or at least diminished to the point of insignificance. This is indeed difficult to do. It is possible to find instances in which additional circumstances so favor the Germans that the American advantages are offset entirely, such as in the Hürtgen, or the initial phases of the Ardennes counter-offensive. But this again is misleading, and merely substitutes one type of historiographical astigmatism for another. What is needed is the opportunity to study the combat operations of the American and German armies in a situation in which tactical air power is absent or its effectiveness obviated, a situation in which American logistical advantages are nullified by higher headquarters' alternative priorities or by the realities of weather and terrain, and a milieu in which the manpower circumstances of both sides are adequate for the fulfillment of their respective doctrinal requirements and expectations. In other words, it is necessary, for accurate appraisal of the relative combat proficiency of the German and American armies in the ETO, to find a time and a place when the odds were even.

The time? Autumn and winter, 1944–45. The place? The Vosges Mountains.

Summary of the Study

The detailed study of tactical and operational-level events that composed the campaign in the High and Low Vosges from 15 October 1944 to 15 January 1945 provides a significant opportunity to examine both armies in situations wherein the usual mitigating factors played few, if any, significant roles. One can derive a truly accurate picture of the comparative combat proficiency of the two adversaries from a careful and detailed analysis of this campaign. The unique nature of this opportunity is revealed by a statement of the peculiarities of the circumstances under which the Americans of the U.S. Seventh Army and the German *Army Group G* fought the Vosges battles.

The broad-front strategy adopted by Gen. Dwight D. Eisenhower in western Europe called for pressure all along the western front in the late summer and autumn of 1944. Driving across France after the spectacular battles of the breakout from Normandy, the U.S. Third Army effected a linkup with elements of the Seventh Army attacking up the Rhône valley from the Riviera in late September. Once this continuous front was formed from the English Channel to the Swiss frontier, it fell to the divisions of Lt. Gen. Alexander Patch's Seventh Army to advance through the Vosges Mountains in consonance with the overall strategy of Supreme Headquarters, Allied Expeditionary Forces, Europe (SHAEF).

Never before in the history of modern warfare had an army fought its way successfully through opposition in the Vosges. The French Revolutionary armies of the late eighteenth century had gone around the mountains, to the west in Lorraine, to the east near Woerth, and to the south across the Rhine, whereas the Germans had bypassed these formidable obstacles by sweeping past to the north during the Franco-Prussian War. The French and the Germans had become hopelessly entangled in trench fighting in the western foothills of the Vosges during the first and last days of World War I. The Maginot line garrisons in the Low Vosges, built in the 1930s specifically to take further advantage of the already excellent qualities of this very defensible terrain, in large part surrendered only after the rest of the French army capitulated in 1940. The Germans simply bypassed the strongest part of the Maginot fortifications, the part lying between Montmédy in the west and Wissembourg in the east, by driving through the Ardennes and crossing the Meuse at Sedan.

When approached from the south, as they were by the Seventh Army in 1944, the Vosges Mountains first present terrain featuring the highest altitudes of the entire range. These mountains, high hills, and ridges south of the Saverne Gap are appropriately called the High Vosges, and they vary from fifteen hundred to well over four thousand feet in elevation. They also present considerable but relatively gentle slopes to the west and south, allowing for the construction of excellent fields of fire for direct-fire weapons, and facilitating good observation for the direction of artillery and other indirect-fire weapons. It was in the High Vosges, therefore, that Oberkommando der Wehrmacht (OKW—the German Armed Forces High Command) ordered the winter defensive lines to be constructed. Engineers of *Army Group G,* under the recently appointed General der Panzertruppen Hermann Balck, began fortifying the area in September with the assistance of German workers and Alsatian forced labor.

The combination of terrain, well-sited and sturdily constructed fortifications, and extensive obstacles created a difficult series of objectives for the Seventh Army's VI and XV Corps. Yet the combat elements of these units succeeded in penetrating the objectives in only a few weeks of fighting, despite the fact that several of the American divisions committed were brand-new to the theater and to combat of any kind, whereas others had only recently been pulled out of the line in Italy after months of ferocious and costly campaigning.

The German units, on the other hand, were largely made up of combat veteran leaders and troops who, although lacking in armor and in air support, were fighting in mountainous terrain where armor was easily defeated and where fighter-bombers were of limited usefulness. Although sometimes outnumbered, most German units still had their full complement of mortars and machine guns, by far the most important infantry weapons used in mountainous and hilly terrain. The Germans' own doctrine called for them to be able to fight outnumbered and win under such circumstances and in such terrain; hence OKW had ordered *Army Group G* to hold in this area until the spring of 1945. The failure of experienced German combat leaders to fulfill their own doctrinal requirements in the face of a mixed bag of American units that were simultaneously exceeding their own similar expectations illustrates the superior combat proficiency of the Seventh Army in this, the first phase of the battle for the Vosges.

After being outmaneuvered and after sustaining considerable casualties in the High Vosges, the *First Army* elements of *Army Group G* withdrew to a second line in late November and December, with the German lines anchored, in the east, in the *Westwall* (Siegfried line) and in the west in the Low Vosges. The fight by Seventh Army elements in the Low Vosges provides even further evidence of the Americans' combat superiority. During this period (late November to mid-January 1944–45), the largely cloudy, foggy weather allowed very limited air support. Furthermore, the mountainous terrain of the Low Vosges, although not as high as that of the High Vosges to the south, provided even steeper and less approachable slopes, which, in combination with the heavy snowfall, severely limited or even completely nullified the usefulness of armor. Finally, the Maginot line fortifications in the XV Corps sector provided all-around defense and, especially in the area known as the Ensemble de Bitche, presented some defenses so formidable that the Germans had not dared to attack them in the 1940 campaign. Incorporated in the German defensive lines, they were penetrated by the combat echelons of XV Corps in appalling weather in December 1944, in a series of brilliant infantry attacks that drew the grudging praise of Generalmajor Friedrich-Wilhelm von Mellenthin, the *Army Group G* chief of staff. Significantly, all this was accomplished during a period when the Seventh Army was literally the last American army in the ETO in priority for logistical support and personnel replacement.

Indeed, it was in this same area of the Low Vosges that the western prong of the German counteroffensive known as Operation Nordwind fell at midnight on the last New Year's Eve of the war. Attacking elements of the *XC* and *XIII SS Corps,* attaining local numerical superiorities of four to one and more, made only limited gains at best against the Americans in this area. On the eastern end of the Seventh Army's line in the Low Vosges, in the VI Corps sector, *LXXXIX Corps* attacks gained considerably more ground. But, despite the heavy German numerical superiority, these attacks ground to a halt after well-executed American counterattacks. The OKW mission had specified the seizure of Strasbourg and Saverne as requirements for this effort, but even after considerable personnel and materiel expenditures, *Army Group G* came up well short of its objectives due to the Americans' tenacity and skill in the defense.

When the Seventh Army resumed the offensive in March 1945, it was against a German enemy of vastly decreased effectiveness, due to the German withdrawal of considerable numbers of troops belonging to some of the finest units in *Army Group G.* The tactical balance after January 1945 changed so far in favor of the Americans that the validity of this study cannot be continued beyond that point.

Historiography and Available Sources

Comparisons of U.S. and German tactical combat proficiency have recently been made by several widely read authors. Most of these works, unfortunately, suffer from serious drawbacks.

Some authors, most notably Trevor N. Dupuy in his *Numbers, Predictions and War,* have attempted to analyze historical examples of ground combat with an incredibly complicated series of parameters describing the availability of ammunition and fuel, the effects of weapons and morale, the quantities of troops available, et cetera ad infinitum. Although the parameters are indeed comprehensive and technically well thought out, two problems exist that tend to nullify the usefulness of this type of work. First, none of these parameters existed as such during the period when the battles being analyzed were fought; they are artificial and ex post facto at best, irrelevant at worst. As Edward Filiberti pointed out in his monograph "Developing a Theory for Dynamic Campaign Planning," the chief flaw of Dupuy's Quantified Judgment Model is that battle results are used to explain the unquantified factors that led to the victors' success. Thus, says Filiberti, Dupuy's methodology and combat effectiveness factors suffer from a logic error stemming from trying to tie temporal sequence to causal relation.[2]

Second, Dupuy has built in fudge factors that he calls "intangible variables," and which he admits are "almost impossible to assess in absolute terms with complete objectivity."[3] The usefulness of this work as anything more than an interesting collection of conceptual ideas for commercial war games is thus extremely limited.

Other studies, one of which is often cited by well-intentioned but uninformed admirers, are limited by even more basic flaws. These works, which frequently cite each other, contain gross historical inaccuracies, and represent the worst kind of revisionist history. The most notorious of these is Martin van Creveld's *Fighting Power*. So many factual flaws regarding the U.S. Army exist in this book that it is impossible to list them all here. A single example should suffice. Contrary to one of van Creveld's typically bizarre allegations, no U.S. combat divisions used pigs, bees, monkeys, centipedes, or belligerent dogs for their unit insignia; no such "whimsical" designs embarrassed American troops or adversely affected their morale.[4] Less strange but more pernicious are these authors' assertions that American doctrine stifled initiative, whereas that of their German adversaries facilitated it; that American replacements were little more than barely trained cannon fodder, whereas German units trained and fought together from the outset; and, perhaps most dangerous of all, that the German doctrines for operations and tactics were so far superior to those of their bumbling *Ami* opponents that the contemporary U.S. Army should emulate the practices of the very foe their forebears so soundly defeated! Such books are actually most useful mainly for instruction in how *not* to write comparative history.

A far more sophisticated approach is that taken by Allan R. Millett, Williamson Murray, et al., in *Military Effectiveness*. In this three-volume work, various authors analyze the combat effectiveness of several armies from 1914 to 1945 using a multilevel methodology (political, strategic, operational, and tactical) that integrates the sociological, organizational, and technological aspects of each. Unfortunately, Volume III, which concerns itself with World War II, does not analyze the combatants in the Vosges campaign.[5]

Interestingly, despite the great deal that can be learned from the study of combat operations in the Vosges, very little effort has been expended on the campaign by the historical community. The only independent attempt to chronicle the Seventh Army's ETO campaigns is a rather short work by John F. Turner and Robert Jackson entitled *Destination Berchtesgaden.*[6] This book provides a readable but rather sketchy summary of Seventh Army operations all the way from the planning of Dragoon through the end of hostilities in Europe in May 1945. Much of the book clearly reflects the authors' heavy reliance on the official Seventh Army operational after-action report. Entitled *Report of Operations,* this important primary source document was published in 1948 and was subsequently declassified in 1958. It provides a solid overview of the operational endeavors of Patch's army, but understandably provides precious little comparative analysis.

The official U.S. Army Historical Series volume on the Seventh Army's campaigns in the ETO, titled *From the Riviera to the Rhine,* was not published until the spring of 1993, nearly a half century after the fact![7]

Russell F. Weigley included a short analysis of the Seventh Army's situation during offensive operations in the Vosges in his classic work *Eisenhower's Lieutenants.* Although Weigley recognizes that "in manpower, the Allied advantage was not all that great, especially against enemy soldiers shielded by the pillboxes and dragon's teeth of the West Wall,"[8] he does not explain in detail the significance of the Allied penetration of the Vosges strongholds, nor does he credit the Seventh Army combat units with many significant accomplishments. Understandably, Weigley chose to concentrate his effort on First and Third Army units, because they numbered in their ranks the most flamboyant and personally remarkable general officers. This, after all, was the purpose of the book, as its title implies.

More recently, an Alsatian teacher and member of the Cercle d'Histoire de l'Alsace du Nord, published a comprehensive descriptive work on the Nordwind counteroffensive.[9] Unfortunately, this work concentrates overwhelmingly on that portion of Nordwind that occurred on the Alsatian Plain, although the author does include excellent background and, happily, used multiple American and even some German primary sources.

Fortunately, primary source material is available in great quantities for a proper in-depth study of the Vosges campaign. On the American side, there exist official unit histories on the division and separate regiment or cavalry group level for practically every major unit committed during the period. Most of these are excellent and thorough works, compiled and edited immediately after the war (and some *during* the war by specially appointed divisional historical sections) by bright enlisted men and junior officers who had immediate access to the daily staff journals kept during combat, as well as to the men who fought the campaigns themselves. The researcher must, of course, be prepared to cut through a certain amount of propaganda or bias endemic to these writings. But, largely because these histories were written by enlisted men and officers awaiting discharge, they are generally accurate representations of their respective units' endeavors. Exceptions to this rule are the histories of the 70th and 63d Infantry Divisions, which are extremely sketchy, and the history of the 36th Infantry Division, which is long on photographs and very short on meaningful text.

This shortcoming can be more than made up for, however, by studying the divisional command and staff journals, which exist not only for these divisions, but all of the Seventh Army divisions, at the National Archives in Washington, D.C., and at the Records Annex in Suitland, Maryland. The original documents are available at these locations, and include detailed records down to and including pencil-sketched battalion position overlays and coffee-stained operations logs that were, no doubt, scribbled in the dead of night by the light of a gas-fueled lantern.

Dozens of U.S. regimental and even battalion histories also exist, but these vary wildly in quality and are too numerous to mention here. Nearly all infantry regimental operations and intelligence journals are also available at the National Archives.

Of immense importance to the study of this (or any) World War II campaign are the unit strength reports available at the National Archives Annex in St. Louis, Missouri. Virtually *every* morning report, listing exactly how many soldiers were present for duty in each company-sized unit in the entire U.S. Army, is available on microfilm there. Although St. Louis is not primarily a public research facility, existing mainly for support of the U.S. Army Reserve Personnel Center and efforts to reconstruct veterans' service records, it is possible, with time, patience, and perseverance, to gain access to these invaluable resources.

On the German side, some histories of *Army Group G* units are now available in published form, but they also vary considerably in quality. Most of them have been published since 1970, as interest in the war has gradually burgeoned in Germany since that time. Many are long on excuses (*"die verdammte Jabos"*) and short on analysis. Like their American counterparts, they must be carefully read and digested to ensure separation of fact and would-have-been-fact. But they too are generally accurate representations of the wartime endeavors of their respective units.

More useful than these later works, however, are a series of monographs commissioned by the Twelfth Army and, later, U.S. Army Europe (USAREUR) in the 1946–49 period. They were written in German and, sometimes, translated to English, by former officers of various *Army Group G* units. The monographs comprise firsthand accounts of the activities of many of the most important German units present in the Vosges. Although many were written by former battalion- and regimental-level officers, some, such as Friedrich Wiese's "19th Army in the Belfort Gap, in the Vosges, and in Alsace" and von Mellenthin's "Army Group G Operations in the Vosges," are by army- and corps-level officers with a broader perspective. These works, which number more than fifty, are available in several places, but the most complete collection is in the National Archives.

Many captured German unit daily journals, mostly at the corps level and above, are also available at the National Archives, although only a few from the 1944–45 era survived. Most of these are on microforms, because the originals, which were seized by U.S. Army elements during and after the war, have long since been returned to the Bundesmilitträgeschichtlichesarchiv (Federal Military Historical Archives) in Freiburg, Germany.[10] Ironically, there seems to be somewhat more respect for U.S. tactical fighting abilities in some of these wartime journals than in postwar unit histories.

Unfortunately, nothing approaching the wealth of American personnel strength documentation exists for the units of *Army Group G*. However, it is possible, by meticulously screening available U.S. intelligence reports, to develop an accurate appraisal of German personnel and equipment strengths and verify them against the estimates provided by *Army Group G* veterans in their postwar USAREUR manuscripts. Cross-referencing with German tables of organization and equipment yields accurate hard quantities or numbers.

To allow full comprehension of the doctrine against which the performance of both German and U.S. units must be judged in this study, a set of both American and German prewar and wartime field manuals is available at the Military History Institute at Carlisle Barracks. Much of the German doctrine is striking in its similarity to the U.S. doctrine of 1943–44.

One more source of information can prove valuable for the student of this campaign.[11] French author Francis Rittgen has produced two interesting works that add local color and depth to certain features of the Vosges campaign. These books include the recollections and observations of many Frenchmen who lived through the campaign. Another French-language publication that provides information important for understanding the formidable nature of the Maginot line in the Low Vosges, especially in what became the XV Corps sector, is Roger Bruge's *On a Livré La Ligne Maginot*.[12] This book details the layout and design of every major Maginot fort from Wissembourg to Longuyon, including the important Ensemble de Bitche.

Conclusion

The detailed study of combat operations in the Vosges Mountains in the fall and winter of 1944–45 provides an important opportunity to compare the relative tactical combat proficiency of the German and American armies of the period. This appraisal is possible because of such factors as terrain, weather, and the strategic priorities that placed the opponents in this area on a comparable operational and tactical footing. That the Seventh Army's combat elements were more successful than their Wehrmacht counterparts in *Army Group G* provides strong evidence of the superior combat proficiency of American units.

The areas to be examined here, drawing largely on evidence abundantly available in primary sources, include not only the conduct and results of combat actions during the campaign, but also the training, equipment, personnel, and leadership provided to each major unit. The purpose of this comparison is to determine, as fairly as possible, which side most frequently and successfully fulfilled its doctrinal requirements.

CHAPTER 1

THE BATTLEGROUND

When will blood cease to flow in the mountains?
When sugar cane grows in the snows.
—*Caucasian Warriors' Proverb*[1]

The Vosges Mountains have always been a refuge and a great defensive bastion. They rise dramatically from the Rhine Valley near Belfort to peaks of four thousand feet or more. Running parallel to the Rhine along the broad, flat Alsatian Plain for about ninety miles, they become even more rugged as they descend to their northern terminus near the Lauter River. Generally, geomorphologists divide the thirty-mile-wide range into two parts: the High Vosges, to the south, made up mainly of granite and gneiss, and the Low Vosges (which many Germans call the Hardt), composed mainly of sedimentary rock such as red sandstone. The High Vosges were formed by titanic terrestrial upheavals during the Paleozoic era, but were somewhat smoothed by glaciers later on; thus, their slopes are somewhat even and they allow easy east-west crossings at a few passes. The Low Vosges to the north of the Saverne Gap were never affected by the vast, abrading seas of ice that planed the higher formations to the south. Thus, although these more northerly mountains do not reach elevations much in excess of three thousand feet, they afford even fewer places to cross due to their steeper, more dramatic crescendos and diminuendos in relief.[2]

During the dim prehistory of Alsace, several hundred years before Christ, a still-unidentified Celtic people inhabiting the Vosges attempted to supplement their mountain fastness with the construction of a ten-kilometer-long, three-meter-high wall around a mountain peak (the modern *Fliehburg*) near contemporary Obernai. Known as the *Heidenmauer* (Heathen Wall), due to its pre-Christian origins on the site of the shrine of Saint Odilia, patroness of Alsace, it represents one of the earliest known fortification systems in the Vosges.[3]

In the first century before Christ, the frightened Sequanians, Aeduans, and other Celtic tribes retreated to the craggy protection of "Mons Vosegus" when Ariovistus and his Suevi (Swabians) crossed the Rhine and threatened to subjugate them and occupy their territory. When Caesar marched northeastward to Alsace from southern Gaul, he and his proud legions successfully ejected the Germans from the area by defeating them in battle near Vesontio (modern Besançon). Fortunately for the Romans and their Gallic allies, Ariovistus chose to retreat northeastward across the Alsatian Plain toward the area that is today Sélestat in an attempt to link up with reinforcements; had he and his Germans withdrawn to the Vosges, Caesar may never have crossed the Rhine, however briefly.[4]

After later defeating the Belgae in northern Gaul and consolidating Roman control of the entire area, the Romans built numerous roads, including several through the greater and lesser Vosges passes.[5] Indeed, the Vosges became militarily significant again before the end of the Roman period in the fifth century, as they provided a refuge for Alsatians threatened by the successive invasions of Burgundians and Huns. By the time the tribesmen returned to the valleys and plains from the safety of the highlands, Roman rule had been swept away and the chaos that was the early Middle Ages in Europe descended.[6]

During the medieval era, the Vosges became an oft-contested barrier between empires. By the Treaty of Verdun in 843, the heirs of the ruler of the First Reich, Charlemagne, or Karl the Great, divided up the Frankish Empire. The Vosges and all of Alsace fell within the sphere of Lothair, whose name was given to his "Middle Kingdom" between the realms of his victorious brothers, Charles the Bold and Louis the German. As with so many "middle" lands throughout history, Lotharingia (from which the modern name "Lorraine" is derived) became a battleground for the armies of subsequent disputing rulers. Although the Vosges region was never crossed by force of arms during this period, it and all of Alsace eventually (by 925) became a part of the German duchy of Swabia, and as such was absorbed by the Holy Roman Empire.

Far from the home of the Houses of Hohenstaufen and Hapsburg, Alsace remained very much a distant border region to these great and powerful rulers. It is not surprising, therefore, that Alsace should have been governed through an extremely complicated system of vassalage that became so confusing even to the nobles of the time that armed bickering became inevitable. Indeed, the history of Alsace during the later Middle Ages is a troubled one, marked by frequent conflicts between various landed overlords, the holders of minor fiefs, and the guildsmen of the ten free cities of the region. Suffice it to say, however, that no outsider ever conquered Alsace, much less crossed the Vosges by force during this period. Even Charles the Bold purchased, rather than conquered, Alsace to bring on the brief period of Burgundian domination in the late fifteenth century.[7]

The Peasants' War swept through Alsace from southwest Germany in 1524–25, adding more pages to the growing chronicle of armed conflict in the Vosges. The craggy, compartmented nature of the area gave rise to a fascinating mosaic of Calvinist, Lutheran, and Roman Catholic pockets, often separated by only a ridge or a valley.[8] The region remained a bloody but indecisive battleground for the forces of religious reaction and reform, of French aspiration, and of Hapsburg domination as the Thirty Years' War brought the Vosges and the rest of western Europe into the early modern age.

Throughout the Middle Ages, the peaks of the southern portion of the range became crowned by numerous fortresses, which blocked the passes from east to west. To the north, more castles appeared, and the likes of the Fleckenstein (near modern Lembach) and the Falkenstein (near modern Philippsbourg) were built, preventing easy transit between France and the lands of the Holy Roman Emperor.

Illustrative of the Vosges Mountains' military history of this period were the fortunes of the château that came to be known as Haut-Koenigsbourg. Sitting atop the Staufenberg at an elevation of 2,484 feet, the château looked out over the vast, flat Alsatian Plain to the east toward the Black Forest. Erected upon the ruins of walls originally built by the Romans to protect the approaches to a high pass in the southern Vosges (today called the valley of Ste. Marie-aux-Mines), the fort had a long and complicated history between the time of its construction as a medieval military edifice in the twelfth century and its destruction in 1633.

Mirroring the stormy history of Alsace, the château passed from the ownership of the House of Hohenstaufen to the House of Lorraine, and eventually from the House of Württemberg to the Hapsburgs. It served at various times as a fortress-residence of vassals of the Dukes of Lorraine and the Bishops of Strasbourg, as a haven of the robber barons who preyed on traffic through the nearby pass, and as a bastion of the Holy Roman Empire. In fact, its garrison was under the command of an Imperial officer, Capt. Philippe de Lichtenau, when it was besieged in May 1633 during the "Swedish" phase of the Thirty Years' War.

The stubborn and valiant de Lichtenau managed to hold out for more than three months within the battered redans of the château, refusing all of the dire surrender ultimata of the attacking Swedes of the Hubalt Regiment. Finally, out of food and ammunition, with troops of the garrison mutinously evaporating into the night, de Lichtenau surrendered and the structure was sacked and burned by the Swedes. The siege marked the height of Protestant venture into Alsace, however, and no further advance through the Vosges was made from Haut-Koenigsbourg.[9]

The Vosges continued to prove impenetrable in the early modern era. When Alsace officially became a part of France under the terms of the Treaty of Ryswick in 1697, Vauban, Louis XIV's chief military engineer, went to work improving the damaged and increasingly obsolete defenses of this new border region. The massive red sandstone citadel originally constructed according to his plans at Bitche, in the Low Vosges, for example, was again strengthened with typical bastioned outworks in 1714. Nearly eight decades later, in the autumn of 1793, it was attacked by Prussians under the Duke of Brunswick, but it never fell.[10]

Indeed, during the first war of the modern era to be fought in Alsace, the 1870–71 Franco–German War, the attacking Germans wisely chose to make their main effort away from the barrier of the Vosges. Attacking from the Palatinate, the Germans drove in the direction of Metz, in Lorraine, and on toward Sedan with two field armies, while a third army, under the crown prince of Prussia, pinned down mobilizing French troops in Alsace.

Although the Germans gained a significant tactical victory over the French at Woerth and Elsasshausen, towns in the eastern foothills of the Low Vosges, they never had to face much in the way of serious opposition in the mountains and hills themselves; Marshal MacMahon withdrew his recently defeated troops well beyond them through the Saverne Gap to the east in an attempt to link up with the French armies massing around Metz. The only real resistance met by the German Third Army while pursuing the French to Lorraine was offered by the garrisons in a series of fortresses that blocked the east-west roads in the Low Vosges. Interestingly, the Prussian crown prince *did* leave Bavarian troops behind to invest the French garrison of about a thousand in the 156-year-old citadel at Bitche, but they never succeeded in capturing the place. The proud tower was not surrendered until after the general armistice several months later.[11]

Alsace and Lorraine were, of course, ceded to the Germans after 1871, becoming known as the Reichsland. Recognizing the new military realities of this dramatic territorial alteration, the French during the interbellum years conducted a massive buildup of their aging defensive fortifications in the Champagne region. Taking advantage of both the successive series of escarpments and the rivers (Meuse, Moselle, and Meurthe) that run north-south in this area, the French created a formidable set of man-made barriers that protected the remainder of their homeland from further German conquest. To avoid what surely would have turned into a pointless slugging match, the German General Staff decided upon a holding action along the eminently defensible Vosges and a vigorous main attack through neutral Belgium and Luxembourg—what became known, somewhat inaccurately, as the Schlieffen Plan.

Because this plan called for a complete change of combat venue from that of 1870–71, the Vosges were spared much bloodshed in World War I. The French First Army attacked in the southern High Vosges across the crest of the range toward Guebwiller and Thann during the opening days of the conflict, and succeeded in seizing Mulhouse on the Alsatian Plain. The German Seventh Army attacked toward Épinal through the Saverne Gap, but never got far beyond the Meurthe. The relatively static warfare that characterized the conflict in the rest of France also occurred in the Vosges. Some of the fortifications in the Parroy Forest and along the northeast side of the Meurthe, created after the stabilization of the lines in the autumn of 1914, were so sturdy that they were used by the Germans in 1944. Although fighting certainly took place in the Vosges region, and Mulhouse was eventually recaptured by the Germans, neither side tried seriously to force the Vosges passes during the course of the conflict.

The Maginot Line

After the provisions of the Treaty of Versailles brought Alsace and Lorraine back into French hands, it was not long before the French government decided to take strong defensive measures to make those long-disputed provinces a permanent part of France. In the 1930s, under the leadership of the Alsatian-born World War I veteran and war minister André Maginot, the French embarked on the most ambitious project of permanent fortification in modern times. Named after this badly wounded zealot, the Maginot line consisted of a series of state-of-the-art fortifications and improved existing positions. This system barred the way along the Franco-German frontier for 192 miles, starting at the Swiss border and continuing northward along the west bank of the Rhine. In the vicinity of the antique Vauban fortress of Fort Louis (fought over heavily in 1793), the line turned northwest across the Alsatian Plain toward Hatten. From there, it continued in roughly the same direction toward the northern terminus of the Low Vosges, where it ran basically due west to the Saar. It formed a salient to the south in the vicinity of Sarreguemines that terminated just south of Sarralbe, whence the line turned northwest again and continued to Longuyon. There the major fortifications ended, and only an irregular series of lighter pillbox-type defensive works continued to the English Channel.[12]

The experience of the French army in the trenches during World War I showed heavily in the design of the Maginot fortifications. The works were built of steel-reinforced concrete designed to withstand heavy bombardment and machine-gun fire, and were emplaced to provide mutually supporting fires out to tremendous ranges over bristling antipersonnel and antivehicular obstacles. Indeed, the creation of the Maginot line permanently altered the geography of Alsace and parts of the Vosges. Nearly the entire front, from Fort Louis to Longuyon, with the exception of the Saar region, contained layered belts of interlocking fortifications, which ensured that flanking fires could be brought to bear on any local breakthrough. Basically, there were four types of Maginot works, namely the casemate, or *blockhaus;* the *abri d'intervalle;* the *observatoire;* and the *ouvrage.*

The casemate was a small (generally less than a hundred feet in any dimension), multichambered pillbox consisting of two levels. The *étage superieur,* or ground level, contained the firing positions for machine guns, antitank guns, and grenade launchers and/or small (50mm) mortars. The *étage inferieur,* located below ground level and accessible by staircases hidden behind armored doors, included the living quarters and generators providing power for the facilities.[13] These casemates constituted the great majority of the Maginot fortifications along the Rhine and also filled the gaps between the larger fortifications throughout the remainder of the line. Typically, the casemates' machine guns and antitank guns were enclosed in armored embrasures set into the concrete walls and had largely unobstructed fields of fire and observation over heavily mined and barricaded fields out to the maximum effective range of the weapons.[14] Additionally, their mortars, usually of the short-range 50mm variety, were capable of placing accurate indirect fires into all folds in the ground that might otherwise have provided cover and concealment for an attacker. These mortars were emplaced in armored turrets, often with coaxially mounted machine guns, allowing them to fire through 360 degrees traverse, thus covering all approaches to the casemate.

Many casemates, especially in the vicinity of the larger fortresses, were constructed with their weapons facing in directions other than directly at the frontier, that is, to the flanks or rear (south) to ensure all-around protection of these more important defensive edifices. In this way, not only were the *petit* and *gros ouvrages* (described below) protected from all geographical aspects, but the enemy was also presented with a confusing maze of successive belts of fortifications that were capable of continually engaging him even if the first lines of Maginot positions were overrun.

The second type of Maginot fortification was the *abri d'intervalle.* These were essentially underground barracks that served as protective shelters for the units, mostly infantry, waiting just to the rear of the main line of fortifications for orders to counterattack or reinforce threatened segments of the line. Up to eight stories deep, each barracks contained all the facilities usually associated with military quarters, including mess halls, latrines, aid stations, ammunition magazines, and sleeping and recreational rooms, all ventilated and lighted by self-contained diesel-powered electrical generators. Since these fortifications were essentially passive in nature, their armament usually consisted only of machine guns for self-defense, and their above-ground facades usually faced away from the expected enemy route of advance.[15] This, of course, made them useful as auxiliary fortifications for the protection of the rear of the other works; to this end, some of them had heavily barricaded and mined rear-facing entrances.[16]

The third type of Maginot fortification was the *observatoire.* This was also an essentially passive defensive work (usually protected by one or two organic machine guns) that served simply as an observation post for the surveillance of otherwise concealed enemy avenues of approach, such as large ravines, which did not warrant protection by a casemate or *ouvrage*.[17]

The fourth type of Maginot line emplacement, the *ouvrage*, was the backbone of the system. There were five official classifications of *ouvrage*, according to the size of the garrison, but basically only two categories—infantry and artillery—and two classifications—*gros* (designed for garrisons of more than 450 men) and *petit*—were commonly used.[18] These massive edifices gave rise to the Maginot line's legendary invincibility. Each fortress included its own quarters, similar to those of the *abri d'intervalle,* all located up to fourteen stories *below* ground, as well as massive facilities for the storage of months' worth of rations, water, and diesel fuel for the continuous operation of the huge electrical generators that powered the lights, turrets, and other electromechanical machinery in each *ouvrage.* Also reflecting the World War I heritage of the Maginot line was the installation of an atmospheric overpressure and filtration system designed to protect troops from the types of wind-borne chemical agents that wreaked so much havoc in the trenches from 1915 to 1918. Run by immense bellows located in the barracks/headquarters/magazine complex that was the heart of every *ouvrage,* this system also was powered by the tremendous generators located in the depths of each fortress.

These facilities were connected by deep tunnels to the fighting *blocs,* often located two to five kilometers from the barracks and headquarters area. Through these tunnels ran electric trains that rapidly transported troops from their living quarters to their fighting positions—again demonstrating how the World War I experience affected the French army, which found that distance from battle was needed for the proper rest and refreshment of combat troops. These trains also carried ammunition for the guns and mortars of the *blocs* from the magazine area. The final movement of the shells from tunnel to turret was performed by electric elevators.

Indeed, these trains performed a critical function, for it was the potent offensive weapons of the *ouvrage,* encased in several different types of nearly invulnerable steel and concrete emplacements, which composed the raison d'être for these mighty edifices. The weapons ranged from 75mm guns and 81mm mortars to 135mm howitzers, all sited to provide withering indirect fires against likely enemy avenues of approach.

Many batteries were mounted in fixed concrete and steel embrasures in the general direction of the German frontier. Such structures allowed only relatively minor changes of azimuth, but they fully protected their guns and gunners because the structures were essentially invulnerable to enemy bombardment due to their location on reverse slopes and extremely thick concrete and steel shells. Moreover, in most *ouvrages*, numerous guns were mounted in heavily armored, fully rotating, retractable steel turrets, which afforded defense against bombardment and close assaults from every point of the compass. These ingeniously designed mounts, which fitted flush with the ground between firings, allowed extremely accurate indirect fires to be delivered on targets through 360 degrees, with range and deflection adjusted by forward observers securely sheltered in *observatoires*, casemates, or the forward *blocs* of the *ouvrages* themselves.

All of these fortifications shared one common characteristic: They helped transform the naturally difficult Vosges and Alsace into a death trap for any invader.

The 1940 Campaign

The Germans, well aware of this situation, planned and conducted their 1940 campaign in France so as to nearly totally bypass André Maginot's creation. As they destroyed a large portion of the French air force on the ground in the first few days of the fighting, the Germans moved large armored formations through the Ardennes Forest, practically unopposed, toward the Meuse River at Sedan. German assault echelons crossed the Meuse under the cover of literally thousands of Luftwaffe fighter and fighter-bomber (*Jagdbomber*, or "*Jabo*" for short) sorties. This exercise of massive air superiority simultaneously warded away the remnants of the numerically devastated and technologically inferior French air force and softened up the defenses and morale of the disorganized poilus attempting to stem the tide of massed *Panzer* formations. The beautiful French spring weather allowed constant Luftwaffe support and facilitated the rapid movement of the German armored and motorized formations. The slashing spearheads of the German army completely unhinged the French defense plans as they raced to the Channel. The fate of the best French army units, located in Belgium and northern France, was decided in a few short days.

This totally unexpected maneuver trapped dozens of French second-line and fortress divisions in and around the Maginot line, cutting them off from supplies or effective means of aiding their comrades-in-arms to the west. These French fortress units, although possessing heavy firepower, lacked the mobility to conduct any but the most local of counterattacks, and were therefore practically useless for the rather short duration of the campaign.

The entire German operational concept was a tribute to the potential effectiveness of the Maginot defenses and the formidable nature of the Vosges massif. It was not until the rest of the French army was effectively hors de combat, leaving only the defenders of the Maginot fortifications to uphold the worthy traditions of French armies of more glorious eras, that the Germans mounted any serious assaults on these defensive works.

Several of the *petits ouvrages,* such as Haut-Poirier and Welschoff in the salient formed by the fortifications in the Saar region, surrendered to assaulting German and Austrian troops after being surrounded and bombarded at close range with heavy artillery.[19] Others, however, particularly in the so-called Ensemble de Bitche (a series of several geographically close *gros ouvrages* belonging to both the Secteur Fortifie de Rohrbach and Secteur Fortifie des Vosges, deeply ensconced in the forbidding forests and jagged hills of the Low Vosges), held out even beyond the armistice, shelling German units within range and machine-gunning those German troops unfortunate enough to be assigned the task of probing the stubborn French defenses. Although severe damage was inflicted on a few of the *ouvrages* by Luftwaffe dive-bombers and army heavy artillery, the German reluctance to conduct concerted assaults on most of the die-hard garrisons again reflected the high regard in which the Germans held the Vosges-Maginot defenses.

Impact of Terrain and Weather on the 1944–45 Campaign

If the defenses and terrain of the Vosges and Alsace provided a formidable obstacle to the Wehrmacht's blitz in the spring of 1940, in many ways they offered an even more daunting countenance to the advancing American troops of Lt. Gen. Alexander Patch's Seventh Army in the autumn of 1944. Unlike the Germans four years before, the Americans faced a naturally imposing Vosges barrier reinforced by recently constructed fieldworks. Worse, thanks to General Eisenhower's broadfront strategy, the Seventh Army faced the task of crossing the entire Vosges chain, not just the Low Vosges. This unprecedented feat would have to be followed by a penetration of the most formidable of the Maginot fortifications and a Rhine River crossing in what promised to be winter conditions—although the Germans planned to hold their Vosges positions until at least the spring of 1945!

The peaks of the mountains in that southern portion of the range called the High Vosges afford outstanding long-range fields of observation and fire in all directions. In clear weather, visibility from the geographical crests of the ridges and hills is limited only by the curvature of the earth or by the presence of intervening terrain features; in foul weather, this advantage is attenuated but in no way affords any reciprocal advantage to the attacker, who must close to nearly point-blank range to identify his objectives. Most of the Vosges high ground overlooks either concave or at least constantly graded slopes, preventing approaching troops from using the base of mountains for cover and concealment.

The vegetation present in the Vosges also compounded the Americans' difficulties. Much of the range is heavily forested, both with deciduous hardwoods and, at higher elevations, by coniferous evergreens. These vast forests provided concealment to the Germans, as well as a ready source of barrier and field fortification materials. Although the deciduous vegetation at lower altitudes became barren by early November, thereby providing defenders at lower altitudes with somewhat less concealment as the campaign progressed, it also exposed the attackers to earlier discovery and long-range engagement. Since the Germans were generally ensconced on the commanding high ground and the Americans were advancing from the low areas, the vegetation clearly favored the defender in infantry combat.

The great ranges at which fighting could be joined favored long-range, flat-trajectory, direct-fire weapons—namely, machine guns. Machine guns, however, are most effectively employed when they can achieve "grazing fire." This term refers to fires that skim over the surface of the ground at about waist level out to the maximum effective range of the weapon. This optimizes the weapons' high volume of fire by increasing the probability of hitting advancing soldiers throughout the depth of their formations. Since a machine gun's bullets move on a relatively flat trajectory, those that miss the intended target will continue on to hit undetected targets. Even if hits are not achieved, the leaden death spraying out at lethal heights suppresses unprotected movement and halts advances. In ruggedly hilly terrain such as that in the Vosges, achieving grazing fire is much less common than "plunging fire." Plunging fire results when bullets are fired from an altitude considerably above the target; this affects only the engaged targets by impacting immediately behind, beside, or before them, and causes no damage to targets arrayed in depth. Clearly, machine guns with great ranges are most effective in such an environment, as are ones with relatively slow rates of fire, such as the .30-caliber medium and heavy models used by the American infantry (M1919A4 and M1917A4, respectively). High rates of fire, in the nine hundred to twelve hundred rounds per minute (fifteen to twenty per second) range, such as those achieved by the standard German infantry machine guns (MG34 and MG42), simply place many more bullets into the turf in and around the target, thus wasting ammunition.

High-angle, indirect-fire weapons are also very effective in heavily wooded, mountainous terrain. The ability to engage the enemy from masked positions of relative security with well-observed and adjusted fire control teams is critical to success. Weapons such as howitzers are therefore extremely potent; mortars are even better, because they can be far more easily manhandled into positions inaccessible to towed or self-propelled artillery. Additionally, the lethality of high-explosive projectiles such as those fired from these weapons can be greatly enhanced by fuses that are hypersensitized or ones that are time or proximity actuated. This causes the shells to detonate upon striking a branch or treetop (or times them to do so), scattering shell and tree fragments over a wide area. Fortified positions, especially well-prepared ones incorporating effective overhead cover, can do much to protect against artillery and mortar fire. Attacking troops, on the other hand, must rely on rapid movement and obscuration by terrain to avoid taking heavy casualties. Neither of these were options for American infantry moving on foot through densely vegetated, rugged terrain under the watchful eyes of German hilltop defenders.

The steep slopes and the vegetation in the region affected vehicular operations as well. In 1944, most of the major roads ran east-west through the mountain passes on the short axis of the range. Therefore, much of the traffic supporting the U.S. logistical effort had to negotiate unpaved secondary roads that were very narrow and winding. This caused considerable driver fatigue and wear and tear on the vehicles themselves, because the supplies for the forward units came from Marseilles—more than four hundred miles to the south.

Rivers, too, generally run east-west in the Vosges, following the natural contours of the slopes. The greatest of these, the Meurthe, is a major obstacle, especially to vehicles, in the path of an army attempting to force the range from south-southwest to north-northeast. Defending the commanding high ground on the north side of this river affords any defender a marked advantage for obvious reasons.

The effects on combat vehicles attempting to operate in the rough Vosges terrain were even more serious and more complicated. Although both German and American tanks of the period were capable of negotiating slopes of 57 to 70 percent, depending on the model, the speeds attained while climbing steep grades were practically glacial—between five and ten miles per hour.[20] This made columns of armored vehicles sitting ducks for German antitank gunners, especially those manning the excellent 88mm triple-purpose (antiaircraft, antiarmor, and antipersonnel) artillery piece. Furthermore, the dense vegetation and large hardwood trees characteristic of the Vosges greatly limited off-road mobility. Essentially, tanks and other armored fighting vehicles in this campaign were restricted to narrow, easily blocked thoroughfares that could be kept under constant surveillance and accurate fire from positions on the surrounding high ground. Even short-range weapons such as the rocket-launching German *Panzerfausts* and *Panzerschrecks* could be effective in such terrain, especially if employed in ambushes at the many curves along the serpentine mountain roads. In summary, the Vosges Mountains constituted extremely poor tank country, prohibitive of slashing armored thrusts and conducive to antiarmor defense.

Communicating in mountains is also difficult, particularly by radio. All radio sets used up through regimental level, on both sides, were of the frequency-modulating (FM) type and were therefore principally line-of-sight devices. Clearly, in such terrain as the Vosges, this limited the range and effectiveness of radio combat communications. The advantage in this category also clearly went to the defender, who, by virtue of his ability to pick the place of combat, could more easily install and rely upon wire communications. In the fluid situations created by offensive maneuver, where having flexible means of communications is of the utmost importance, many American commanders had to rely upon messengers, one of the least responsive and most cumbersome of all methods of communicating.

The exceptionally rugged nature of the Vosges has many other implications for ground combat as well. It is not uncommon to find grades of 15 to 25 percent or more on the slopes of the High Vosges; to the north in the Low Vosges are hills with grades of 30 percent or even greater. Traversing such slopes on foot, carrying sufficient ammunition and equipment to both fight effectively and to survive the increasingly severe weather on a sustained basis, had devastating effects.

According to a recently conducted scientific study at the United States Military Academy at West Point, the demands of mountainous terrain on the body are indeed great. It was discovered that the metabolic response of a well-conditioned male carrying forty-two pounds of equipment (about right for a World War II American infantryman with M1 Garand rifle, steel helmet, basic load of .30-caliber ammunition, and personal gear) increases *exponentially* with vertical slope.[21] In other words, maneuver up the 15 to 30 percent slopes of the Vosges range induced physical stress that was literally hundreds of times greater than that created by fighting in the relatively flat terrain of Normandy, Belgium, or central France.

Such a situation clearly favored the comparatively sedentary and sheltered conditions of the defense. Conversely, the attacker needed to maintain a much higher level of physical fitness, as well as more durable morale and tenacious leadership.

Because two combatant armies must endure the same climatic conditions simultaneously, it has been said that the weather favors no one. But from mid-October 1944 to mid-January 1945, the weather clearly assisted the dogged defenders of the Vosges. Although temperatures in the Vosges that winter were not extreme (ranging from 38 to 68 degrees Fahrenheit in October, 25 to 60 degrees in November, 15 to 43 degrees in December, and consistently below freezing in January),[22] daily rain and considerable winds during the period created conditions that made living in the open an extremely hazardous and miserable experience for the frequently exposed American infantrymen.

Wet, cold conditions are highly conducive to the following disabling injuries: immersion foot, which results from contact with water or moisture under 50 degrees for twelve hours or more; trench foot, which results from the same conditions for forty-eight to seventy-two hours; and frostbite, which is the crystallization of tissue fluids in the skin resulting from exposure to temperatures of 32 degrees or less for periods that vary with wind velocity and humidity.[23] Diseases such as pneumonia are also a constant threat in cold and humid weather. During the second half of the month of October in the Vosges, it rained every day save one.[24] November brought much more rain and, in the higher elevations, the first snows. December and January were snowy and frigid.

During cold weather, soldiers need more food because their bodies consume more calories. Troops in the attack, living in the open, more often lack facilities to cook rations than soldiers who are defending towns or are in fixed fortifications. The fluid, ever-changing requirements of the offense often prevent commanders from bringing hot food forward to the frontline combat troops who need it most. Soldiers consuming cold rations, such as the American C or K rations, expend as much heat digesting the food as the nutrients themselves provide, so no net heat production results.[25] This problem in turn often creates lethargy, requiring exceptionally inspirational and conscientious leadership to overcome it if attacks are to be executed with sufficient vigor.

Cold weather, mud, and snow also affect vehicular performance. Operations in deep snow, slush, or mud require up to 25 percent more fuel per unit of distance traveled.[26] Because vehicles generally move much more during offensive operations than while in the defense, this had a serious impact on the Americans, who had to shuffle vehicles to refueling points much more frequently. This, in turn, retarded the momentum of attacks. Indeed, in early December, as the attackers grinding through the Vosges mud began to encounter the first snows, they often had less than a day's fuel reserves on hand. Availability of cold weather lubricants also became a problem during that month.[27]

The increase in fuel consumption brought on by the weather was probably the only factor of the Vosges terrain and climate that adversely affected the Germans as much or more than it did the U.S. forces. Due partially to the effectiveness of Allied strategic bombardment and partially to Red Army advances in Romania in the fall of 1944, German fuel production fell off drastically during the Vosges campaign.[28] The Wehrmacht's supplies of all classes of petroleum products were greatly diminished, thereby affecting not only gasoline and diesel quantities, but also the availability of special winter lubricants essential for cold weather operations.

The effects of the losses of German aircraft fuel production capacity in this same period, however, were actually lessened by the Vosges weather. Whereas in other areas of Europe, U.S. Army Air Forces (USAAF) tactical fighter-bomber elements were able to conduct close air support operations largely unopposed by the Luftwaffe, and U.S. ground units had little cause to fear aerial attack, this was not the case in the Seventh Army sector. There were only ten flyable days in all of October in this area (all but one in the early part of the month), and no sorties were flown in support of ground operations from 5 to 19 November.[29] The poor weather also completely frustrated American aerial photoreconnaissance efforts.

By December, when conditions aloft had improved, many of the U.S. efforts were targeted on Germans ensconced in the Maginot line fortresses around Bitche, against which bombs had no decisive effect. By the middle of December, the weather closed in again, allowing the Germans to conserve their fuel to mount both air interception and ground attack missions themselves. There were even instances of Luftwaffe pilots flying captured U.S. P-47 "Thunderbolt" fighter-bombers, an effective *ruse de guerre* that resulted in successful attacks on U.S. positions.[30] Generally, the weather, when it came to aerial operations, was something of an equalizer for the two otherwise grossly imbalanced opponents.

From the middle of October 1944 to the middle of January 1945, the U.S. Seventh Army and the German *Army Group G* slugged it out over the ancient battleground of Celts, Romans, Burgundians, Huns, Austrians, Swedes, French, and Prussians. The campaign was bitterly contested, because Alsace lay on the doorstep of the Reich, and the Vosges constituted the last great geographical barrier before the Rhine itself. Nearly every conceivable advantage of terrain was conceded to the defender, who, though sometimes empirically outnumbered, was required by his own doctrinal precepts to fight outnumbered and win in such situations. An examination of the tactical and operational doctrines under which both sides fought this campaign is therefore essential for a full understanding of the course of events that led to its dramatic conclusion: the first successful opposed crossing of the Vosges Mountains in history.

CHAPTER 2

The Opposing Forces

In regard to mountain warfare in general, everything depends
on the skill of our subordinate officers and still more on the
morale of our soldiers. Here it is not a question of skillful
maneuvering, but of warlike spirit and wholehearted
devotion to the cause.
—Clausewitz, *Principles of War,* 1812[1]

On the surface, much about the tactical and operational doctrines of
the opposing forces in the Vosges appears to be similar. Both of the
armies involved owed much to Clausewitz and *Vom Kriege (On War)*,
although for different reasons. In Germany, Clausewitz and his teachings
had long been popular due, of course, to his nationality, but also to
Helmuth von Moltke (the Elder) and his lionization of Clausewitzian
principles as he interpreted them.[2] Many Germans during the era of
the Third Reich also viewed Clausewitz as one of the fathers of German nationalism, which further fueled enthusiasm for his teachings.[3]
   In the United States, where military thought had been dominated
by the more pragmatic and less sophisticated concepts of Henri Jomini
since the antebellum period, Clausewitz's ideas had nevertheless been
incorporated by a sort of osmosis. Before the American Civil War, Jomini's
writings had been the natural choice for officers in an army that had
not faced a major opponent since 1815. After all, Napoleon's successes
were the envy of every commander, and Jomini was Napoleon's direct interpreter and critic. Furthermore, since the Union won the conflict on which its officers had embarked with a tactical education
grounded in Jomini's *The Art of War,* it was only natural that the army
would cling to the precepts that had worked for it in battle. After the
Civil War, although a few officers, such as the prolific Col. Emory

Upton, became enamored of the army of the German Empire and all its works and all its ways, tactical thought in the U.S. Army remained fixed on the fading glory of Gettysburg and the immediate realities of the campaigns against the Plains Indians.

As the results of World War I were analyzed by the officers of an army that had finally faced the Germans and their Clausewitzian tactics on the battlefield, the reading of Clausewitz by American officers became more commonplace.[4] By the time *Field Manual (FM) 100-5, Field Service Regulations,* was published in 1941, Clausewitz's influence was evident in the document setting forth the doctrine by which the U.S. Army would fight the ground battle in World War II.[5]

What made up the doctrines of the two belligerents who faced each other across the deep valleys and high ridges of the Vosges in the autumn of 1944? Since the concepts of both sides had Clausewitzian roots, it is best to describe and analyze them within a framework of the principles set forth in *Vom Kriege*. It may then become clear that both sides possessed basically sensible, appropriate tactics and operational techniques for the conduct of a campaign such as the one conducted in the Vosges. Furthermore, to truly grasp the impact of these respective doctrines, one must understand the organization of formations and the training conducted by both sides, which was intended to enable soldiers and officers to undertake and execute required tasks. Finally, the impact of these doctrines and the training associated with them on the morale of the combat troops on both sides must be examined. Only then can one properly analyze the actual conduct of the campaign so as to determine which side was superior at translating doctrine into action.

THE GERMANS

German Army Operational and Tactical Doctrine in Late 1944

The basic document describing German operational and tactical doctrine during World War II was *Die Truppenführung* of 1933. According to the principles set forth in this work, the attack was the most effective means of destroying enemy forces, and was therefore the preferred mode of operations.[6] The defensive was to be assumed only as a means of allowing preparation for further offensive operations or offensive operations in another sector.[7] This clearly reflected

Clausewitz's theories on attack and offensive operations. In *Vom Kriege,* Clausewitz insisted:

> The act of attack, particularly in strategy, is thus a constant alternation and combination of attack and defense. The latter, however, should not be regarded as a useful preliminary to the attack or an intensification of it, and so an active principle; rather it is simply a necessary evil, an impeding burden created by the sheer weight of the mass. It is its original sin, its mortal disease.[8]

In the attack, the Germans emphasized the destruction of the enemy's forces over the attainment of geographical objectives. This is not to say that geographical considerations were given short shrift. On the contrary, German doctrine required extremely acute terrain appreciation and encouraged commanders to take maximum advantage of opportunities afforded by geographical realities. It is, however, accurate to conclude that German doctrine followed Clausewitz's dictum that, "In war, the subjugation of the enemy is the end, and the destruction of his fighting forces the means."[9]

The need for knowledge and appreciation of the effects of terrain were reflected in the heavy emphasis the Germans placed on reconnaissance. Doctrine identified three types of reconnaissance: operational, tactical, and battle. All reconnoitering was to be carried out aggressively and in sufficient strength to deal effectively with enemy security elements.[10] Clearly, such doctrine reflects an understanding for the need to reduce what Clausewitz referred to as "friction," or "the force that makes the apparently easy so difficult."[11] Through superior reconnaissance in depth, the Germans hoped to foresee and thus avoid much of the unexpected and otherwise unpredictable obstacles that cause this friction.

Operational reconnaissance was to be carried out by high-altitude aircraft or by motorized units on the ground. Such mobile elements were usually equipped with armored cars, although some had light tanks and motorcycles as well. The reconnoitering units conducting operations at this level were usually assigned only specific points or closely defined areas for observation. Frequently, the ground reconnaissance forces were given only a direction and an objective when tasked with operational reconnaissance missions.[12] The objective of such activities was usually to gain information about enemy dispositions in great depth, allowing planning for operations and contingencies up to the corps level.

Tactical reconnaissance was intended to discern enemy dispositions in the immediate battle area and to afford the commander intimate, up-to-date information on the local terrain and enemy dispositions to facilitate the formulation of appropriate battle plans.[13] This type of reconnaissance was usually conducted up to thirty kilometers (a day's march in fair weather and easy terrain) in front of the attacking main body by divisional reconnaissance battalions using motorcycles, armored cars, and half-tracks. Patrol reports were collated at a forward message center for accurate and rapid transmission to the appropriate regimental or division commander.[14]

The thorough and aggressive conduct of these types of reconnaissance efforts reflected adherence to Clausewitzian concepts regarding advance guards and outposts as well. Clausewitz pointed out that "On the one hand, they [advanced guards and outposts] shape the engagement and ensure that the tactical plan is carried out; on the other, they often lead to separate engagements."[15] The German practice of carrying out reconnaissance efforts with armored vehicles reflects this view of probable engagement.

Battle reconnaissance fulfilled yet other Clausewitzian precepts. Carried out at all levels throughout the actual conduct of combat operations, this type of reconnaissance was executed constantly to obtain timely, accurate information about the enemy's activities and to ensure absolute mastery of the nature of the terrain in the battle area—by direct observation, the taking of prisoners, the capture of documents, and so on. Units conducting such efforts could form simple battle reconnaissance patrols, ordered to avoid contact with the enemy, or larger, more heavily armed combat patrols capable of carrying out raids of every type.[16]

The performance of such battle reconnaissance provided the German commander with the information necessary to avoid, or at least minimize, the dangerous condition that Clausewitz referred to as "imperfect knowledge of the situation." Such a defect could "bring military action to a standstill," Clausewitz warned, with all of the concomitant perils of loss of momentum, divergence of effort, et cetera.[17] Additionally, accurate and timely battle reconnaissance helped to lessen the friction of war that threatened to doom to failure even the best of plans, for "accurate recognition" of the realities of battle by the commander was enhanced by unceasing reports from combat patrols.[18]

Beyond reconnaissance, German doctrine for the conduct of attacks demanded swift, coordinated combined arms strikes designed to demoralize the enemy by encircling him, cutting his lines of communication, and denying him freedom of maneuver. Such offensive action was most effectively carried out by armored or, at least, motorized forces that could rapidly penetrate the enemy's weakest points, fan out behind his main defensive positions, and wreak havoc deep in his rear areas. To reduce the inevitable effects of Clausewitzian friction, the Germans encouraged independent action by their combat leaders, depending on their astute judgment to allow the German operational (corps or division level) commanders to retain the initiative in the rapidly developing situations encountered in the offensive.[19]

Army tactics and operations (both offensive and defensive) were generated by field orders, the format and general content of which were described in the *Truppenführung* manual. The Germans stressed allowing subordinates maximum flexibility in the conduct of tactical and operational activities, and their format for combat orders reflected this emphasis. The *Truppenführung* manual recommended the following sequence for the issuance of combat operations orders: information on the enemy—to include an estimate of his intent—and friendly forces in the area that could have an impact on the upcoming operation; the commander's intent; missions for all combat elements in the command; instructions for supporting elements; and command post locations and communications instructions.[20]

Orders could be issued either verbally or in writing (although it was required to write down even verbal orders after they were given),[21] but they were always to be concise. As the *Truppenführung* manual expressed it:

> An order should contain all that the receiver must know to independently accomplish his mission, and no more. Correspondingly, the order must be brief and clear, definite and complete, and should be understandable to the receiver and should take his circumstances into account. [Author's translation.][22]

Of course, such principles assumed a high level of competence and responsibility on the part of subordinate commanders. The *Truppenführung* specifically pointed out that although the commander should give his subordinates the greatest possible freedom of action, he must nevertheless not allow subordinates' activities to endanger the success of the whole operation.[23] In addition, the manual warned that the commander must not delegate those decisions for which he alone was responsible.

German doctrine originally identified five distinct types of attacks.[24] All were intended to accomplish or at least significantly contribute to the ultimate mission of the destruction of the enemy's forces. The type eventually chosen by a commander depended upon enemy dispositions, terrain (hence the criticality of reconnaissance), and what friendly forces were available. Each type of attack reflected Clausewitz's teachings on the value of maneuver: cutting the enemy's supply lines, preventing the enemy from reinforcing, paralyzing the enemy by preventing coordinating communications, threatening the enemy or preventing his retreat, and retaining the flexibility to attack individual enemy positions with superior forces.[25] Eventually, seven different types of attacks were developed. The two additions were variations on the themes of flank attack or encirclement, and were developed during the war. They will be addressed after the original five.

Each type of attack also called for the execution of a main effort in a narrow sector (*Schwerpunkt*), normally directed against the enemy's flank or rear, and several diversionary or supporting efforts. In all cases, combined arms cooperation was stressed and thorough coordination was considered essential.[26]

The Germans considered the flank attack to be the most effective type of offensive maneuver. By taking on the enemy from the side, it maximized surprise and diminished the retarding effects of enemy fortifications, which were usually oriented to the front. Enemy forces could be rapidly cut up and destroyed by "rolling up" his defensive line without the danger of exposing one's own rear to counterstrokes.

The envelopment involved both a supporting frontal attack, designed to fix the enemy in place, and a main effort consisting of a flank attack from the side or, preferably, the rear to destroy the immobilized enemy. The coordination of such an offensive maneuver was difficult because it involved maneuver from two directions simultaneously. But the benefits were also considerable. To avoid being split by enemy counterattack, reserves had to be employed in depth, and this further compounded the complexity of the maneuver. Of course, as complexity increases, so do the factors leading to friction.

The most potentially costly of all attacks was the frontal attack. From their experience in World War I, the Germans knew that this type of offensive operation required a clear superiority of forces and firepower if enemy positions were to be overwhelmed by direct assault.

Because of this difficulty, when faced with the impossibility of any type of attack other than frontal, the Germans preferred the penetration and breakthrough. By concentrating overwhelming force against the enemy in an extremely narrow sector, the Germans hoped to cause a rupture in the enemy's line that would then, in effect, create two new unprotected flanks. Once the penetration was achieved, the breakthrough took on the characteristics of a flank attack, with all of the advantages described earlier.

The limited objective attack was intended to fix the enemy in place or to gain a specific piece of ground. Usually, such attacks took place as part of a greater maneuver designed to bring about more decisive results. For example, the unit executing a flank attack could require that the enemy be immobilized or tied down to successfully move against his weak flank. The unit conducting the supporting attack would therefore conduct a limited objective attack to facilitate the flanking unit's maneuver.

During the war, two other types of attacks evolved, both of which were variations on two preexisting themes.[27] Attacking an enemy wing was preferred when the enemy's flanks were initially unassailable due to terrain or manner in which his forces were arrayed. An attack on the extreme end of an enemy position might possibly cause his forces to bend back, thus exposing a flank. Such a success would then be followed by a flank attack.

Encirclement was a variation on envelopment. This maneuver required only a weak, if any, supporting attack, and was designed to totally isolate the enemy. The development of this maneuver probably had its origins in the experiences of the 1940 campaign in France and the initial stages of the 1941 campaign in the Soviet Union. If the enemy chose to fight rather than succumb to the pressures and fears induced by being cut off, then there would clearly be problems for the attacker: With unsubdued enemy left in the rear, the encircler could easily become the encircled!

Each of these attacks was preferably conducted by highly coordinated combined-arms teams. The composition and disposition of enemy forces generally dictated the roles to be played by the maneuver elements of armor *(Panzer)*, mechanized infantry *(Panzergrenadier)*, and infantry *(Grenadier* or *Infanterie)* elements, all of which were to be supported by flexible, responsive artillery fires. In this regard, German doctrine could only hope to roughly correspond with the precepts of Clausewitz, because technological advances—the likes of which were spurred by World War I and were, therefore, unimaginable in the early nineteenth century—had vastly changed the character of the various combat arms. Still, Clausewitz had insisted that

> only corps . . . or divisions should be made up of a permanent combination of all arms. In the case of less significant units, temporary combinations made to meet the needs of the moment should suffice.[28]

Interestingly (and probably without purposely doing it), in this regard the Germans' doctrine closely followed the master's guidance. The lowest level at which a permanent combined-arms team could be found was indeed the division; below that level, only battle groups *(Kampfgruppen)*, organized on an ad hoc basis for the accomplishment of a specific mission, were formed. As a result, there was limited opportunity for the commanders and soldiers of these different units to become accustomed to working together. (The temporary and ad hoc nature of these battle groups would have a seriously negative effect on the conduct of many German operations as World War II continued, as will become evident later.)

If the enemy had well-prepared positions around which it was impossible to maneuver, these were to be battered and broken by artillery barrage and then assaulted by tank-led infantry formations until a penetration had been achieved. The armored element would then storm through and rampage behind enemy lines, and the infantry would mop up remaining pockets of enemy resistance with the help of artillery.

In the event the enemy had not yet formed a solid, coherent defense (again, the need for thorough reconnaissance can be seen here), then the initial attacks were to be made by armored and mechanized infantry elements, allowing a rapid breakthrough and subsequent pursuit, with the infantry echelons following in the van for the conduct of their unenviable but inevitable mopping up tasks.[29]

If the enemy was routed, the German pursuit maintained contact with the retreating enemy units with armored or armored reconnaissance elements so as to keep him from halting, consolidating, or catching his breath. More armored and motorized infantry formations followed as quickly as possible, deployed in depth, with the forward elements of even these units constantly attacking the backpedaling enemy. Whatever enemy forces remained were bypassed, to be destroyed later by those friendly echelons constituting the "depth" of the pursuit effort.[30]

This concept of pursuit is Clausewitzian in every sense. In *Vom Kriege,* Clausewitz addresses the pursuit of retreating forces at length, and makes clear that only a violent, prolonged, and tenacious pursuit will suffice, "thereby speeding up the enemy's retreat and promoting his disintegration."[31] Few more stark examples of Clausewitz's final argument can be found: If the enemy's forces "disintegrate," then his subjugation to the will of the victor can only quickly follow.

The Germans' experiences during the war served to lessen their prewar and early war tendency toward spectacular, slashing thrusts. After 1940, faced by enemies who did not lose their will to fight when cut off or bypassed by German armor, their tactics became more conservative. The authoritative compendium of American and other Allied experience and intelligence, the *Handbook on German Military Forces,* published by the U.S. War Department in March 1945, states:

> The original German *Blitzkrieg* tactics were based on the belief in the irresistible power of tank formations operating independently with the support of dive-bombers. Considerable modifications have taken place in this theory over the past few years. At the present time, the offensive tactics of the Germans are less spectacularly bold than they were in 1939, *but the fundamental theory behind them has changed remarkably little* [emphasis added], though in their armored tactics they stress more tank-infantry coordination since unlimited air support is no longer at their command.[32]

Ironically, although both Clausewitz and his followers preferred the attack, Clausewitz saw the defense as the stronger form of warfare.

If successful, the attack allowed active pursuit of the destruction of the enemy's forces on friendly terms, and facilitated conquest and the enhancement of the ability to wage war by the capture of enemy supplies, equipment, et cetera. The defense, on the other hand, had a "passive purpose": to preserve what was already possessed.

Yet Clausewitz insisted that "the defensive form of warfare is intrinsically stronger than the offensive," for numerous reasons.[33] This concept, as he himself grandiloquently points out in *Vom Kriege,* is one of the least understood of all his dicta; even Clausewitz believed that the depth of intellectual comprehension required to grasp this concept is beyond many superficial readers of his work.

Conduct of the defense allows the commander to choose terrain and thereby make optimal use of whatever is available. It turns the passage of time to greatest advantage as defenses are prepared in greater and greater depth and complexity. The defense allows orchestration of the counterattack at the moment when the enemy's thrust has been parried, when he has taken unforeseen casualties, and when he is, logically, least prepared for a defense of his own. The defense is, in the final analysis, stronger because it facilitates the destruction of the enemy's forces while providing maximum opportunity for both protecting friendly forces and launching an attack under the best possible circumstances.

Accordingly, German doctrine called for the organization of defenses in great depth. The Germans organized the battlefield into three areas: the advanced position, the combat outposts, and the main battle line.

Reconnaissance elements usually occupied the advanced position about five thousand to seven thousand meters forward of the main battle line, with the triple mission of gaining intelligence (information about the enemy's attacking strength, intent, direction of advance, et cetera), delaying the enemy's progress (though not halting it at the expense of serious loss to friendly units), and deceiving the enemy as to the location of the main line of resistance. To these ends, advanced positions were usually placed on hilltops, ridges, or at crossroads, where reconnaissance elements were afforded optimal fields of fire and observation. From these locations, German forces in the advanced position could observe and report enemy activities, call for and adjust artillery fires, and engage attackers with antitank weapons and machine guns at maximum ranges before withdrawing along preselected covered and concealed routes to the protection of the main battle line.[34]

Infantry, tank, and antitank units occupied the combat outposts, usually located two thousand to five thousand meters forward of the main battle line. These elements had the mission of breaking up the enemy's attack before it struck the main battle line, and so were dug in and concealed to the greatest extent possible. Here the mission also entailed deception, trying to make the enemy believe he had encountered the main defensive belt so he would deploy his units on line for the final assault—thus dissipating his momentum long before he hit the strongest part of the friendly defenses. The troops occupying the combat outposts would then fall back under the cover of friendly artillery fire, assemble behind the main line of resistance, and prepare to counterattack.[35]

At the main battle line, all rearward movement of friendly forces ceased and positions were held at all costs. Positions were organized in depth with interlocking fields of fire designed to halt the enemy as far forward as possible. Obstacles such as barbed wire, land mines, and antitank ditches were employed both to impede the enemy's advance and to channel his forces into areas where maximum friendly fires could be brought to bear from well-protected, entrenched, and camouflaged positions. When the enemy had dashed his last reserves against this line and begun to fall back in bloody disarray, the counterattack would be launched, perhaps directly into the pursuit mode, to complete the destruction of his forces.[36] For this purpose, it was critical to have a designated reserve (in the event that the combat outposts had been rendered ineffective or had been eliminated altogether), and that this reserve be positioned so that a swift and effective counterattack could be launched.

As the war continued, German defensive practices changed, even if their *doctrine* did not. Greater reliance was placed on linear "passive" defenses and, frequently, only scaled-down counterattacks were launched. Like the changes to offensive doctrine, this alteration of original prewar concepts was due largely to wartime exigencies. As the 1945 *Handbook on German Military Forces* put it:

At present more emphasis is placed on the construction of defensive positions, and counterattacks are frequently local in character. It is most likely that this passive type of defense is only an expedient due to German shortages of mobile equipment and manpower.[37]

In mountainous regions, German doctrine called for maximum use of reverse-slope defenses—those prepared on the side of hills away from the approaching enemy. Such positions afforded the greatest amount of protection and allowed far better concealment as the foe advanced. They also allowed engagement of the enemy from the flanks and rear as he passed by unaware, and thus allowed greater damage to be inflicted.[38] The disadvantage of such positions, of course, is that they can be surrounded and cut off if the enemy advances one terrain feature beyond them, so it was imperative that this be prevented by a stout, unyielding defense.

Clausewitz issued stern warnings about the use of mountainous areas in the defense. He claimed that such regions constituted excellent positions for the conduct of delaying actions, or *relative defense,* because they slowed the enemy, disorganized him, channelized his attacks, diminished his troops' morale, and provided superb opportunities for inflicting tremendous damage on his forces. At the same time, as in all defensive activities, friendly forces would be able to preselect and use routes of withdrawal and subsequent defensive positions.

Clausewitz warned against the use of these regions for what he called absolute defense. It logically followed, Clausewitz pointed out, that movement in mountains for the defender is just as difficult as for the attacker, and that "therefore the defender has a clear advantage so long as movement is only up to the attacker; the advantage vanishes as soon as the defender has to move as well."[39] Such movements, essential for the maintenance of the greater strength of the defense, would include not so much the preplanned, unresisted withdrawal of advanced positions or combat outposts, but rather the execution of counterattacks and, in the event of a rupture in the main battle line, the withdrawal of the greater part of the friendly forces. In other words, mountainous terrain could turn against the unsuccessful defender with the same disadvantages it presented to the attacker.

The conduct of a delaying action was not only a classically Clausewitzian use of mountainous terrain, but was inherently easier to execute in such areas, given German doctrine for these maneuvers. Delays enabled units to disengage from the enemy, move to the rear, and establish a defensive position before the enemy could effectively pursue and annihilate them. To accomplish this, lines of resistance were designated to coordinate the orderly movement of units to the rear.

Rear-guard units were to take maximum advantage of long-range machine-gun, mortar, and artillery fires to delay the enemy advance, and obstacles such as minefields and roadblocks were to be integrated into the scheme of maneuver to allow delaying units the maximum time possible to establish new defensive positions before the arrival of the pursuing enemy.[40] Clearly, the conduct of such operations would be enhanced in mountainous terrain, where limited avenues of advance could be easily blocked by small forces, and artillery fires could be effectively adjusted from higher elevations.

German Army Organization

At the time that hostilities commenced in 1939, the army was organized at the operational level in a fairly simple and straightforward manner. As pointed out earlier in this chapter, the lowest echelon at which the various branches (that is, armor, artillery, infantry, and engineers) were organized together on a permanent basis was the division. There were a few standardized types of divisions, and at the outset, most German divisions were uniformly equipped, trained, and organized. Such uniformity allowed commanders to understand the capabilities of subordinate echelons and enabled them to plan appropriately for their operational and tactical employment.

In 1939, there were basically six types of divisions: the infantry division *(Infanteriedivision),* the armored division *(Panzerdivision),* the motorized infantry division *(Infanterie Motorisiertesdivision),* the mountain infantry division *(Gebirgsdivision),* the cavalry division *(Kavalleriedivision),* and the light division *(Jägerdivision).* Additionally, the Luftwaffe fielded parachute infantry divisions *(Fallschirmjägerdivisions).*

An infantry division was organized with three infantry regiments of three battalions each, and totaled about 9,750 men in these regiments. (See Figure 1.) The regiments were supported by three battalions of horse- or truck-drawn light artillery, equipped at full strength with thirty-six 105mm howitzers each, and by a battalion of medium artillery equipped with eight 150mm howitzers and four 105mm rifles; the divisional artillery regiment carried a total of 2,500 men on its personnel rolls at full strength. No tanks, tank destroyers, or assault guns were organic to this type of division, but such units could be attached according to the requirements of a given situation. (The antitank battalion was equipped with towed antitank guns.) There were about

FIGURE 1
GERMAN INFANTRY DIVISION

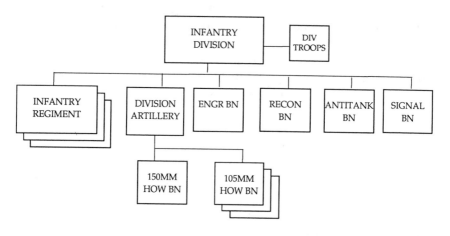

5,000 more men manning the division armored reconnaissance battalion and the antitank battalion, as well as support troops, including signal, engineer, quartermaster, military police units, and the like.[41]

With three major subordinate maneuver units (infantry regiments), each possessing three of its own maneuver units (infantry battalions), the commander of an infantry division had considerable flexibility when planning for the deployment of his troops. When conducting a penetration and breakthrough attack, for example, he could choose to weight his main effort at the *Schwerpunkt* with two regiments while conducting a limited objective attack with his remaining regiment. In the defense, he could defend his assigned terrain with two regiments while keeping one in reserve for a counterattack. Each of the regimental commanders could then choose to defend their assigned sectors with two battalions, while holding one in reserve for their own counterattacks.

The armored division was organized with a tank regiment of two tank battalions (about 1,700 men total) and with two mobile infantry regiments, one motorized and one mechanized, each with about 2,200 men. (See Figure 2.) Each tank battalion had about fifty tanks, which

FIGURE 2
PANZER DIVISION

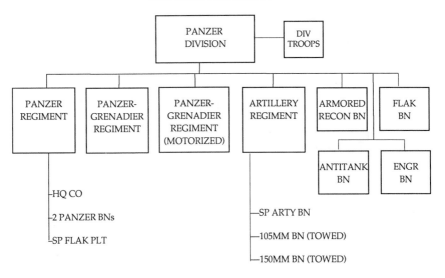

by 1944 would have been either *Pzkw IVs* or the more mobile and better-armed *Panthers*. These maneuver elements were supported by an armored artillery regiment (with about 1,600 men) made up of one battalion of twelve truck-drawn 105mm howitzers, one battalion of twelve self-propelled 105mm howitzers, one battalion of truck-drawn 150mm howitzers and six additional self-propelled 150mm howitzers, and one battalion of towed 170mm heavy guns. The divisional armored reconnaissance, antitank, and engineer battalions, all of which were mobile due to the presence of motorized and/or armored transportation assets, and divisional support troops made up the remainder of the division's roughly 13,500 soldiers.

In the attack, these tank formations would be accompanied by mechanized infantry in their own armored personnel carriers. These units would be followed by truck-borne motorized infantry who would consolidate on objectives seized by the armored echelons, or who could begin the task of mopping up bypassed enemy pockets of resistance.

For operations in mountainous terrain, such as that found in southern Germany and numerous other parts of Europe, the Germans raised a number of mountain divisions. (See Figure 3.) Generally, such orga-

FIGURE 3
GERMAN MOUNTAIN DIVISION

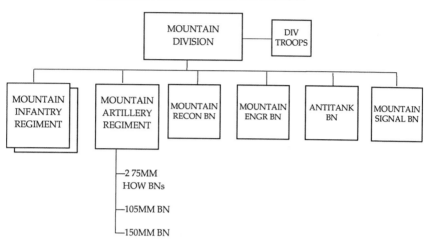

nizations' maneuver elements included only two infantry regiments, because mountain warfare did not call for the kind of maneuver required of conventional units. The equipment used was specially tailored to mountain environments, as typified by the lighter artillery found in the mountain artillery regiment.

The other types of divisions were similarly organized for optimal flexibility; details of their organizations are not covered, because these types did not participate significantly in the Vosges in 1944–45.

Although division organizations were, indeed, fairly flexible and manageable, even from the beginning there were some inconsistencies of organization and purpose that portended an ominous later trend. For example, the light divisions never had clearly defined organizations. In 1939, these were motorized divisions with some armored battalions included, but by 1940, these divisions became *Panzer* divisions. In 1941, four infantry divisions were redesignated as light divisions when they received motorized transport, and these units were in turn eventually converted to *Panzergrenadier* divisions.[42] In fact, after 1941, many of the motorized infantry divisions received larger quantities of armored troop carriers (of a wide variety of types) and these were subsequently renamed *Panzergrenadier* divisions as well. (See Figure 4.)

FIGURE 4
PANZERGRENADIER DIVISION

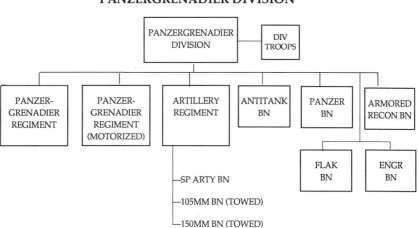

Each type of division differed in organization, equipment, and purpose, but through uniform organization and equipment within a type, each could be employed to fulfill a clearly understood doctrinal requirement. In the attack, for example, a *Panzer* division would lead a flanking attack and, followed by *Panzergrenadier* formations, would continue to roll up an enemy's flank, while remaining pockets of enemy resistance (if any) would be engaged and destroyed by more slowly moving infantry divisions. Since each division was uniformly organized and had been similarly trained, such a maneuver could be carried out by any division in a universally understood manner. The flexibility thus enjoyed by German operational-level commanders was great, and the friction resulting from misunderstandings or miscalculations of unit abilities or mission requirements was low.

As the war continued, the different types of German divisions proliferated. By 1942, the Waffen SS began fielding divisions that generally received the best equipment and more of it than army formations—despite the reality that many of their leaders were not trained to the same standards of tactical proficiency as those of the army.[43] Waffen SS divisions also were frequently oversized; that is, their organizational structures included elements such as assault gun battalions and rocket launcher battalions, which the army equivalents simply did not possess.[44] This not only prompted resentment among army officers, but also contributed in other ways to the increasingly strained relations between the army and the SS at all levels. Frequently, due in part to the considerably different ideological, political, and social backgrounds of the SS and Wehrmacht officer corps and in part to the differentials in training (particularly of the officers), quarrels arose between commanders of adjacent army and SS units—all adding to totally unnecessary friction on the battlefield.[45]

By 1944, much of the French coast was being guarded by yet another new type of division, namely the Coastal Defense division *(Küstenverteidigungsdivision)*. Such units had differing organizations but were largely manned by older troops, convalescing wounded, or somehow otherwise physically disabled soldiers of little value in a field environment. The units' transport capacity for their two fortress infantry regiments (often organized into separate battalions without a real regimental unity) instead of the usual three infantry regiments was practically nil, since they were intended for the static defense of Festung Europa, thus seriously limiting their operational utility. Still, they were equipped with larger quantities of machine guns and other heavy weapons, so their effectiveness in the defense could be considerable under certain circumstances, even away from the coast.

By September 1944, OKW had decided to stop replenishing certain badly mauled infantry divisions and to instead replace them altogether with new, differently organized and equipped formations called *Volksgrenadier* divisions. (See Figures 5 and 6.) Although these new units usually retained the number and, when appropriate, the name of previous divisions, their three infantry regiments had only two battalions each. Some of these divisions had two infantry regiments of three battalions each. Additionally, they had diminished reconnaissance capabilities (a *Füsilier* company with bicycles and perhaps a few armored cars replaced the half-track and heavy armored car–equipped reconnaissance battalions of the 1939-pattern divisions) and reduced (by more than 30 percent) artillery assets. These *Volksgrenadier* divisions eventually numbered fifty in all, and usually trained together for only about ten weeks before being deployed to the front.[46]

In an attempt to compensate for the reduced numbers of combat troops in these divisions, *Volksgrenadiers* were supplied with higher proportions of automatic weapons such as submachine guns and machine guns;

FIGURE 5
VOLKSGRENADIER DIVISION (TYPE I)

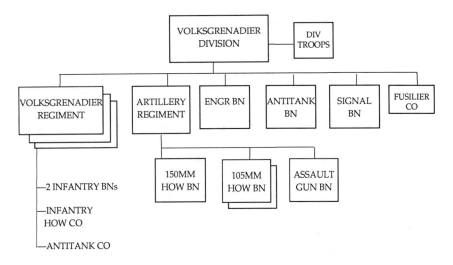

FIGURE 6
VOLKSGRENADIER DIVISION (TYPE II)

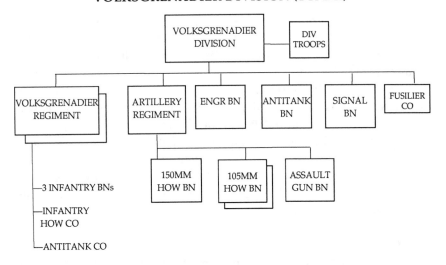

they were also frequently supported by corps-level *Nebelwerfer* units firing multibarreled rocket launchers, which, although not as accurate as conventional artillery, nevertheless delivered an extremely high volume of high-explosive fires.

Still, although these fortress and *Volksgrenadier* divisions' organizations were designed to make up in firepower what they lacked in manpower, their mobility and tactical utility at the operational level were hampered by lack of training and the almost total absence of organic transportation assets. Further, by reducing the number of infantry regiments to two (or the number of battalions within three regiments to two), the ability of such units to mount the counterattacks called for by doctrine and by necessity became severely limited. By opting for such expedient solutions to strategic problems, OKW was practically forcing its field commanders to rely on what Clausewitz pointed out as the stronger but less preferable mode of operations—the defense. As mobility, maneuverability, and tactical options became increasingly limited by the introduction of new types of divisions, it became increasingly difficult for commanders to estimate the capabilities of these units. Misunderstandings of such capabilities could only be furthered by the terse, mission-type orders favored by the Germans. As the multitude of new types of units increased, so also would the need for specificity of instruction. Either way, the structure of the German military organization did not fit with its decentralized system of tactical orders.

Although the production of armaments such as armored vehicles actually grew until the middle of 1944, according to Albert Speer,[47] the number of experienced tankers was vastly reduced by the disastrous (for the Germans) battle of the Falaise pocket. To compensate for these losses, the Germans created separate *Panzer* brigades—an altogether new size and level of organization. A *Panzer* brigade was smaller than a division but larger and better supported than a regiment. But there was no established doctrine for the employment of such formations, nor was there any operational experience upon which to draw for their use. As with the other organizational changes initiated in 1944, the result was a loss of operational flexibility and increased friction in battle.[48]

German Army Training

Before the continuous ground combat phases of World War II in Europe were initiated by the Germans with the execution of Operation Barbarossa in June 1941, the organization and training of the soldiers and officers of combat formations followed a logical and highly effective pattern. Units were raised with recruits and, so far as possible, cadre, from discrete geographical areas of Germany, trained sequentially from individual skill instruction through corps-level maneuvers, and then committed to battle. This ensured not only a high level of technical and tactical proficiency, but also created a bond of camaraderie and trust between the officers, noncommissioned officers, and lower enlisted men that would pay great dividends of cohesion under the Sturm und Drang of battle conditions.[49]

Typically, in peacetime, German regiments trained their own recruits during a sixteen-week period each year. When World War II began, this obviously became impractical, but each regiment maintained its own training battalion at the regimental home depot, and the soldiers of each regiment were, as much as practicable, drawn from the same geographical area within Germany. The positive impact of such a system was considerable, particularly in a country where geographical origin corresponded so directly to ethnicity and religious background. Additionally, such a system ensured that each soldier felt that he was a member of his regiment from the outset, with all of the associated positive effects on cohesion.[50]

As the war developed and lasted much longer than originally envisioned, however, the German replacement system required radical changes to keep up with the demands of attrition. After the autumn of 1942, the training of replacements for particular regiments was no longer performed by those regiments' respective training battalions. Beginning at this time, the best that could be hoped for was that a training battalion from a particular military region *(Wehrkreis)* would be able to supply troops as replacements for several regiments from the same geographical area. The breakdown here is obvious, and, as a result, the cohesion derived from a feeling of belonging to a specific unit from the outset of a soldier's military service was diminished if not altogether lost.[51]

Without a coherent strategy for mobilization, the German manpower replacement system developed in an even more erratic manner as the war progressed. By 1944, as the quantity of trained pilots and available fuel waned, Luftwaffe ground support personnel were organized into infantry battalions, regiments, and even divisions for combat deployment to the fighting front. Often, these units had received scant training in infantry combat techniques.[52] As the German surface fleet declined drastically in usefulness and size, naval ratings were also often pressed into combat as individual or small-unit replacements in army formations—with practically all of the problems of training, conditioning, and cohesion one might expect from such a policy.

As the Anglo-American Allies prepared for the invasion of France and the Soviets pressed ever closer to Germany's frontiers, even more pronounced changes to the German manpower and replacement system were instituted. By the time of the Normandy invasion in June 1944, there were a considerable number of "ethnic German" *(Volksdeutsche)* troops serving in German army units. What exactly constituted ethnic "Germanness" is difficult to ascertain, for such a designation apparently was derived from the inconsistent and often bizarre National Socialist theories of race. At the outset of the war, Austrians and Sudetenlanders (ethnic Germans from western Czechoslovakia, annexed in September 1938) were included in units raised in the traditional way in the newly created *Wehrkreise XVII* and *XVIII* (Austria) and *Wehrkreis Böhmen* (western Czechoslovakia). By the time the Allies invaded western Europe, Nazi doctrine had been expanded or reinterpreted to include Alsatians and non-Sudeten Czechs as ethnic Germans eligible for duty in army *(Heer)* combat formations.

Oddly, the Waffen SS had even more liberal standards. By 1944, the ranks of the Waffen SS included whole divisions of Albanians, Ustachi Croats, Poles, Ukrainians, Dutch, Danish, Belgian, and other types previously (and, undoubtedly still, behind their backs) classified as *Untermenschen* (subhuman). Of course, these units were usually officered by Germans and were employed, as much as possible, against the most appropriate enemies. For example, the Croatian divisions were employed in antipartisan roles against Tito's Communist guerrillas in Yugoslavia; the Dutch, Danish, and Belgian units, recruited heavily from particularly anti-Communist sectors of the political right, were sent to the eastern front; and the Ukrainian and other Russian troops (often turncoat prisoners) usually fought in the west.[53]

The degree of ferocity with which such ethnic German units fought—in the west, anyway—was not particularly high, and often resulted in the wholesale or nearly wholesale surrender of such organizations. Equipment furnished to such units was practically thrown away in these cases. In situations involving the amalgamation of *Volksdeutsche* replacement troops with bona fide German *(Reichsdeutsche)* soldiers, or in cases of ethnic German units being brigaded together with all-German outfits, differing language, customs, and traditions played havoc with cohesion. What a far cry from the pre- and early war situations of ethnic and regimental homogeneity!

In addition to these variations from prewar norms, other replacement and manpower practices were adopted by the autumn of 1944 that only added to the troubles of the German army. In addition to the arrangement by which a single training battalion supported several regiments with replacements, by this late stage in the war, often the training units themselves were committed as tactical fighting entities. This situation left the supported units without a training and replacement base, and from that point on, there was only the most tentative, if any, relationship between field units and the organizations providing them with replacements.

Worse, in the fall of 1944 the German army instituted a system of straggler control that effectively destroyed unit cohesion altogether. Military police *(Feldgendarmerie)* operated straggler control points at which members of shattered units, troops who had been cut off or otherwise lost touch with their parent organizations, and other stragglers were herded together, placed under the command of a lieutenant or captain, and sent as a "unit" to the front. Obviously, this deprived some units of their returning troops; placed together soldiers of no particular region, unit, or even skills or ranks; and allowed no time for the bonding process of training so valuable and necessary for unit success on the battlefield. The effects this policy had on morale and cohesion were devastating, as will be observed later.

Summary of German Army Doctrine, Organization, and Training by Late 1944

German tactical and operational doctrine was theoretically sound and battle proven, but this doctrine was not always reflected by the organization of army units for combat by 1944. For a variety of reasons, many new types of units were introduced by late 1944, each with varying organizations and types of equipment. Many of them were unsuited for the execution of doctrinal tactical or operational maneuvers, and this only added to the Clausewitzian friction always present in war. Further, the growing disparity between Waffen SS and army units caused counterproductive rivalries that detracted from the common effort against the Anglo-American Allies and the Soviets.

By late 1944, these units, already handicapped by doctrinal and organizational inconsistencies, were often manned by ill-trained and sometimes unmotivated soldiers. In attempting to deal with the rapidly worsening battlefield situation, the German army adopted measures that often redounded to its disadvantage. The failure to prepare a replacement system that could adequately cope with the demands of a protracted, high-intensity conflict resulted in the adoption of increasingly counterproductive stopgap measures. The most brilliant of tactics and operational techniques are useless if they are not carried out by formations suited to the accomplishment of the required tasks; by late 1944, the German army in the west was suited neither by organization nor by personnel and training for the execution of its mission to hold back the Allies from the gates of Germany.

THE AMERICANS

U.S. Army Tactical and Operational Doctrine in Late 1944

The primary document prescribing tactical and operational doctrine for the U.S. Army in late 1944 was *FM 100-5, Operations,* which was revised and updated in 1941 and again in mid-1944. The operational and tactical tenets and teachings of this manual were supplemented by a variety of others, the most important of which for the purposes of this study was *FM 100-15, Field Service Regulations for Larger Units.* Additions and corollary practical hints were communicated to field commanders in training and in combat from July 1944 on through the distribution of a series of circulars known as "Battle Experiences." These publications consisted of dos and don'ts contributed by officers and soldiers in combat against the Germans and edited for publication by officers at SHAEF. The published American tactical and operational doctrine was so similar to the German army's that it shared its Clausewitzian validity almost point for point.

Like that of the Germans, American doctrine placed heavy emphasis on reconnaissance. United States doctrine also classified reconnaissance operations into three categories, namely distant, close, and battle; these corresponded in their essentials to the Germans' categories of operational, tactical, and battle reconnaissance.[54] As with that of their German foes, the Americans' doctrine called for "constant and intensive" reconnaissance efforts conducted by forces heavily enough equipped to allow protection and exploitation of the situation.[55] To reduce friction, the reports of these units, as well as other intelligence gathered from sources such as prisoners of war, signal intercepts, and aerial reconnaissance, among others, were collated, analyzed, and distributed as quickly as possible.[56]

Like German doctrine, American doctrine stressed independence of action and the use of initiative at all levels. Indeed, the wording of *FM 100-5* on this point is extremely close to that of the *Truppenführung* manual. Orders should be "clear and concise" and should not "trespass upon the province of a subordinate."[57] Further,

> Orders must be as clear and explicit and as brief as is consistent with clarity. Short sentences are easily understood. *Clarity is more important than technique.* The more urgent the situation, the greater is the need for conciseness in the order. Any statement of reasons for measures adopted should be limited to what is necessary to obtain intelligent cooperation from subordinates. Detailed instructions for a variety of contingencies, or prescriptions that are a matter of training, do not inspire confidence and have no place in an order.[58]

To stress the importance of initiative, *FM 100-5* went on to emphasize that subordinates' orders should be original and not mere parrotings of their superiors' orders.[59] Indeed, in the words of this manual,

> In spite of the advances of technology, the worth of the individual man is still decisive. The open order of combat accentuates his importance. Every individual must be trained to exploit a situation with energy and boldness and must be imbued with the idea that success will depend upon his initiative and action.[60]

Given the experiences of previous generations of the U.S. Army in the years of conflict on the western frontier and in the mountainous jungles of the Philippine archipelago, it should not be surprising that initiative was so highly prized. Indeed, an army operating over the vast distances of the western plains and in the densely vegetated, compartmentalized terrain of the Philippines had to develop a tradition of individual thought and action in order to succeed. As pointed out in *FM 100-5,* such attributes were ideal for success in the fast-paced environment of modern battle as well.

The recommended format for operations orders under U.S. doctrine was extremely close to that of the Germans. Although not specified in *FM 100-5,* it was outlined in *FM 101-5, Staff Organization and Operations,* and consisted of the following paragraphs: "Situation," which described the friendly and enemy units that could have an impact on the impending operation, as well as the weather and the terrain and their possible effects; "Mission," in which the mission of the whole unit was clearly and succinctly stated; "Execution," which included the overall concept of the operation and the missions (but not detailed instructions) for the subordinate echelons; "Service Support," which delineated logistical responsibilities; and "Command and Signal," which gave information concerning locations of headquarters and communications instructions.[61]

As in German doctrine, the preferred mode of wartime operations was the offensive. *FM 100-5* cites essentially the same justifications as the *Truppenführung* manual: decisiveness, maintenance of initiative, et cetera.[62] Unlike the German classification of such maneuvers, however, the U.S. Army identified only two types of attacks, namely, envelopments and penetrations[63] (although there were two distinct types of envelopments specified, that is, turning movements and double envelopments). In each type of operation, attacking troops would be divided into two or more groups. One of these groups would constitute the main attack, into which the "greatest possible offensive power is concentrated to bring about a decision."[64] The other group, or groups, conducted secondary attacks designed to "render maximum assistance to the main attack."[65] This simplified classification may have allowed greater flexibility in the formulation of plans for offensive action, but basically paralleled German doctrine.

Main attacks were to be characterized by narrow zones of attack; heavy fire support from artillery, tanks, and aviation assets; and deep echelonment of reserves. Such attacks were made to secure terrain objectives that facilitated the destruction of hostile forces.[66] As with German doctrine, attacks were to be made by combined-arms units, and thorough coordination between attacking echelons was stressed.[67] Although the importance of firepower was emphasized, the decisive factor contributing to the success of any attack was the "intelligent, energetic, and coordinated execution" of such assaults.

Envelopments involved a secondary attack against the enemy's front to prevent reactive maneuver, and a main effort directed against the flank or rear of the enemy's forces.[68] One type, the turning movement, sought to hold the enemy with a supporting attack and to maneuver around a hostile flank with the intent to seize a vital objective in the enemy's rear.[69] This tactic was very similar to the Germans' envelopment. The other type of envelopment that was specified in *FM 100-5* was the double envelopment, which sought to simultaneously envelop both enemy flanks while preventing enemy reaction by the execution of a supporting attack.[70] The successful conduct of such an attack required a considerable superiority of combat power, and was similar in concept to the Germans' encirclement.

The other basic type of attack described in *FM 100-5* was the penetration. The objective of a penetration was the "complete rupture of the enemy's dispositions," and the subsequent roll up of the enemy's lines.[71] Again, the character of such operations was clearly almost identical to the Germans' equivalent.

Interestingly, American doctrine did not call for frontal attacks, except when penetrations were usually to be made from the frontal aspect of enemy positions. Wing attacks and flank attacks also received no recognition in the American manual; after all, a wing attack is only a penetration through the extreme end of an enemy line, designed to facilitate a subsequent envelopment. A flank attack is nothing more than an envelopment that does not require a limited objective attack to prevent enemy reactive maneuver. Although the American lexicon of attacks may seem, at first glance, more limited than that of the Germans, it is, in fact, only less complicated.

If friendly attacks resulted in the enemy's withdrawal, American doctrine called for the conduct of pursuit operations. Such operations required the exertion of constant, direct pressure on retreating enemy units while highly mobile, combined-arms teams attempted to envelop them and cut their line of retreat. Annihilation of fleeing enemy forces was the goal, just as it was in German doctrine.[72]

The American doctrinal concept of the defense also closely resembled that of their German foes. The Americans organized their defenses in depth, and their doctrine called for responsive, violent counterattack.

The defense sector was organized into four areas: the covering force area, the outpost line, the main line of resistance (MLR), and the reserve area.[73]

The mission of the units in the covering force area was to delay the attacking enemy, deny him forward artillery observation, and permit the strengthening of the defenses of the other friendly defensive echelons. After the covering force fell back, the mission of the units on the outpost line was not only to delay the enemy, but impede his advance in such a way that he would be deceived into thinking he had found the MLR. This would hopefully cause the attacker to deploy his units for the assault and thus dissipate the greatest force of his attack before it reached the main defenses.[74]

After completing their mission, units on the outpost line would retire to the main line of resistance to occupy reserve positions or, possibly, act as part of the defense. Under no circumstances were the positions along the MLR to be abandoned without permission from higher headquarters: Defense required that battle positions be "held at all costs."[75] Positions on this "line" (*FM 100-5* was very careful to point out that the MLR was only a rough line, and really consisted of positions at irregular intervals in some depth) were to be sited to assure interlocking fields of fire, mutual observation, and mutual support in every way. Indirect fires were to be carefully coordinated to ensure maximum destruction of enemy forces in front of the MLR.[76]

The units occupying the reserve area were to conduct counterattacks "without delay, on the initiative of the local commander."[77] Since combined-arms operations were so stressed, it was expected that these reserves would conduct their counterattack supported by tanks and other mechanized vehicles. Interestingly, *FM 100-5* emphasized that mechanized forces were not suited to the defense of positions, but rather to the role of counterattack.[78] Holding ground remained a strictly dismounted infantry affair.

Overall, the American concept of defense closely resembled that of the Germans; the precepts of Clausewitz were held to as closely as they were in offensive doctrine.

U.S. Army Organization

Although U.S. Army doctrine closely resembled that of the Germans, U.S. Army organization differed in several key respects. Unlike the

Germans, who had many different divisional organizations, the Americans essentially developed only three, and stayed with them throughout the war.[79] This uniformity eased supply and other logistical support problems, and, most importantly, diminished the friction in command and tactics so prevalent on the German side. For an American corps commander and his staff, what they saw was what they got, and they knew that each of their divisions and subordinate elements would be fully capable of executing doctrinal requirements. Of course, the quality of leadership and amount of experience always introduced variables, but that was as true for the Germans as it was for the Americans.

The three types of divisions disposed by the Americans were the infantry division, the armored division, and the airborne division. Since no airborne divisions took part in the Vosges campaign, only the organization of the first two will be addressed here.

The U.S. Army infantry division was organized in a fashion somewhat similar to that of the Germans' early-war organizations. (See Figure 7.) The maneuver elements of the infantry division consisted of three infantry regiments, each with three infantry battalions. This allowed the "two-up, one-back" arrangement so conducive to the execution of both offensive and defensive doctrine. For example, in the attack, two regiments could conduct the main effort while one conducted a secondary attack; in the defense, two regiments could defend forward while one regiment remained in reserve to counterattack. These regiments of approximately 3,300 men each were supported by three battalions of 105mm howitzers with twelve guns each, and by one twelve-gun battalion of 155mm howitzers; the total authorized personnel strength of the "division artillery," as these four battalions and their ancillary support group were called, was 2,230.[80] A total of 2,123 troops made up the remainder of the division, including combat support troops such as engineers, armored reconnaissance, and signal units, as well as service support units such as quartermaster, ordnance (maintenance), and other logistical groups.[81] No tanks or tank destroyers were organic to a U.S. Army infantry division, but there were habitual relationships developed that assured combined-arms operations.

These relationships were prescribed in *FM 100-5,* which called for the formation of task forces known as regimental combat teams, or RCTs. (See Figure 8.) The U.S. Army adhered to a system of pooling of assets such as tank battalions, tank destroyer battalions, heavy artillery

FIGURE 7
U.S. INFANTRY DIVISION

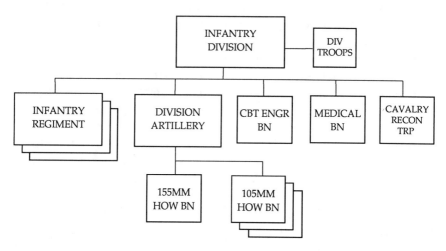

battalions (155mm rifles, 8-inch howitzers, 8-inch rifles, and 240mm howitzers), and specialized engineer units at the corps and even field army level. Supposedly, these units would be assigned on an as-needed basis to infantry divisions in combat, and then released and reassigned upon completion of a particular mission for which their presence had been required. By mid-1944, it was common to assign particular tank and tank destroyer battalions to a specific division for the duration of combat, however, because it was recognized that combined-arms operations were always superior to operations without such benefit. Furthermore, a habitual working relationship encouraged the development of trust, mutual understanding, and cohesion—which paid off on the battlefield.

Typically, an RCT would include a company of tanks (M4-series Shermans), a company of tank destroyers (these could be M18 Hellcats, M10 Wolverines, or M36 Sluggers, all of which were designed to carry a heavier gun than a Sherman at the expense of a degree of armor protection), a company from the divisional combat engineer battalion, and a battalion of 105mm howitzers from the division artillery. With the possible exception of the tank and tank destroyer units, all of these

FIGURE 8
REGIMENTAL COMBAT TEAM

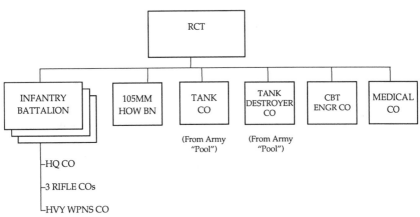

component outfits had trained together extensively in the United States prior to deployment, and a high degree of cohesion and cooperation was thus attained.[82] The RCT system guaranteed that the combined-arms operations so heavily emphasized in the tactical and operational doctrine of the day would be carried out regularly. Although American doctrine also allowed the formation of battalion task forces, this practice of building semipermanent RCTs provides a marked contrast to the German system of temporary, ad hoc *Kampfgruppen,* established and dismantled on a strictly situational basis.

The post-1942 U.S. armored division provided another exceptional contrast to the German organization of units for combat. (See Figure 9.) Each armored division consisted of three "combat commands," designated Combat Command A, Combat Command B, and Combat Command R, for "reserve." (See Figure 10.) These divisions, the personnel strength of which totaled roughly eleven thousand soldiers, were superbly organized for the conduct of mobile, combined-arms warfare. Organic to each of these combat commands was a tank battalion (with three companies of M4 mediums and a company of M5 light tanks for reconnaissance), an armored infantry battalion (with three rifle companies mounted in

FIGURE 9
U.S. ARMORED DIVISION (1943–45)

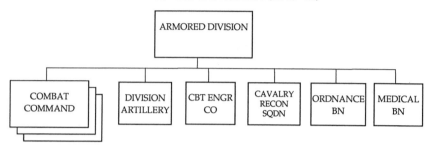

FIGURE 10
COMBAT COMMAND

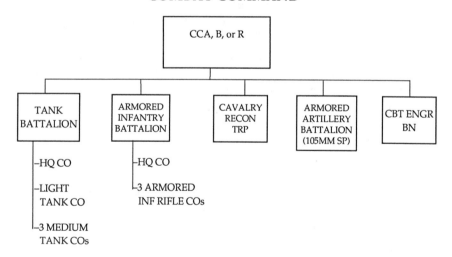

M3-series half-tracks to enable them to keep up with the tanks), an armored medium artillery battalion (with M7 self-propelled 105mm howitzers, which were really nothing more than M4 chassis carrying the standard M1 105mm howitzer, thus easing the logistics and maintenance requirements), and a mechanized cavalry reconnaissance troop with M8 armored cars and M5 light tanks. Additionally, an armored combat engineer company was usually attached to facilitate mobility; these troops were also carried into combat in armored half-tracks. Clearly, this organization, marked by complete mobility and armored protection for all combat units, surpassed anything established by the German army during World War II.

Simplicity—of command, supply, and maneuver—was characteristic of American organization for combat in 1944. Units were identically organized and equipped to achieve a considerably greater capacity for combined-arms warfare than their German counterparts. In addition, the cohesion inculcated by the American system of regimental combat teams in infantry divisions and combat commands in armored divisions far exceeded that of opposing German formations.

U.S. Army Training

Unlike the Germans, whose training system changed considerably during the course of the war, the U.S. system was largely fixed in 1941 with the introduction of the Mobilization Training Plan (MTP) by Army General Headquarters (GHQ). Although the quantity and number of types of divisions to be created diminished as the war progressed, the basic plan for the activation, training, and deployment of divisions remained unchanged throughout the war.

The MTP called for the activation of infantry divisions from three sources: the Regular Army divisions, already in existence at the outset of the war; the National Guard divisions, which consisted of reservists who trained for about thirty-nine days per year until mobilization; and the "new," or Army of the United States (AUS) and Organized Reserves (OR) infantry divisions, the soldiers of which were activated, trained, and deployed together according to a uniform plan.

Starting with the mobilization of 1940, the Regular Army and National Guard divisions participated in a series of exercises designed for the large-scale testing of doctrinal techniques and organizations that had been previously impossible under the fiscal constraints of the

Depression-era American economy. By the time of deployment to combat theaters, these divisions had trained together for the better part of at least two, if not three or more, years. Although numerous officers and noncommissioned officers (NCOs) were removed to serve as cadre in the AUS divisions in mid-1942, the cohesion thus imparted was considerable.

Beginning in the middle of 1942, GHQ implemented the MTP to build an army that eventually included eighty-nine divisions, of which thirty-nine were AUS or OR infantry divisions built according to the standard plan. This plan included a process by which recruits were brought to a training post and subsequently trained in basic and advanced individual techniques for seventeen weeks by a cadre of fifteen hundred experienced regulars. These regulars had themselves already served together for up to two months in various higher-level schools designed to prepare them for their upcoming assignment. The regulars in the training cadre then became the higher-level chain of command upon completion of individual training. By the time that a division embarked on its phases of unit training, then, the soldiers had already served together for more than four months, and been reduced in number as a result of training attrition by about 20 percent. By this process, the mentally and physically unfit or injured were reassigned or discharged prior to the commencement of unit training.

Unit training through the regimental level was conducted at the activation post for thirteen weeks. During this time, platoon, company, and battalion teams were built in both dry-fire and live-fire training exercises. This phase was followed by fourteen weeks of combined-arms exercises, in which each division was deployed as part of a corps to a maneuver area away from the activation post. As a result, this training was conducted solely in the field, with the goal of mentally and physically acclimating the men to protracted operations in a field environment.

Following the combined-arms phase, during which regimental combat teams were formed and thoroughly tactically drilled in the field, there followed a movement to a garrison (usually a different one than had been used for activation and earlier training phases) for eight weeks' training in coordinated air, mechanized, and antimechanized warfare techniques. Upon the completion of this fifty-two-week training program, the division was available for deployment to a combat theater.

Eleven of the sixteen armored divisions ultimately created by the Americans during the war followed a similar training scheme, tailored appropriately for their different needs.[83]

Although the American system for creating and training divisions was effectively organized and systematically carried out, the problem of providing replacements to units already in combat caused significant turbulence for numerous divisions prior to deployment. Various replacement training centers had been established by branch (infantry at Fort Benning, Georgia; field artillery at Fort Sill, Oklahoma, among others) for the provision of individual replacements for units that were sustaining casualties in combat. These centers never provided sufficient quantities of troops for the adequate replenishment of manpower to committed formations. Two factors influenced the decision to strip units already in various phases of training of certain percentages of their personnel rather than to increase the output of the replacement training centers.

First, commanders in the field overwhelmingly preferred replacements who had been trained as part of a division. Such soldiers already understood the importance of teamwork and were generally more highly motivated.[84] Second, replacements to units already in combat clearly needed to know the basic skills associated with their assignment (as an infantryman, artilleryman, et cetera), whereas units still in training would have some time left to incorporate replacements who required additional training.

As a result of this reasoning, soldiers (mostly privates; commanders generally preferred to promote NCOs from within their own organizations) who had been with a division since activation were sometimes pulled out and sent to units already in combat. They were often replaced by reclassified soldiers who had previously been trained to be technicians or specialists of some sort under the Army Specialized Training Program (ASTP), by former USAAF trainees, or by soldiers who had originally been trained as antiaircraft gunners. (Army estimates of the number of soldiers needed for these programs had been much too high.) The Supplemental Training Period was thus added to the divisional MTP in recognition of the need to integrate these troops into the division's combat echelons. Divisions usually created Provisional Training Battalions to teach basic combat skills to these newly arrived troops. After several weeks of such individual training, these replacements would be sent to the units with which they would deploy for integration into the fighting team.

Essentially, this program affected about one-third of the infantry divisions that took part in the Vosges campaign, namely the 63d and 70th (both of which participated only as separate battalions and regiments at the very end of the period studied), the 100th, and the 103d. Still, no more than 33 percent of these two latter divisions' infantrymen had been with their units for less than a year.[85] This means that the majority of the soldiers, and an even greater majority of the officers and NCOs, had been together for a year or more when these units reached combat in the autumn of 1944.

To effectively integrate replacements received during combat, all divisions conducted extensive training when rotated into reserve or during lulls in combat action. The 36th Division, for example, regularly published training memoranda describing such training as might be most useful in upcoming operations, and directed its conduct accordingly.[86]

Summary of U.S. Army Doctrine, Organization, and Training by Late 1944

American tactical and operational doctrine closely resembled that of the Germans in its essentials by late 1944. As such, it adhered closely to those Clausewitzian precepts that were still valid. It stressed the importance of combined-arms operations in both the attack and in the defense, and made considerable demands for initiative and good judgment on the part of its soldiers.

Unlike the Germans, however, whose organization for combat sometimes failed to accurately reflect the needs of tactical and operational doctrine, the Americans' organization was admirably suited to the task. By uniformly organizing and equipping their units and by the institution of carefully tailored regimental combat teams in their infantry divisions and combat commands in their armored divisions, the Americans ensured flexibility and cohesion in the execution of their doctrine.

Although American unit training was not ideally conducted due to the need for replacements for units already in combat, it nevertheless basically satisfied the requirements of cohesion and bonding by ensuring that most of the soldiers in combat formations had served and trained together for a considerable amount of time prior to deployment to a combat theater. In marked contrast to the Germans, the Americans integrated replacements from other branches and specialties into their new units, rather than the wholesale creation, in short periods of time, of units from personnel originally trained for duty other than ground combat. During lulls in the action, U.S. units conducted training designed to sharpen combat skills and to fully integrate replacements for men lost in combat.

Of course, strategic considerations dictated many of the differences in organization and training of the respective foes' armies in the Vosges by the autumn of 1944. It should be remembered, however, that both nations were conducting two-front, coalition warfare, and that their strategic situations were mostly of their own making. Nevertheless, the fact is that, by 15 October 1944, American doctrine was more clearly reflected in the organization of its troops for combat, and U.S. soldiers were far better trained and led than most of their Wehrmacht counterparts. The result of these differences was the success of American arms in the Vosges campaign.

CHAPTER 3

THE BATTLE FOR THE HIGH VOSGES

The enemy had every conceivable advantage but he lost and maybe it was because he was home and we had to get there.
—*History of the U.S. 397th Infantry Regiment*[1]

BACKGROUND

In early October 1944, less than two months after the U.S. Seventh Army landed in southern France by amphibious and airborne assault, its combat elements arrived at the southern base of the High Vosges Mountains. The linkup its troops effected with Lt. Gen. George Patton's Third Army in late September created the continuous line essential for Eisenhower's broad-front strategy.

The character of combat in which Seventh Army soldiers engaged during the late summer of 1944 differed dramatically from what they had experienced in Italy or elsewhere. Unlike the slogging matches and continual frustrations of VI Corps efforts in Italy, after its successful landing on the south coast of France, the corps pursued the rapidly fleeing units of the *Nineteenth Army,* commanded by General der Infanterie Friedrich Wiese.[2] In the process, the Germans lost 88,900 prisoners to the Seventh Army[3] and arrived at the southern base of the Vosges without much in the way of armor or other heavy equipment, with the exception of Generalleutnant Wend von Wietersheim's *11th Panzer Division.* (This unit had been nicknamed the "Ghost Division" due to its exploits during its extensive experience in the Soviet Union.) In an economy of force measure, the *Nineteenth Army* fell back to the

Vosges and the Belfort Gap in an attempt to hold fast there with the help of the most defensible terrain west of the Rhine. Here, the Reichsland of Alsace, annexed again in 1940, would be held by a variety of forces from *Nineteenth Army* in the south and *First Army* farther north toward Lorraine, both under the control of *Army Group G.* This formation was commanded until 21 September by Generaloberst Johannes Blaskowitz, a superb tactician and veteran of forty-three years of military service. Although sixty-one years old at the time of the campaign, Blaskowitz was among the Germans' most capable senior commanders. A Prussian who entered service at age seventeen, he had extensive World War I combat experience as commander of both an infantry company and a battalion, and he had served continuously in the *Reichswehr* during the interbellum years. Blaskowitz commanded the *Eighth Army* in the invasion of Poland, and had destroyed the Polish Lodz Army; afterward, he negotiated the surrender of Warsaw. He missed direct action in the French campaign, mainly because he was in disfavor with Hitler and the Nazi party over his protests against SS atrocities in Poland, but he commanded the *First Army* during the occupation of France from 1941 to 1944.[4] Not long after the disaster on the Riviera, Blaskowitz was replaced in command of *Army Group G* by General der Panzertruppen Hermann Balck.

Balck commanded *Army Group G* through most of the Vosges campaign. This fifty-one-year-old Prussian entered the army in 1913 and served as a junior officer, experiencing extensive combat in World War I, including command of a cavalry troop. Serving in the *Reichswehr* continuously between the wars, Balck commanded armored formations in both France and Russia, including a brigade group in 1940, the *11th Panzer Division* from May 1942 to March 1943, the *Panzergrenadier Division Grossdeutschland* in mid-1943, *XL* and *XLVIII Panzer Corps* in 1943–44, and the *Fourth Panzer Army* in mid-1944.[5] Although obviously an able and highly experienced combat commander, Balck's flair for offensive, fluid operations did not fit the character of his mission and his assigned subordinate units in the Vosges Mountains.

The Allied forces arrayed against the Vosges defenders were controlled after early September by the U.S. 6th Army Group, commanded by Lt. Gen. Jacob L. Devers. A classmate of Patton's (United States Military Academy [USMA] Class of 1909), the fifty-seven-year-old Pennsylvanian was a field artilleryman by experience. Like many of his American peers, he had missed combat experience in World War I. In fact, his mid-career assignments included instructor tours at his alma mater (1912–16 in the Department of Mathematics and Military Engineering, 1919–24 in the Tactical Department, and 1936–39 in the Athletic Department) and at the Field Artillery School at Fort Sill, Oklahoma (1917–19). Although he briefly commanded the 9th Infantry Division in 1940 and 1941, his major wartime post had been service as commanding general of the American component of the European theater of operations staff in England from May 1943 until Eisenhower's assumption of that position in 1944. Devers's appointment to command of the 6th Army Group in mid-1944 resulted more from Gen. George Marshall's recognition of his talents than Eisenhower's desire to work with him again, and this situation would later lead to a degree of friction between Devers and the supreme commander.[6]

The 6th Army Group's order of battle included the Seventh Army and the Free French First Army as its principal combat maneuver elements. In addition to the three infantry divisions of VI Corps, on 29 September 1944, Seventh Army's combat power was increased significantly by the transfer of XV Corps from the triumphant Third Army, which had recently completed its dramatic dash across France. The principal combat formations of this corps at the time were the 79th Infantry Division, the Free French 2d Armored Division *(2ème Division Blindée),* and the 106th Cavalry Group (Mechanized). These elements had been in continuous combat since the battle for the Normandy *bocage* four months earlier, and had essentially no combat experience with mountain warfare.

Devers's concept of operations for this most southerly zone of SHAEF's broad front called for a massive single envelopment of the German defenders. While the Seventh Army attacked through the Vosges as the 6th Army Group's main attack, the French First Army conducted a supporting attack toward the German defenses in the Belfort Gap. This effort, by threatening to burst through the shortest and fastest route to the Rhine and Germany, tied up a considerable portion of the *Nineteenth Army*'s strength, but it still left the *338th Volksgrenadier Division* of the *IV Luftwaffe Field Corps,* the *LXIV Corps,* and the *XLVII Panzer Corps* (replaced by the *LXXXIX Corps* headquarters shortly after the beginning of the campaign) to deal with the Seventh Army. Additionally, Blaskowitz, and later Balck, deployed elements of *Army Group*

G's other field army, the *First,* including the *LVIII Panzer Corps* in the vicinity of the Parroy Forest, northeast of Lunéville, to oppose the XV Corps thrust toward the Saverne Gap. Against these forces, Devers planned to conduct a single envelopment in accordance with the doctrinal tenets of *FM 100-5.* As the Free French fixed a large number of German defenders in the Belfort Gap with their assault against that "gate" to the Rhenish plain, the Seventh Army would break through the Vosges passes and onto the Alsatian Plain beyond. Once accomplished, the Allied superiority in armored and other mobile assets could be brought to bear on the flatlands between the Rhine and the eastern Vosges, and the destruction of German army forces west of the Rhine could be vigorously pursued.

Lieutenant General Alexander Patch, the Seventh Army commander, developed a plan for rupturing the Germans' Vosges defenses that called for the main attack to be made by VI Corps in the High Vosges and the supporting attack to be made initially by XV Corps on the Seventh Army's left flank in the north. The VI Corps's three divisions were to penetrate the German defenses and drive deep into the Vosges to seize the passes leading to the Alsatian Plain, Strasbourg, and the Rhine. Supporting attacks were to be carried out by XV Corps against Rambervillers, Baccarat, and Badonviller, near the boundary between the two corps. Simultaneously, XV Corps was to protect the right flank of the Third Army, its neighbor to the north, as Third Army drove into Lorraine.[7]

Patch understood implicitly the necessity and nuances of aggressive maneuver in difficult terrain. A veteran of the 1916 Punitive Expedition against Mexico and campaigns of the American Expeditionary Force (AEF) in France in World War I, the 1913 West Point graduate commanded the Americal Division in the Pacific from May 1942 until January 1943. During that time, Patch's division—an amalgam of National Guard units from North Dakota, Illinois, and Massachusetts—distinguished itself during offensive and defensive operations in the dripping jungles of Guadalcanal. Patch gained even further useful experience when he assumed command of XIV Corps in the Solomons following his stint with the Americal. Although the Vosges were half a world away from the islands of the southwestern Pacific, the lessons Patch absorbed in a combat command in difficult terrain against an experienced foe enhanced his ability to succeed in his European endeavors.

During its drive up the Rhône Valley, Seventh Army's primary combat element had been the VI Corps, commanded by Maj. Gen. Lucian K. Truscott, Jr. Truscott was one of the most combat-experienced American commanders by that stage of the war. As head of the American segment of the British Combined Operations Headquarters, he was present as an offshore observer at the Dieppe raid in 1942; later in the same year, he commanded the 9th Infantry Division's 60th Infantry Regiment in the Torch landings near Port Lyautey, French Morocco. A 1911 graduate of the Oklahoma Normal School, the forty-nine-year-old Truscott had been commissioned in the horse cavalry in 1917 from the U.S. Army 1st Officers' Training Camp. He had, thanks to his outstanding polo abilities, become a friend and protégé of George Patton. After serving under Patton in the Sicilian campaign as commander of the 3d Infantry Division, Truscott had taken the division ashore in the amphibious assaults at Salerno and Anzio before replacing Maj. Gen. John P. Lucas, who was relieved of command of VI Corps during the long, bitter fight to break out of that beachhead. Few commanders were better suited to launch the American drive into the Vosges. In the words of Russell Weigley, "No American commander drove harder than Truscott, and none clung more steadfastly to the principle that destroying the enemy army was the goal."[8] Truscott recognized the dangers inherent in the Vosges mission. In a letter to Lieutenant General Patch on 15 September, he wrote, "With the approach of weather in which rain and snow are to be expected, operations will be most difficult. As demonstrated in Italy during [the] last winter, the Boche can limit progress to a snail's pace and even stop it entirely, even against superior strength." As a result, Truscott suggested that the "time available to [the Germans] should be reduced to the minimum," and planned his operations accordingly.[9]

The 3d, 36th, and 45th Infantry Divisions made up the combat echelons of VI Corps. All were battle-experienced formations. In fact, all three had been heavily committed in the hill and mountain fighting of the Italian campaigns.

The 3d Infantry Division, commanded by World War I combat veteran Maj. Gen. John "Iron Mike" O'Daniel, had seen combat from the Torch landings in North Africa onward. The "Rock of the Marne" Division (so called for its World War I accomplishments) was originally a Regular Army unit at Fort Lewis, Washington, before the United States's entry into active hostilities. Although the division had deployed from the continental United States mostly intact in the autumn of 1942, personnel of its subordinate combat units, especially the 7th, 15th, and 30th Infantry Regiments, had been heavily replaced before the landings in France due to attrition sustained in the division's battle between Casablanca and Rome. Still, because casualties amongst headquarters and support personnel are nearly always much lighter than those in line units, the 3d Division's command structure was highly experienced in combat, especially fighting in mountainous terrain.

The 36th Infantry ("Texas") Division was commanded by Maj. Gen. John Dahlquist, who had supervised the division's preparation for Operation Dragoon after assuming command just two months before. Unlike the 3d Division, the 36th had been a Texas National Guard division before the United States entered the war. As a result, many of its members drew their cohesiveness not from the common bonds of Regular Army prewar soldiering, but rather from the close ties of territorial, civilian occupational, or even familial association. Of course, eight months of savage fighting in Italy had taken its toll, especially in the three infantry regiments (the 141st, 142d, and 143d). To replace the considerable losses incurred during the Italian campaign from Salerno to Anzio to Rome, replacements were funneled into the division without regard for their regional origin. Still, the bonds of regional loyalty combined with the cohesive effects of nearly three years of training together at various locations in the United States and North Africa to give the units of the 36th Infantry Division the resilience essential for success in the crucible of Vosges Mountains warfare.

The 45th Infantry Division, or "Thunderbird" Division (so called because of the distinctive American Indian mythical bird prominently displayed on its shoulder patch) had also been a National Guard division during its prewar days. Commanded by Maj. Gen. William Eagles, a forty-nine-year-old West Point graduate (Class of 1917) and former regimental commander and assistant division commander in the 3d Infantry Division under Truscott, the division had originally been made up of National Guardsmen from Oklahoma (the 179th and 180th Infantry Regiments and Division Artillery), Colorado (the 157th Infantry Regiment), Arizona, and New Mexico. Like the Texas Division, it derived its cohesion from extensive prewar ties typical of the American National Guard establishment, and also from nearly three years of training together at such diverse locations as Camp Barkeley, Texas; Fort Devens, Massachusetts; Pine Camp, New York; Camp Pickett, Virginia; and the Blue Ridge Mountains of Virginia and North Carolina.[10] This extended period of training helped to weld together those non–National Guard replacements brought in to bring the division to full strength and keep it there in the predeployment phase. Especially important for its later role in Italy was the training the division underwent in the Blue Ridge country, where its soldiers learned about the special demands of mountain combat.

Indeed, all three divisions had seen more than their share of mountain fighting by the time they reached the foothills of the Vosges. For the 3d Infantry Division, most of the Sicilian campaign had required conquest of the parched Mediterranean mountains of the central and northern coastal regions of that island. In Italy, aside from the invasions at Salerno and Anzio, nearly all of the fighting by the Rock of the Marne, the Texas, and the Thunderbird Divisions had been confined to the craggy Apennines, where the German army had built successive lines of formidable fortifications. The reduction of these German strongholds had called for vicious, bitter assaults by the divisions' infantrymen and engineers. The resulting casualties had been heavy, and had induced considerable personnel turnover.[11] Still, there remained a large cadre of soldiers of all ranks who understood the complex and often unique requirements of mountain warfare against a tenacious and wily foe. Furthermore, they understood all too well the dire implications of frontal assaults against enemy troops entrenched in mountain defenses.

Not all of the experience gained had been directly combat related, either. The necessity of dealing with nonbattle casualty-inducing factors, such as cold weather injuries and the exhaustion brought on by the difficult negotiation of mountain terrain, had also prepared the 3d, 36th, and 45th Infantry Divisions for the next round in the Vosges. Also, the aggressive logistical support essential for successful operations, made tedious and exhausting by rural mountain tracks and muddy, winding roads, had already been a daily reality for these divisions' support echelons throughout their first two years of combat.

Even with their considerable experience, however, VI Corps soldiers required some time to prepare for the invasion of southern France. For two months, from mid-June to mid-August 1944, all three had been pulled out of the line in Italy and were subsequently shipped south to various locations on the southwest coast of Italy to rest, integrate replacements, and train for both the general and specific tasks inherent in the Dragoon mission.

XV Corps, commanded by Maj. Gen. Wade H. Haislip, had a considerably different character and background. Activated during the breakout from the Normandy beachhead in late July, its subordinate units had seen extensive offensive action in the subsequent race across France. Haislip, a 1912 West Point graduate, was a career infantryman who had seen action in World War I. Before assuming command of XV Corps, he had been a member of the War Department General Staff and had served as commander of the 85th Infantry Division from its activation through its unit training.

The 79th Infantry Division had been assigned almost from the beginning of XV Corps's existence, so there was a significant degree of cohesion between corps and division headquarters, just as there was between the commanders and staffs in VI Corps.

Although the 79th Infantry Division did not take part directly in the initial assault on the High Vosges, it nevertheless played an important role in the Seventh Army's autumn campaign by attacking through the Parroy Forest west of the Saverne Gap. The division was commanded by Maj. Gen. Ira T. Wyche, a 1911 West Point graduate, and had been organized and trained under the Army of the United States (AUS) concept. The "Cross of Lorraine" Division (so called for the shoulder insignia it had adopted and worn since its service in that area in World War I), and its organic 313th, 314th, and 315th Infantry Regiments, were activated and underwent basic and small-unit training at Camp Pickett, Virginia, and Camp Blanding, Florida, in the summer and autumn of 1942. The division later took part in army-level maneuvers in the Cumberland Mountains of Tennessee in the winter of 1942–43. Additional training was conducted in California, Kansas, and England prior to landing in France eight days after the Normandy invasion in June 1944.[12] Major General Wyche was originally commissioned in the infantry, and had served in Europe with the American Expeditionary Force in 1918; he later transferred to the field artillery. Although fifty-seven years old, he remained vigorously in command throughout the European campaign.

After four consecutive months of combat as part of First and Third Armies, the 79th Division had sustained considerable casualties, yet it was allowed no time for rest or reorganization. Immediately following the seizure of Lunéville as part of the Third Army, the division had been thrust into the battle for the Parroy Forest, where Hitler himself had fought as a corporal in World War I. Four days after the 79th plunged into its first major forest action, it and the remainder of XV Corps were transferred to the Seventh Army.

The XV Corps's part in this stage of the Vosges effort was to conduct supporting attacks for the penetration operation being carried out by VI Corps. Although not part of the Vosges massif, the thickly wooded Parroy Forest proved to be a major obstacle in the path toward the Vosges mountain barrier and the Saverne Gap. The intense combat in this sector caused more than two thousand casualties in the division in less than a month, and when the 79th was pulled out of the line on 22 October, it needed every bit of the sixteen days that XV Corps could give it to prepare for subsequent operations. In addition to a rest program, "an intensive training program was begun with particular attention paid to the new replacements the division had received," thus ensuring the continued combat effectiveness of its subordinate echelons.[13]

As the 79th Division withdrew from the line, it was relieved by the green 44th Infantry Division. When it had been called to active duty in September 1940, the 44th was composed of men from the New York National Guard (the 71st and 174th Infantry Regiments and 156th Field Artillery Regiment) and the New Jersey National Guard (113th and 114th Infantry Regiments and 157th and 165th Field Artillery Regiments). When the 79th switched to the 1942 triangular organization, half of the division artillery battalions were replaced with U.S. units, and two of the infantry regiments (the 113th and 174th) with one from the AUS (the 324th). The division spent most of its first four years at such diverse locations as Fort Dix, New Jersey; Camp A. P. Hill, Virginia; Camp Claiborne, Louisiana; Fort Lewis, Washington; and Camp Phillips, Kansas, training soldiers and officers as replacements for other units. As a result, the division's regional bonds with the National Guard establishment all but disappeared, replaced by the cohesion born of common training experiences.

During most of this time, the division was commanded by Maj. Gen. James Muir, a 1910 West Point graduate. But shortly before sailing for Europe, Muir was given a corps command, and Maj. Gen. Robert L. Spragins, West Point Class of 1913, took over the 44th. Spragins, a fifty-four-year-old infantryman, had extensive combat service as the chief of staff of the 24th Infantry Division in the Pacific, where he had been wounded. As a junior officer, he had been cited for valor by the Coast Guard during the Vera Cruz expedition of 1914. Fortunately for both the division and its new commanding general, after arriving at Cherbourg in mid-September 1944, the 44th was allowed to train for a full month in Normandy before relieving the 79th Division.[14]

While the 79th Infantry Division and XV Corps artillery gradually wrested the Parroy Forest from elements of the German *11th Panzer* and *15th Panzergrenadier Divisions* and, later, the *553d Volksgrenadier Division*, VI Corps's leading echelons began the slow grind into the High Vosges. Meanwhile, German *First* and *Nineteenth Armies* were preparing defensive positions intended for occupation throughout the winter along the Meurthe River and on the high ground behind that obstacle.

Lieutenant General Patch ordered VI Corps to advance on the axis St. Dié–Molsheim-Strasbourg, with the ultimate goal of taking Strasbourg or assisting the First French Army on his right in doing so. In a terse, two-page field order issued to subordinate units on 29 September, Patch simply delineated the general direction that he desired the attack toward Strasbourg to take; it was up to Truscott to decide exactly where and how to attack.[15] In turn, Truscott allowed his division commanders maximum freedom in developing their attack plans, but oriented the corps' advance on those few passes through the Vosges that would allow the Americans to break out onto the Alsatian Plain.[16]

Seventh Army was directly supported in these endeavors by XII Tactical Air Command (TAC), commanded by Brig. Gen. Gordon P. Saville. The principal combat element of XII TAC during the battle for the High Vosges was the 64th Fighter Wing, which initially included only a single group of thirty-six Republic P-47 Thunderbolt fighter-bombers. This unit, the 324th Fighter Group, based at Tavaux after 20 September 1944, included the 314th, 315th, and 316th Fighter Squadrons, each with twelve Thunderbolts.[17] Although these aircraft were probably the best close-support machines in Europe at the time, even if the weather had been ideal, this small number could hardly have been decisive.[18] Furthermore, since these were the only combat aircraft at XII TAC's disposal, they were required to fulfill the deep interdiction air support role as well, attacking targets such as rail and road junctions, bridges, and tunnels. After mid-October, as the weather worsened in the Vosges, these relatively paltry assets (compared to the multiple wings assigned to support the First and

Third Armies farther north) would be of practically no use for close air support to Seventh Army anyway, because fog, cloud cover, and diminishing periods of daylight would curtail their usefulness. With its few aerial support assets limited by weather and its armored units hampered by the mountainous terrain, Seventh Army would have to rely on its infantry for success in the Vosges. On 15 October, VI Corps counted 17,695 infantrymen in the 120 line and heavy weapons companies in its three divisions and the attached 442d Regimental Combat Team.[19]

General der Panzertruppen Balck nominally had ten to twelve divisions at his disposal for the defense of Alsace, but most of these formations were considerably understrength. In opposition to VI Corps, Balck arrayed elements of the *Nineteenth Army* under the command of General der Infanterie Friedrich Wiese with approximately 13,100 infantrymen and *Panzergrenadiers*.[20] Wiese, a fifty-one-year-old Schleswiger, enlisted at the outbreak of World War I, was commissioned during the war, and served with infantry units in combat. He was forced out of the service by the Versailles treaty restrictions, and served with the Hamburg police. When Hitler abrogated the treaty, Wiese returned to the army and, from 1935 on, commanded infantry units of regimental size and larger. In the east, he commanded *XXXV Corps* before being assigned to command the *Nineteenth Army* in late June 1944.

The *Nineteenth Army* elements with which Wiese sought to defend the Vosges included *IV Luftwaffe Corps*'s *338th Volksgrenadier Division, LXIV Corps*'s *198th Infantry Division* and *716th Volksgrenadier Division,* and *XLVII Panzer Corps*'s *16th Volksgrenadier Division* and *21st Panzer Division*.[21] In all, these formations fielded about 12,200 infantry combat troops. In addition to these, Wiese was able to deploy an additional 900 infantry belonging to an assortment of *Kampfgruppen* and separate fortress machine-gun battalions opposite the VI Corps zone, boosting his total to the aforementioned 13,100 infantrymen.

These units were deployed forward of the Meurthe in strongpoint positions to delay the American advance and to give the formations attempting to defend along the Vosges defensive lines time to prepare their defenses on the northeast side of the river and along the military crests of the western Vosges. Construction work on the Vosges positions began on 1 September 1944 under the supervision of Generalleutnant Gustav Höhne. Gauleiter Rehm of Strasbourg coordinated the provision of labor for this construction. Many of the laborers were drafted locally in Alsace and put to work under the auspices of Organisation Todt, but there were also considerable numbers of workers from the German Labor Service (Reichsarbeitsdienst, or RAD) and the Hitler Jugend from nearby Baden and Württemberg. Additionally, numerous army units of up to regimental strength were also committed to this task, including the *360th Cossack (Ost-Reiter) Regiment* (consisting of captured Soviet troops who had defected to the Germans), which performed yeoman work.[22]

About the middle of September, reconnaissance staffs consisting of infantry, artillery, and engineer officers from the *Nineteenth Army* divisions defending the Vosges joined the engineer and labor elements already at work since the beginning of the month to coordinate the construction of fortifications in their divisions' envisioned sectors and to provide tactical advice. The work progressed well until the VI Corps's attacks in mid-October forced the withdrawal of many of the army units for combat duty. Even after this, though, work continued until early November, resulting in the completion of most of the projected fortifications, with the exception of the intended works in the immediate vicinity of the Vosges passes.[23]

According to General der Infanterie Helmut Thumm, *LXIV Corps* commander during the period, the construction staffs paid little attention to the requests or advice of the tactical liaison groups.[24] As a result, two belts of fortifications were constructed, although hardly in consonance with German defensive doctrine. The first, in the western High and Low Vosges, consisted mainly of strongpoints and trenches for the delay and deception of attacking Allied units, all constructed for 360-degree defense. While these positions may have been suitable for use as combat outposts, they were much more than the two thousand to five thousand meters in front of the second belt prescribed by German doctrine.[25] The second echelon of defensive works, useful as the main line of defense, consisted of multiple rows of trenches and strongpoints, thick belts of barbed-wire obstacles, deep minefields, abatis, antitank ditches, and log-crib roadblocks, all integrated into the natural obstacles so prevalent in the Vosges, such as streams and rivers, thick woods, steep inclines, and villages. Their ten- to twenty-kilometer distance from the first belt, however, prevented the mutual support and sequential defensive dynamic that a more doctrinally correct arrangement would have afforded. Their placement would have allowed them to be used effectively as delay lines, perhaps, but this was neither the builders' intent nor the army's mission. Still, although not wisely placed, these defenses significantly compensated for the Germans' initially slight numerical inferiority. In addition to providing a tactical advantage, the existence of prefabricated fieldworks allowed a measure of relative comfort for the *Nineteenth Army*'s defending troops in the face of the increasingly severe autumn weather, and at least partially relieved them of the exhausting labor required to prepare positions themselves. Their *Ami* opponents had no such good fortune, and had to dig in each day to shield themselves from the effects of German artillery, rockets, mortars, and infantry counterattacks.

The disparity in the training and organization of the respective sides' combat echelons was what made the difference in the High Vosges, however. The premier German unit deployed in front of the intended winter line was indisputably the *21st Panzer Division*. This division was commanded by Generalleutnant Edgar Feuchtinger, a native Lothringer (born in Metz) who had commanded the division throughout its participation in the Normandy campaign. Feuchtinger was a fifty-year-old artilleryman and *Reichswehr* veteran who had seen action in World War I and commanded an artillery regiment in the early phases of World War II. His combat experience in the latter, however, was extremely limited; he had seen no action as a *Panzer* commander. In fact, he had a reputation among his peers for high living and among at least some of his subordinates for being a Nazi party toady.[26]

Feuchtinger's division had been briefly refitted near Molsheim in Alsace after being badly mauled during the Allied breakout from the *bocage* country. By the time of the Vosges campaign, the division was still organized conventionally with an armored reconnaissance battalion of tanks and armored cars, a *Panzer* regiment (the *22d*), and two *Panzergrenadier* regiments (the *192d* and the *125th*). In the second half of October, the division's strength had been increased considerably by the absorption of the *113th Panzer Brigade* and half of the *112th Panzer Brigade* as reinforcements.

The division had also received a considerable number of replacements, and by late October was in the best shape it had been in since the Normandy campaign. The *Panzergrenadier* regiments and attachments included about twenty-eight hundred combat effectives, and the tank battalions of the division's *22d Panzer Regiment* disposed about half the normal number of *Mark IV* and *Panther* tanks. The divisional artillery, composed of the *155th Panzer Artillery Regiment* and the *200th Assault Gun Battalion,* provided direct and indirect fire support with thirty-two 105mm and 150mm guns and howitzers, both towed and self-propelled, and eighteen 75mm and 88mm antitank guns. The division was periodically reinforced by fortress machine-gun units, with up to eighteen heavy water-cooled machine guns each, and by the inevitable "march companies," or company-sized groups of hastily gathered replacements, which Feuchtinger usually tried to distribute to the more experienced, established units.[27] As a result, according to Oberstleutnant Helmut Ritgen, who served with the *21st Panzer Division* from Normandy on, morale remained high in this division until the spring of 1945.[28]

Generalleutnant Lüttwitz, commander of the *XLVII Panzer Corps,* assigned Feuchtinger's division a large sector—twenty-seven kilometers—consisting of mostly open, rolling hills interspersed with small forests from Gerbeville in the north to Girecourt in the south. This allowed Feuchtinger to take advantage of his unit's inherent capabilities and to fight a highly mobile delay falling back from the prepared defenses of the Vosges winter line. Additionally, the *21st Panzer Division* could use the two principal north-south–flowing rivers in the sector, namely the Mortagne and, farther east, the Meurthe, to organize its defensive sector and slow the advancing Americans. It was a challenging but by no means impossible task for a division that had retained a fair amount of cohesive leadership and organization at the regimental level and below.

Although the leadership at division level may have been consistent, a blow to the cohesion of operational command and control was struck just as the fight for the High Vosges was beginning in earnest, when Generalleutnant Werner Albrecht Freiherr von und zu Gilsa and his *LXXXIX Corps* headquarters assumed command of the *21st Panzer* and *16th Volksgrenadier Divisions* on 20 October. Replacing the commander and staff of *XLVII Panzer Corps,* who were called on to help prepare for operations being planned by OKW for mid-December in the Ardennes, this headquarters switched to the control of *First Army,* with different subordinate units, ten days later. Clearly, friction resulted from the changeover, and the command and control of the units fighting an already complex series of maneuvers was complicated still further.[29] Fortunately for the Germans, von und zu Gilsa, a fifty-five-year-old Prussian nobleman, was a highly experienced and brave commander. A World War I infantry veteran, he had commanded the *216th Infantry Division* in Russia and was awarded the Knight's Cross for his leadership there.[30] Every bit of his talent would be needed for the conduct of the campaign into which he and his staff were thrown.

Although the *21st Panzer Division* possessed sound leadership and at least a modicum of cohesion, the ad hoc character of most other German division-sized units in *Nineteenth Army* contributed greatly to their downfall in the battle against the Americans. Prisoners taken by the U.S. VI Corps during this period indicated that low morale existed due "to the fact that most of these men belonged to different units until recently and represent a motley crew without team spirit."[31]

The *16th Volksgrenadier Division,* for example, conducted operations in the sector to the left of the *21st Panzer Division,* west of the winter line from Girecourt to Bruyères. Some of the division's cadre came from the former *16th Infantry Division,* which had seen extensive action in central France during the summer. The division had been surrounded and largely destroyed by elements of Patton's Third Army in September. Most of the division's approximately twenty-two hundred infantrymen, however, were drawn from units that had been shattered in the American drive across France and collected in the area around Nancy.[32] The division's three organic subordinate regiments included the *221st, 223d,* and *225th Volksgrenadiers.* These were composed of troops from numerous destroyed remnants, often of *Volksdeutsche* (ethnic German) origins, meaning Sudetenlanders, Austrians, et cetera.[33] Also part of the *16th Volksgrenadier Division* during this period was the *19th SS Polizei Regiment,* composed of about 50 percent former German police and about 50 percent survivors of destroyed units.[34] This unit was eventually disbanded and the soldiers dispersed to other *16th Division* units. Also attached were the *49th Fortress Machine-gun Battalion* and the *38th Reserve Light Infantry (Jäger) Battalion.* Clearly, this division's tactical organization was chaotic, only detracting from cohesion while contributing to friction for the higher staffs and commanders attempting to direct it. Still, its commanding general, Generalleutnant Ernst Häckel, was a reliable, experienced commander. A Bavarian with World War I combat experience, he had commanded regiments and divisions in combat on the eastern front.[35]

The sector allotted to Häckel and his men was a little more than five kilometers wide, and consisted of heavily wooded Vosges hills between twelve hundred and fifteen hundred feet high. Only one high-speed avenue of approach bisected the area: the Girecourt-Grandvillers-Bruyères road, which led to St. Dié on the Meurthe beyond. If Häckel and his *Volksgrenadiers* could hold that road, the Americans would have no means of supporting an attack across the Meurthe at or near St. Dié.

The units of *LXIV Corps* in the sector to the south of the *16th Volksgrenadiers*, namely the *716th Volksgrenadier Division* and the *198th Infantry Division*, also had organizational and cohesion problems. This corps, too, was commanded by a highly capable officer, General der Infanterie Thumm. Thumm was a forty-nine-year-old Württemberger who had served as an enlisted man and as an infantry officer during World War I. Captured by the British army just three months before the Armistice, Thumm was repatriated after the end of the conflict and served with the *Reichswehr* continuously between the wars.[36] The composition of Thumm's subordinate units would make great demands on his command abilities, but generally he handled them well, taking advantage of the terrain and weather to slow the advancing Americans before attempting to stop them along the Vosges winter line.

The *716th Volksgrenadier Division* included the remnants of a variety of units, including Kriegsmarine sailors and Luftwaffe personnel among its fifteen hundred infantrymen.[37] The *716th*'s two major subordinate maneuver units were the *726th* and *736th Volksgrenadier Regiments*. Their firepower, although already considerable due to the generous issue of machine pistols and automatic rifles, was augmented by the addition of several companies belonging to various nondivisional fortress machine-gun battalions, such as the *1417th* and the *39th*. These latter units were manned largely by older troops whose mission was to defend fixed positions, and by Luftwaffe ground personnel.[38] The *726th Volksgrenadier Regiment* was manned with troops representing the remnants of units that had been destroyed during the retreat from the Riviera, such as the *189th Infantry Division*.[39] The *736th* was manned largely by Kriegsmarine and Luftwaffe personnel who had received only rudimentary infantry combat training.[40] This already disadvantageous situation was made worse by a constant stream of replacements from straggler control points consisting of survivors of smashed units.

Fortunately for the division, it was commanded by an able Prussian World War I veteran, Generalleutnant Wilhelm Richter, who had seen action on the Russian front and was steady and cool under pressure. Richter, a fifty-two-year-old artilleryman, had served continuously in the *Reichswehr* between the wars and had commanded at every echelon from battery on up.[41]

Thumm assigned Richter's division the defense of a relatively small sector in recognition of its weakness. It was still a formidable task, because the *716th*'s area of tactical responsibility extended from just south of Bruyères for thirteen kilometers south along a series of northeast–southwest–running ridges to Laveline-du-Houx and Rehaupal. This terrain facilitated a delay to the extent that the valleys between the ridges contained roads on which to move rapidly to the rear. As the Germans did so, they could cover American units attempting to pursue them from the 2,000- to 2,200-foot heights on either side. This high ground provided superb cover, concealment, and fields of fire for Richter's grenadiers' machine guns, mortars, and artillery.

The *198th Infantry Division,* which was defending the southern flank of the *LXIV Corps* line, also was in a difficult personnel predicament, although the unit's strength, including its artillery regiment, was about up to standard, meaning that it had about thirty-eight hundred infantrymen present for duty at the start of the campaign.[42] The division possessed only two subordinate maneuver elements, the *305th* and *308th Infantry Regiments,* but, unlike certain other comparable units, these regiments' personnel were almost 100 percent *Reichsdeutsche,* or actual Germans. Many of the division's personnel were, however, soldiers who had been previously adjudged unfit for combat duty.[43] Still, as an anonymous GI said about another, similar battle later on, "I don't care if the guy behind that gun is a syphilitic prick who's a hundred years old—he's still sitting behind eight feet of concrete and he's still got enough fingers to press triggers and shoot bullets!"[44] Interestingly, this division was nevertheless rated with the *21st Panzer Division* as among the best German units in the Vosges by the *LXIV Corps* commander during the campaign.[45] This was due in part to the excellent command and staff structure supervised by the division commander, Generalmajor Otto Schiel, a World War I infantry veteran from Baden who took charge in early October.[46] It was also due to the combat experience many division personnel acquired on the Russian front.[47]

The sector in which the *198th Infantry Division* was employed to delay the Americans was also conducive to the mission. From the heights along a line southeast from just south of Rehaupal to Le Tholy,[48] the division's troops could observe the American advance and bring them under fire long before they reached the 1,800- to 2,000-foot heights on which the Germans had ensconced themselves. Like the sector of the *716th Volksgrenadiers* to their north, the *198th Infantry Division* sector also provided a good road net that allowed rapid egress to the main Vosges line to the rear.

To the south of Thumm's corps, General der Flieger Erich Petersen's *IV Luftwaffe Field Corps* held the line from Le Tholy to Plancher. Petersen was a fifty-three-year-old World War I and *Reichswehr* infantry veteran who transferred to the Luftwaffe in 1941 to command paratroopers. This new type of unit was made part of Göring's air forces, which ferried them to their combat destinations. Petersen finally got into the fight as commander of the *7th Flieger* (Airborne) *Division* in Russia after it had been reconstituted following the Crete operation, and brought the division (redesignated *1st Fallschirm-Division* in late 1942) to southern France in March 1943 when the unit was pulled out of Russia for rehabilitation.[49] Although Petersen no longer commanded airborne soldiers, his headquarters was still technically a Luftwaffe organization. The difficulties and friction imparted by an air force corps headquarters being integrated into an otherwise strictly army organization contributed still further to the problems already apparent in *Nineteenth Army*. (This headquarters was eventually redesignated as *XC Corps* and assigned to the army later in the campaign.)

In the U.S. VI Corps zone, the principal combat element of Petersen's corps was the *338th Volksgrenadier Division*, which suffered from many of the same maladies as the other *Volksgrenadier* divisions in the fight for the High Vosges. It possessed only two regiments—the *757th* and the *933d Volksgrenadier*—which, like their counterparts in the *716th Volksgrenadier Division*, were composed of personnel from an amalgam of noninfantry formations. The division was commanded by Generalmajor Hans Oschmann, who had taken the reins from Generalleutnant Rene von Courbiere in mid-September, after the latter's relief for "physical deficiency."[50]

In recognition of the low infantry strength of the *338th* (about five hundred infantrymen per regiment), Petersen assigned it a narrow sector of about five kilometers. He also reinforced its depleted ranks with the addition of at least three of the six fortress machine-gun battalions allotted to his corps, to bring its infantry strength to about eighteen hundred, although probably only nine hundred or so were committed in the American zone.[51] This sector was important because it contained the Remiremont-Cornimont–La Bresse road, which ran on to the Schlucht Pass through the High Vosges to the Alsatian Plain. The high ground on either side of this road provided the same advantages for a delay as the rest of the *Nineteenth Army*'s sector in the High Vosges: superb fields of fire for the many machine guns, excellent long-range observation for adjusting indirect fires, good cover and concealment for the defenders, and so forth.

The *360th Cossack Regiment,* which would be committed later in this sector after its participation in the construction of *Vogesenstellungen,* had an even more dire personnel situation, because it was composed almost exclusively of about a thousand former Russian prisoners of war. Their battle reliability was marginal at best during this stage of the war, because most of the troops had lost the incentive to fight.[52]

Opposing XV Corps, Balck deployed elements of the *First Army,* commanded by General der Panzertruppen Otto von Knobelsdorff. The fifty-nine-year-old Prussian was a member of an illustrious military family, and had served continuously since 1906. He fought in World War I as a junior infantry officer, and was decorated by various German states and the Austro-Hungarian Empire, and served in cavalry, artillery, and infantry units in the *Reichswehr* during the interbellum period. He commanded the *19th Infantry Division* in the invasion of France and *XXXIX, XLVIII,* and *XL Panzer Corps* on the eastern front from 1942 to October 1944, when he assumed command of *First Army* in the west under Balck. According to American intelligence reports, von Knobelsdorff was less than enthusiastic about National Socialism but had nevertheless been awarded the Knight's Cross with oak leaves and swords for his actions on the Russian front.[53]

The German units defending the approaches to the Saverne Gap north of Baccarat and east of Lunéville were of a somewhat higher quality than their *Nineteenth Army* counterparts already ensconced in the outworks of their High Vosges fastness to the south. *First Army* had the dubious honor of defending against Patton's Third Army in Lorraine, as well as elements of Seventh Army's XV Corps. The more dangerous, open terrain in Lorraine, and the German acknowledgment of Patton's operational offensive effectiveness, combined to ensure the assignment of some of the Wehrmacht's best remaining divisions to this army. Although von Knobelsdorff was clearly an outstanding combat commander with extensive operational experience, his arrival on the scene, along with that of his superior, Balck, on the eve of Patch's Vosges offensive did not allow a great deal of time for their familiarization with the situation.

Units of the *First Army* assigned to oppose XV Corps to the north of Feuchtinger's *21st Panzer Division* on the *Nineteenth Army*'s right (northern) flank belonged to the *LVIII Corps* and included the *15th Panzergrenadier Division* and the *11th Panzer Division*. Although these divisions actively defended the vicinity of the Parroy Forest against the onslaught of the 79th Infantry Division in early and mid-October, by the third week of that month, the *15th Panzergrenadier Division* was withdrawn and replaced by the *553d Volksgrenadier Division,* the unit that would be engaged by XV Corps divisions during their drive on the Saverne Gap.

The *553d Volksgrenadier Division* was commanded by a forty-six-year-old Prussian, Generalmajor Johannes Bruhn. An enlisted veteran of World War I, Bruhn was commissioned shortly before the Armistice in 1918, only to be mustered out after the war to serve until 1935 as a police officer in Prussia. Following his return to the army that year, Bruhn served in various command and staff positions in artillery regiments, including better than two years' service on the eastern front. Shortly after his promotion to Generalmajor, Bruhn assumed command of the *553d Volksgrenadiers* and moved with them into the line to defend the most direct approaches to the Saverne Gap.

The eleven-kilometer front for which Bruhn and his *Volksgrenadiers* were responsible presented challenges unknown by *Nineteenth Army* units farther south. At the western gate of the Saverne Gap—the great corridor between the High and Low Vosges—is first the barrier of the Parroy Forest; east of it are a series of rolling hills that are not nearly as heavily forested as the Vosges themselves. No clearly defined ridgelines exist to allow sequential retrograde operations such as delays. Once the ten-kilometer-deep by nine-kilometer-wide Parroy obstacle was breached by XV Corps, the defense of the Saverne Gap would be difficult indeed. In the middle of October, however, there was little cause for

Balck or von Knobelsdorff to worry, since the Parroy deadlock showed little sign of breaking.

Although the Americans had a roughly 1.35 to 1 numerical advantage in the Vosges, the Germans held the advantages of defending known terrain in prepared positions (Clausewitz's "intrinsically stronger form" of warfare), and of living in shelters in increasingly bad weather, which would significantly diminish their cold weather casualties and contribute to higher morale. In addition, the role of air power was obviated by the weather, and the lopsided American advantage in armor (three battalions of medium tanks and two of tank destroyers for the VI Corps to two for the Germans in this sector) was considerably offset by the mountainous terrain and winding, easily mined roads. The victor, therefore, would be decided not by numbers, air power, or armor superiority, but by training and tactical proficiency.

The VI Corps's commanders and staffs knew from bitter experience in Italy that mountain warfare against entrenched German units was costly and slow. On the other hand, the Germans knew that the Vosges terrain was ideal for making a stand throughout the winter months as an economy of force measure; that is, to make up with terrain advantages those shortages identified in equipment and personnel. To avoid a reprise of his Italian winter experiences, Truscott pressed forward as rapidly as possible against the German first-line defenses.

However, just as logistical limitations were forcing the neighboring Third Army to stall, so too were the long lines leading to the Vosges from Marseilles and Toulon stretched to their breaking points. With nearly twice the number of combat formations to support (since the addition of XV Corps), and with ever-growing distances to cover, Seventh Army's supply situation at the time of Patch's 29 September directive simply would not allow an immediate major thrust.

By the first week in October, in fact, the American supply situation had been deemed "critical."[54] Controlled Supply Rates (CSRs) for ammunition were imposed on all Seventh Army units, especially artillery and mortar units. Fifteen to twenty rounds per gun or tube per day were common CSRs; clearly, no major offensive could be undertaken with such constraints.[55] To conserve ammunition, even harassing fires (H & I, or harassing and interdictory fires), important to any operations, were eliminated during the day and curtailed to a maximum of five rounds per gun at night.[56]

By the end of the second week in October, however, these problems had been largely alleviated. A combination of the reorganization of supply channels supporting Seventh Army and the establishment of supply distribution facilities closer to the front at Charmes, Mirecourt, and Épinal caused the logistical situation to improve to the point where Truscott was willing to launch his attack.[57] Unfortunately, the two-week intermission had given the German *Nineteenth Army* additional time to prepare their defenses in depth along the Vosges massif.

The outer defenses against which the VI Corps attack would be launched consisted of strongpoints of the first line of Vosges defenses, occupied by battalion- and regimental-strength units. The key terrain in the U.S. VI Corps zone was initially the town of Bruyères, because it controlled the road net needed to support operations toward St. Dié and the Vosges passes of Ste. Marie-aux-Mines and Bonhomme beyond the Meurthe River.

THE DRIVE ON BRUYÈRES

Responsibility for the defense of Bruyères fell to the *16th Volksgrenadier Division*, but the southern approaches to the town were along the boundary between *LXXXIX Corps* and *LXIV Corps*, so the *716th Volksgrenadier Division* would be engaged by the 36th Infantry Division's assault as well. (See Figure 11.) The subordinate units of the *16th Volksgrenadier Division* around Bruyères included the *2d Battalion* and elements of the *1st Battalion* of the *223d Volksgrenadier Regiment*, as well as the *49th Fortress Machine-gun Battalion*. These units were at about 60 percent strength in personnel but possessed nearly all the heavy weapons (machine guns, mortars, and artillery) of full-strength German units of their types.[58] (See Figure 12.)

Two battalions of the *716th Division*'s *736th Volksgrenadier Regiment* (the *1st* and *2d*) were employed around Champ-le-Duc and Laval-sur-Vologne, along with various other nondivisional units, such as the *38th Reserve Light Infantry (Jäger) Battalion*. (See Figure 12.)

Thus, the VI Corps's assault elements conducting the main attack, the 36th Infantry Division's 143d Infantry Regiment (minus the 2d Battalion, held in division reserve), and the attached 442d Regimental Combat Team (Nisei) would be facing an enemy with only about 50 percent of their American adversaries' personnel strength but with nearly the same amount of long-range firepower, especially at the battalion level. Bruyères is a typical Vosges village in that it lies in a small valley dominated by several major hills. (See Figure 12.) Its characteristically Alsatian stone and masonry structures make ideal defensive positions. Any house can be turned into a pillbox, practically impervious to small-arms fire, within a few hours, let alone the two weeks the Americans' logistical problems had afforded the defenders.[59] To isolate these positions around Bruyères and to prevent German reinforcement from the south, Major General Dahlquist of the 36th Infantry Division deployed the 141st and 142d Infantry Regiments along broad frontages to the south. In a terse two-and-a-half-page division order, Dahlquist directed the regiments to conduct supporting attacks toward the Vologne River. Since his division was augmented by the 442d Infantry Regiment (Nisei) for this particular operation, he massed it and the 143d Infantry Regiment for the main attack within an extremely narrow sector against the *16th* and *716th Volksgrenadier Divisions'* defenses around Bruyères.[60] Under the VI Corps plan, the 45th Infantry Division would simultaneously conduct a supporting attack toward Brouvelieures along the Bruyères–St. Dié road to cut off either German retreat or reinforcement from this direction. Major General Eagles selected the 179th Infantry Regiment for this important maneuver. (See Figure 12.)

This *corps* penetration would be carried out by ordering the *regiments* conducting the attack (the 143d and 442d) to execute an envelopment. Rather than assaulting Bruyères only from the obvious avenue of approach—up the Laval-Bruyères road—Dahlquist chose to make only a supporting attack from this direction. The 442d Infantry Regiment would make the main attack by advancing stealthily through the thickly wooded hills to the west of Bruyères and enveloping the defenders' flank. The regimental commander subsequently chose to attack with the 100th and 2d battalions leading and the 3d Battalion in reserve.[61]

To give the impression that the main attack was to come from the south, the 57mm antitank guns of all three divisional infantry regiments' antitank companies were massed along the Laval-Bruyères road. These short-range guns fired in support of the 143d Infantry Regiment as it advanced, with the 1st Battalion attacking northeastward up the

ORDER OF BATTLE
15–21 OCTOBER 1944

U.S. SEVENTH ARMY
Limited Objective Attacks

GERMAN ARMY GROUP G
Defense of Vosges Outposts

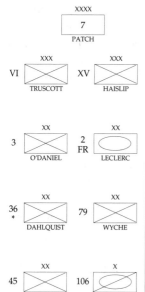

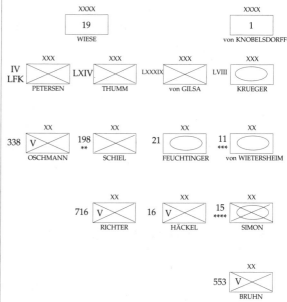

** Reinforced with 360th Cossack Regiment
*** Bulk of division committed in U.S. XII Corps sector (Third Army)
**** Withdrawn 16 October

* Reinforced with 442d RCT

KEY

X	Combat Command or Group	FR	French
XX	Division	LFK	Luftwaffe Feld Korps
XXX	Corps		
XXXX	Army		

- Infantry
- Armor/Panzer
- Mechanized Cavalry
- Armored Infantry/ Panzergrenadier
- Volksgrenadier

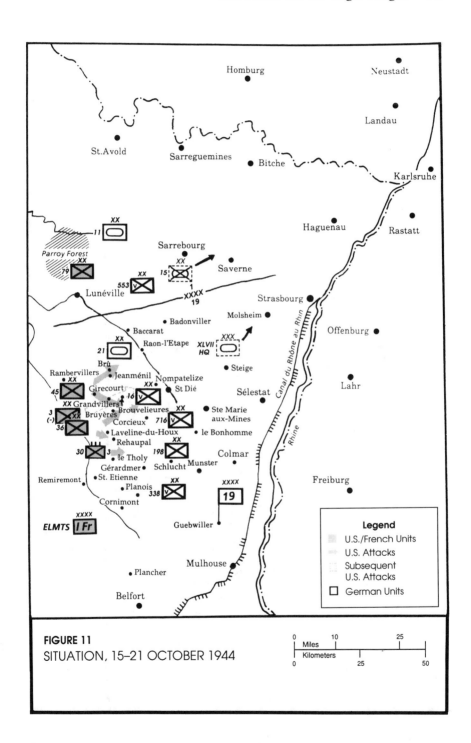

FIGURE 11

SITUATION, 15–21 OCTOBER 1944

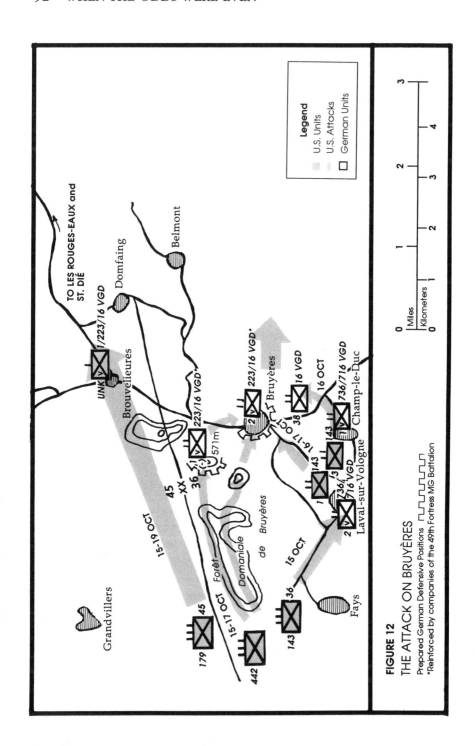

FIGURE 12

THE ATTACK ON BRUYÈRES

Prepared German Defensive Positions

*Reinforced by companies of the 49th Fortress MG Battalion

road and the 3d Battalion attacking first to secure Champ-le-Duc to the east, then turning north to support the 1st Battalion's assault. The 2d Battalion remained in division reserve.[62]

Initially, then, four American infantry battalions assaulted three reinforced battalions of dug-in German infantry. Over mountainous or hilly terrain, machine guns would dominate, and the matchup in machine guns was close. Indeed, the combined machine-gun strength of the four assaulting American battalions was about fifty-six .30-caliber weapons, both water-cooled M1917A4s and air-cooled M1919A4s. The German units defending the Bruyères area employed at least forty-two MG34s and MG42s, which, with their 40 percent higher rates of fire, could put out at least as much lead as their American adversaries' machine guns. The Americans could call on some sixty 60mm and 81mm mortars, whereas the Germans could depend on about two-thirds that number of their own 80mm mortars.[63] The Americans' massed antitank guns would face little more than half their own number, however.

Of course, the Germans could also depend on familiarity with the terrain over which they had had several days, if not weeks, to prepare their defenses. Hundreds of antipersonnel and antitank mines had been skillfully laid along the southerly approaches to Bruyères. Houses and other buildings had been selected to serve both as pillboxes and observation posts, and fields of fire had been carefully selected and cleared.[64] The approaches to Bruyères from the south and southwest are largely open and rolling, providing the defenders with plenty of opportunity for early acquisition and effective long-range engagement of the advancing Texas Division attackers. German doctrine called for designation of landmarks as registration points for indirect fires, and these, too, no doubt had already been chosen and confirmed. The Americans, on the other hand, had to adjust fires as the attack progressed.

The avenue of approach chosen for the main attack was of a very different character. The thickly wooded ridges to the west of Bruyères provided dense primary and secondary growth, thus concealing both attacker and defender until they were relatively close to each other. The one exception to this was the approaches to Hill 571 (its altitude in meters), which dominated the town from the northwest. This hill has a commanding view of all westward approaches from across a hundred-meter-deep, open ravine, the traverse of which would be all but impossible in the face of concentrated small-arms fire by the defenders.[65]

The attack on Bruyères began on the morning of 15 October 1944 in a cold drizzle with considerable ground fog.[66] This weather was both a blessing and a curse for the attackers, because it obscured the initial American advance from German observation but at the same time gave the attackers a miserable time the night before. The Germans no doubt spent a more comfortable night, entrenched as they were in and around Bruyères's stout buildings. In order to launch their attack at 0800, the infantrymen of the 143d and 442d Regiments had to be up and awake in the forty-degree Fahrenheit downpour since 0645, well before dawn that day. Morale was adversely affected; at times like that, the cohesion borne of long association and training together became critical.

The defenders, especially those in the polyglot *16th Volksgrenadier Division* in Bruyères itself, did not share this common cohesive background. Their commander, Generalleutnant Häckel, wrote after the battle that because they hardly knew one another, his commanders and men "often cracked soon after their commitment."[67] In this critical battle, the American superiority in this regard would combine with aggressive and intelligent maneuver to produce an important victory.

The Germans of the *716th Volksgrenadier Division* fiercely contested the 143d Infantry Regiment's assaults on Laval-sur-Vologne and Champ-le-Duc, and the *16th Volksgrenadier Division*'s *223d Regiment* did the same to the 442d Infantry Regiment's advance through the Forêt Communiale de Bruyères. The defenders' strength in machine guns and mortars became apparent during this fight as the stone and masonry structures along each road were skillfully defended. Each time ground was lost to the advancing Americans, an artillery or mortar-supported counterattack was mounted as quickly as possible to recover the yielded territory. Chester Tanaka, a member of the 442d RCT, pointed out that the attacking Americans

did not know then that this was the beginning of a far different kind of fight than the one waged in Italy. Here, the battleground was close to the German border. In Italy, the Germans could afford to trade real estate for time, men and materiel. In the Bruyères sector . . . their fortifications were deeper and more extensive, their firepower heavier and more intense, and their troops grimmer and more determined.[68]

After four days of vicious fighting, however, the Germans found themselves outmaneuvered: The advance of the Niseis of the "Go for Broke" Regiment across heavily wooded and deeply scored terrain had sealed off the *16th Volksgrenadier Division,* and the 179th Infantry's advance to the Bruyères-Brouvelieures road prevented reinforcement from that direction. Although a series of German counterattacks temporarily cut off the 1st Battalion, 141st Infantry Regiment, in the woods to the east of Bruyères (the much-publicized "Lost Battalion" of contemporary newspaper and postwar movie fame), a forceful drive by the 442d RCT brought relief before the supply situation of the stranded battalion became critical.

As the 36th Infantry Division assaulted Bruyères and the 179th Infantry Regiment attacked Brouvelieures, the remainder of the 45th Infantry Division supported the VI Corps's efforts with limited objective attacks in the area east of Rambervillers.[69] (See the northerly prong of the 45th Infantry Division attack in Figure 11.) In this sector, the opposing *21st Panzer Division* skillfully delayed the Thunderbirds' advance with roadblocks, mines, and other obstacles, but the men of the 180th RCT nevertheless made consistent headway. On the northern flank of the division and corps, however, the 157th Infantry Regiment spent most of October in a stationary slugfest with the *21st Panzer Division*'s *Panzergrenadiers* around the twin road junction towns of Brû and Jeanménil. It was not until 29 October that the Germans withdrew from these rubbled villages to avoid being taken in flank by the advancing 180th Infantry Regiment in the south.[70]

To the south of Bruyères, the 3d Infantry Division feinted toward the Schlucht Pass with significant artillery activity. At the same time, the "Rock of the Marne" Division was ordered to quietly withdraw its 7th and 15th Infantry Regiments out of the line near Le Tholy and to attack through the 45th and 36th Divisions toward St. Dié. In this way, Truscott hoped to exploit the direct penetration at Bruyères by massing five of his ten infantry regiments (the 442d, 143d, 7th, 15th, and 179th) in a ten-kilometer-wide corridor toward the Meurthe at St. Dié.

To make the Germans think that the Schlucht Pass, and not St. Dié, was the VI Corps's objective, a complex deception plan was undertaken by the Americans. With radio silence imposed, the 3d Infantry Division unobtrusively withdrew its 7th and 15th Infantry Regiments from the corps's right flank near Gerardmer to assembly areas near the 36th Infantry Division's positions around Bruyères. Meanwhile, radio traffic from the 30th Infantry Regiment and other elements left behind near Le Tholy, on the right flank of the VI Corps zone, simulated the continued presence of 3d Division units. At the same time, 36th Division (141st and 142d Infantry Regiments) troops "lost" helmets and other gear with 3d Infantry Division identification markings while on patrol. The advance elements of the 3d Infantry Division even wore 45th Infantry Division patches on their uniforms so as not to give away their presence to the defending Germans. As a result, the *Nineteenth Army* failed to shift the *198th Infantry Division* or, initially, any other units to the north to defend St. Dié, keeping them instead in place to defend along the 3d Infantry Division's original axis of advance toward the Schlucht Pass.[71] The 3d Division then attacked up the road to St. Dié from Bruyères on 20 and 21 October against disorganized German resistance.[72]

Recognizing too late the dangerous situation represented by the penetration at Bruyères and the true nature of the 30th Infantry Regiment's feint toward the Schlucht Pass, Generalleutnant von und zu Gilsa, commander of *LXXXIX Corps,* on 28 October released newly arrived reinforcements to Generalmajor Häckel. Adding to the already chaotic organization of his division was the assignment of two well-equipped but inexperienced Austrian alpine infantry battalions, the *201st* and *202d,* and two "Special Employment battalions" (*zur besondere Verwendung,* or penal infantry battalions), the *291st* and *292d,* totaling about three thousand combat troops.[73] Additionally, Wiese withdrew the *106th "Feldherrnhalle" Panzer Brigade* from the First French Army sector to the south, and committed it, organized into three combined arms battle groups, to counterattacks in the vicinity of La Salle in an attempt to halt the breakthrough.[74]

Although not even possessing numerical parity with the defenders (3,061 infantrymen in the line and heavy-weapons companies of the 7th and 15th Infantry Regiments[75]) and fatigued by nearly two and a half months of continuous combat, the American infantrymen tore through these fresh German units as they slugged through the thickly wooded hills on either side of the winding Bruyères–St. Dié road.[76] After eighteen days of brutal mountain combat, in subfreezing temperatures, nearly always attacking uphill into the faces of superior numbers of trained alpine troops, *Panzergrenadiers,* and desperate military criminals ensconced in two-thousand-plus-foot heights,[77] the "Cottonbalers" seized Le Haut Jacques pass and Tête de Blainbois (Hill 616—altitude in meters) near the tiny village of Rougiville. Meanwhile, the "Can Dos" of the 15th Infantry fought past German defenses in similar terrain on either side of the road from the hamlet of Bout de Dessous to Nompatelize to seize La Bourgonce, La Salle, and Nompatelize, also by 3 November. Within two days, the leading elements of Maj. Gen. "Iron Mike" O'Daniel's 3d Infantry Division were overlooking the Meurthe Valley opposite St. Dié. As a testament to the ferocity of the fighting and the difficulty of the terrain between Bruyères and the Meurthe, numerous 3d Infantry Division veterans of the Italian campaign called this battle "worse than Anzio."[78]

As Generalmajor Häckel desperately attempted to save the situation in the Bruyères–St. Dié corridor, the commanders of other *LXXXIX* and *LXIV Corps* units attempted to do the same in their sectors. By 28 October, Wiese had begun an extremely complicated response. He shifted Richter's *716th Volksgrenadier Division* to the *LXXXIX Corps* area, where it was inserted north of Häckel's *16th* in the vicinity of La Salle in an attempt to narrow Häckel's sector. Two days later, Thumm's *LXIV Corps* headquarters took control of the battle, as von und zu Gilsa and his *LXXXIX Corps* staff were ordered north to take control of *First Army*'s southern corps, consisting of the *361st* and *553d Volksgrenadier Divisions.* (*LVIII Panzer Corps* headquarters was withdrawn for duty elsewhere.) The *198th Infantry Division* was forced to move north to cover the gap left by the departure of the *716th Volksgrenadiers;* to assist Schiel in covering this sector, Wiese attached the *338th Volksgrenadier Division*'s *933d Volksgrenadier Regiment* to the *198th.* In turn, the *269th Infantry Division* replaced the *198th,* facing elements of the First French Army. (See Figure 13.) Clearly, the friction induced by this complex shuffling of command and control arrangements did not assist German unity of command or cohesion during the raging mountain battle. On the American side, in contrast, the division and corps structures remained constant throughout the operation.

In the conduct of their supporting attacks in the north, Major General Eagles and the Thunderbirds of the 45th Infantry Division's 179th

ORDER OF BATTLE
5 NOVEMBER 1944

U.S. SEVENTH ARMY
Drive to the Meurthe

GERMAN ARMY GROUP G
Delay to the Meurthe Line

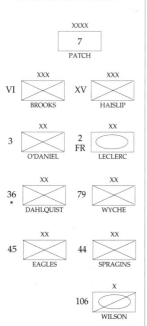

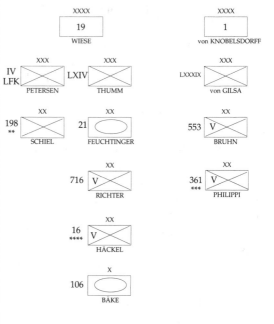

* Reinforced with 442d RCT

** Reinforced with 360th Cossack Regiment

*** Part of division committed in U.S. XII Corps sector (Third Army)

**** Reinforced by 201st and 202d Mountain Infantry Battalions and 291st and 292d zur besondere Verwendung (Penal) Battalions

KEY

X	Combat Command or Group	FR	French	
XX	Division	LFK	Luftwaffe Feld Korps	
XXX	Corps			
XXXX	Army			

Infantry

Armor/Panzer

Mechanized Cavalry

Armored Infantry/ Panzergrenadier

Volksgrenadier

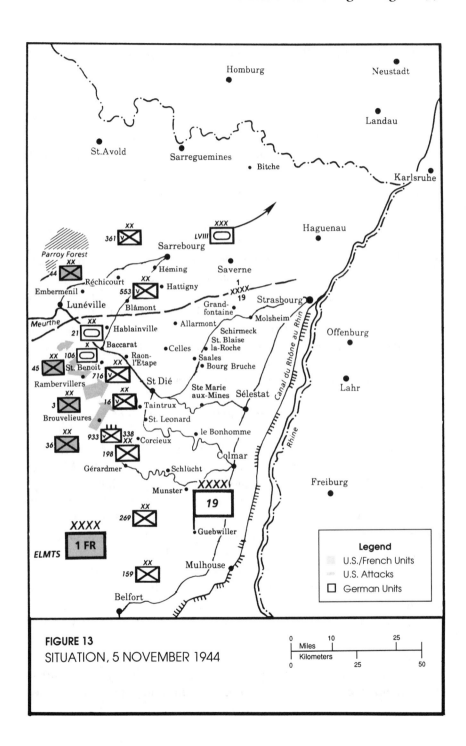

FIGURE 13

SITUATION, 5 NOVEMBER 1944

Infantry Regiment drove into Richter's *Volksgrenadiers,* while the 45th's 180th Infantry Regiment succeeded in pushing through Feuchtinger's *Panzergrenadiers* and an attached battle group of the 106th *Panzer Brigade* near St. Benoit on 30 October. (See Figure 13.) Pushing across the Mortagne River, the 179th and 180th Infantry Regiments steadily drove toward Raon l'Etape on the Meurthe in pursuit of the withdrawing Germans. By early November, however, they were relieved by the 399th Infantry RCT of the newly arrived 100th Infantry Division.

On the VI Corps's southern flank, after the 143d and 442d Infantry Regiments seized Bruyères, Dahlquist's other two regiments launched supporting attacks on 5 November against the overextended *198th Infantry Division* so as to prevent that unit from aiding its beleaguered comrades in the Bruyères–St. Dié corridor. Despite its chaotic organization and command and control arrangements, the *198th* (with the attached *933d Volksgrenadier Regiment*), estimated by Thumm to be the best of his infantry formations, fought stubbornly against the numerically comparable attackers, and succeeded in delaying their progress to the Meurthe. In their wake, however, the Germans left little standing in the Vosges villages from which they withdrew. To make the Texas Division infantrymen's lot even more uncomfortable in the incessant rain, cold, and snow, the Germans burned the sizable towns of Gerardmer, Corcieux, and other smaller villages. Such atrocities did little to improve cooperation from civilians elsewhere in Alsace.[79]

After two weeks of miserable, snowbound fighting, the 36th Division's lead infantry elements arrived at St. Léonard, overlooking the Meurthe valley, on 19 November. (See Figure 14.) Although Schiel's infantrymen made the Americans pay dearly for these gains, their sacrifice was in vain. The VI Corps had crossed the Meurthe River the week before, and its units were driving east and north toward the passes at Ste. Marie-aux-Mines, Bonhomme, and Steige. The American supporting attacks had accomplished their purpose of diverting the best German infantry division in the Vosges, preventing it from taking an active part in halting the main attack toward St. Dié. Most importantly, VI Corps was at last in position to attack the inadequately manned Vosges defensive lines.

The effectiveness of the defense that might have been possible had German reinforcements been committed in a doctrinally sound, organized manner can only be speculated upon, and speculation is not the historian's task. Nevertheless, VI Corps's carefully orchestrated operational penetration, using tactical envelopment and pursuit at Bruyères, and supporting attacks and feints to isolate the main effort, resulted in the near destruction of the *16th Volksgrenadier Division* and valuable reinforcements. It also forced General Wiese to withdraw the *LXIV* and *IV Luftwaffe Corps* to the Meurthe River and Vosges advanced line, and deprived the Germans of thousands of troops for defense of the carefully prepared Vosges positions behind the Meurthe.

Although it is impossible to know the exact number of German casualties sustained during this battle, an idea may be gained from the 7th Infantry Regiment's prisoner count of 1,086 during its drive on Le Haut Jacques alone.[80] During October, VI Corps took over 5,000 prisoners (the total for Seventh Army was 7,122) and killed or wounded thousands more; exact figures regarding German casualties are impossible to ascertain.[81] During October, the three VI Corps divisions involved in the penetration at Bruyères lost 6,189 men killed, wounded, or missing.[82] Even given the usually higher casualties sustained during the conduct of offensive operations, if the Germans lost only half the number of killed and wounded that the Americans did, then their total losses, including those who surrendered to the Americans, amounted to at least 8,100, or approximately 24 percent more than they inflicted on their opposition. Such losses would soon begin to tip the numerical scales in favor of the attackers, and thereby facilitate even greater freedom of maneuver for the Americans.

By massing the better part of three infantry divisions along the Bruyères–St. Dié axis and occupying the high ground on the south side of the Meurthe River against confused and poorly coordinated German opposition, Truscott and Maj. Gen. Edward H. Brooks, who succeeded Truscott as VI Corps commander on 25 October, accomplished their objectives in accordance with doctrinal tenets of mass and narrow frontages during penetration operations. By contrast, Wiese traded space and considerable numbers of troops for only about three weeks of time: time to further prepare the positions that constituted the last barrier before the Vosges passes and the Alsatian Plain, time that would bring the winter snows and fog to completely stymie American air support and superior quantities of armor, and time that would bring relief as a result of the Germans' December Ardennes counteroffensive. Wiese's troops moved into the first Vosges line east of the Meurthe barrier in

ORDER OF BATTLE
12–26 NOVEMBER 1944

U.S. SEVENTH ARMY
*Attack of the Vosges
Winter Line*

GERMAN ARMY GROUP G
Defense of the Vosges Position

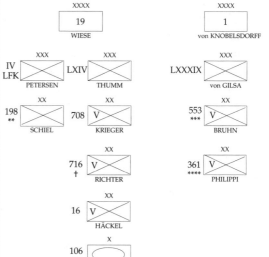

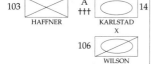

** To Belfort Sector 21–22 November
*** To 19th Army 16 November; back to First Army 19 November
**** Part of division committed in U.S. XII Corps sector (Third Army); part detached to 708th Volksgrenadier Division
† Reinforced with 360th Cossack Regiment
†† Attached to LXIV Corps 25 November

* Seventh Army/SHAEF reserve
††† Attached to VI Corps 26 November

KEY

X	Combat Command or Group	FR	French	
XX	Division	LFK	Luftwaffe Feld Korps	
XXX	Corps			
XXXX	Army			

Infantry

Armor/Panzer

Mechanized Cavalry

Armored Infantry/ Panzergrenadier

Volksgrenadier

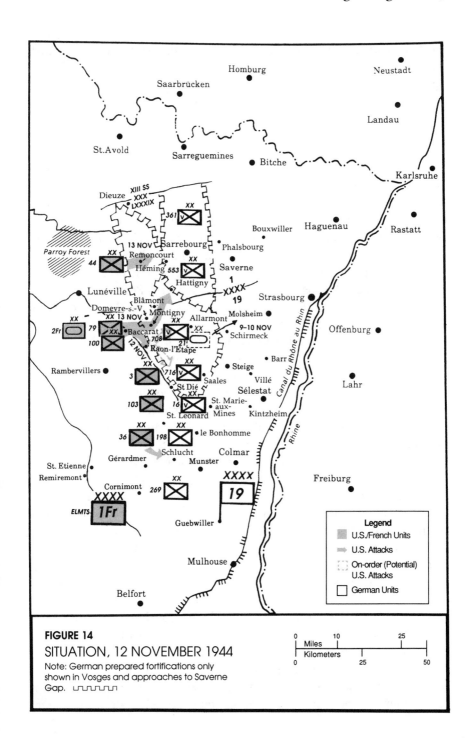

FIGURE 14

SITUATION, 12 NOVEMBER 1944

Note: German prepared fortifications only
shown in Vosges and approaches to Saverne
Gap. ⊓⊔⊓⊔⊓⊔⊓

Legend

U.S./French Units

U.S. Attacks

On-order (Potential)
U.S. Attacks

German Units

0   10   25
Miles
Kilometers
0   25   50

the *LXIV Corps* sector by 5 November and prepared to defend against American attacks toward the Steige, Ste. Marie-aux-Mines, Saales, and Saverne passes. Once at the Meurthe, Major General Brooks faced the challenge of cracking the main German winter lines in the High Vosges.

THE FIGHT FOR THE VOSGES WINTER LINE

In mid-October OKW ordered *Army Group G* to defend the western slopes of the Vosges "under all circumstances."[83] This order further explained the *Führer Befehl* (Hitler's personal order) as meaning that the Vosges positions were to be held to the last man. Successful resistance was to persist until at least April 1945 to allow the *Westwall* to be restored to effectiveness. The German *First* and *Nineteenth Armies* were to hold positions that would prevent American forces from proceeding through the Vosges passes onto the Alsatian Plain, which would then allow them to envelop the German forces holding the Belfort Gap against the First French Army.

In many ways, this plan had considerable doctrinal merit. General der Infanterie Thumm, commander of *LXIV Corps,* pointed out that, with the onset of the Vosges winter, American air superiority would be of limited utility if not altogether nullified by unacceptably low fog ceilings and visibility. In the craggy Vosges terrain, American armor would be confined to the roads and would therefore be more easily handled by German *Panzerabwehrwaffen* such as 50mm, 75mm, and 88mm anti-tank guns and, at the closer ranges made inevitable by crossroads villages, by German *Panzerfaust* and *Panzerschreck,* hand-held antitank rocket launchers prevalent in *Volksgrenadier* and *Festung* battalions.[84]

Even though many of the army units involved in the construction of the Vosges defensive positions were ordered into the line as the Americans broke through at Bruyères and forced the withdrawal of *LXIV, LXXXIX,* and *IV Luftwaffe Field Corps,* improvements to the Vosges defensive positions continued. Alsatian and German civilians, penal battalions, and labor units composed of Russian prisoners persisted in their efforts.[85] Under the auspices of Organisation Todt, they continued to construct positions and obstacles, such as roadblocks, pillboxes, and camouflaged trenches.

A significant number of the German units being used for the defense of the area were new or recently reconstituted. Because the German replacement system called for keeping units in the line until they were "combat ineffective," many of the *First* and *Nineteenth Army* combat units in the Vosges were made up largely of soldiers who had received only four to six weeks of infantry training prior to being committed to battle. Fortunately for them, the terrain and conditions present in the region were optimal for the introduction of such troops, because they had only to occupy and defend static positions with outstanding fields of fire and observation. The German defenders were protected from the increasingly hostile elements of mountain winter weather in the houses they had converted into small forts, as well as the formidable defensive works.

The attacking Americans, on the other hand, were forced to suffer in the open. In the 3d Infantry Division, for example, the increasingly cold and wet weather caused exponential increases in the number of trench-foot cases as the campaign progressed. There were 54 cases of this debilitating condition in September, 160 in October, and 448 in November.[86] Even less mobile soldiers, such as those in artillery and other rear-echelon units, found only limited shelter in some sectors because of the German "scorched earth" policy.

There were, however, certain basic flaws in the German operational concept. As Clausewitz pointed out, once cut off in mountainous terrain, defending units experience great difficulty regaining contact with withdrawing friendly elements. Yet Hitler's personal order made it impermissible even to *plan* for withdrawal or delaying operations from the designated defensive line. Thus, if the attacking Americans were to achieve multiple breakthroughs, defending German commanders could expect the wholesale encirclement and destruction of their units.

Still, the Germans had history on their side. No attacking army had ever forced a crossing of the Vosges. Additionally, the American record in winter mountain fighting in Italy had been something less than spectacular, and all indications were that they were still having problems getting supplies to the front from faraway Mediterranean ports. Although retreat to the stripped Siegfried line positions and the Rhine was unacceptable to Hitler, it would not have mattered if the Führer had permitted a withdrawal. The effectiveness of those positions was questionable; they had been denuded of heavy weapons for reinforcement of the Atlantic Wall fortifications between 1940 and June 1944. A resolute stand at the Vosges barrier was therefore in order.

A reorganization of forces within *Nineteenth Army* and *Army Group G* took place in the second week of November. In recognition of the dangers presented by Patton's Third Army in Lorraine to the north and west, Generaloberst Balck, the veteran *Panzer* commander of *Army Group G,* decided to withdraw Feuchtinger's battle-hardened *21st Panzer Division* from the line in an attempt to form a mobile reserve with which to counterattack in the event of a Third Army breakthrough. With *Nineteenth Army*'s withdrawal to the Vosges positions, such a switch made sense, because German doctrine called for the defense of fortified positions to be made by infantry units. Besides, occupation of prepared defenses would provide an opportunity for the safe commitment of new formations. The relieving unit was Generalmajor Josef Paul Krieger's *708th Volksgrenadier Division.*

The *708th Volksgrenadier Division* had three two-battalion regiments, the *720th, 748th,* and *760th Volksgrenadiers.* Much of the division had been wrecked while fighting Third Army units in September, and the entire division had been pulled back to Czechoslovakia to refit, receive new personnel, and train for six weeks prior to being deployed in the Vosges. Although the cadre consisted largely of experienced Kriegsmarine and Luftwaffe noncommissioned officers, few of them had much experience in ground combat. The greater bulk of the ranks were filled by recruits varying in age from eighteen to forty-five.[87] The infantry companies of this division had about 125 men each, so, including the divisional *Füsilier* company, the *708th Volksgrenadiers* could field about 3,200 men in its combat infantry units.[88]

The division commander was a fifty-one-year-old Bavarian who had commanded infantry companies and battalions in World War I. Like many of his contemporaries, Krieger had been forced out of the army after the war by the Versailles limitations—to serve as a police officer until the repudiation of *der Diktat* brought him back to the colors in 1935. He successfully commanded an infantry regiment in Russia and the Crimea, and assumed command of the *708th* at the outset of its refitting period on 15 September 1944.[89] Although well equipped and close to authorized strength for a division of its type, the *708th*'s training period was hardly adequate for the development of the cohesion so important for success in rigorous mountain warfare.

The fourteen-kilometer sector in which Krieger and his *Grenadiers* relieved the *21st Panzer Division* was a highly defensible one, at least. (See Figure 14.) The first Vosges line ran from just north of Montigny due south to the Meurthe River between the village of Bertrichamps and the more sizable town of Raon l'Etape. In the northern third of this sector, sparsely wooded rolling hills up to 950 feet high afforded outstanding fields of fire and observation. From Badonviller south, however, the terrain becomes more typically Vosgian, with steep, thickly wooded ridges of 1,200 to 1,600 feet squatting perpendicularly across the Americans' avenues of approach. Carefully camouflaged battle positions allowed the defenders to take maximum advantage of this terrain, which would force a close-in fight between infantrymen, without the possibility of armor or effective artillery support. With a breaking-in period in a quiet sector as well prepared as this, perhaps the cohesion required for the *708th Volksgrenadier Division*'s "finishing" could have developed. Krieger and his men were to have exactly the opposite experience, however.

The remaining units of Thumm's *LXIV Corps* defending the Vosges line to the south—the *716th* and *16th Volksgrenadier Divisions*—were still reeling from the beating sustained at the hands of Brooks's VI Corps in late October and early November. Yet the sectors they occupied also constituted highly defensible terrain. (See Figure 14.) Generalmajor Wilhelm Richter's *716th Volksgrenadier Division* defended along the Meurthe from just south of Raon l'Etape to just north of St. Dié, a distance of about twelve kilometers. Although in possession of two large hills that dominate this area, the *716th* was so weak from the pummeling its troops had taken that it was hardly able to do more than defend strongpoints along the Vosges line in this area with its thousand or so remaining infantrymen. The road running east from Le Rabodeau to Senones and the Saales Pass in this sector could afford the Americans a route, although minor, to breach the Vosges and break out onto the Alsatian Plain. Successful defense of the sector near Moyenmoutier was thus critical to German success.

Generalmajor Häckel's *16th Volksgrenadier Division* defended an even smaller sector, in recognition of its strength of barely more than a reinforced battalion. (See Figure 14.) From the northern fringe of St. Dié south to St. Léonard, a distance of about seven and a half kilometers, this broken division defended in prepared positions along the Meurthe, providing superb observation and fields of fire from dominating 1,500-foot heights, albeit at a point on the river where it was barely more than a stream. An important line of communication lay in this sector as well: The road from Ste. Marguerite, just south of St. Dié, leads east to the pass at Ste. Marie-aux-Mines, another route to the VI Corps objective of Strasbourg and the Rhine. Häckel's remnants would concentrate their efforts on securing it.

In Petersen's *IV Luftwaffe Field Corps,* located south of Thumm's *LXIV,* the *198th Infantry Division* continued its dogged defense against Dahlquist's 36th Infantry Division in the fog- and snow-shrouded mountains west of Bonhomme Pass. (See Figure 14.) Unlike the German divisions farther north, which received a brief respite between 5 and 11 November, Schiel's division fought continuously against the unrelenting attacks of the Texas Division. While the *198th* prevented an American breakthrough to the Col du Bonhomme, its constant commitment prevented it from supporting the *LXIV Corps* defense of the passes to the north—either through reinforcement of the brittle line or by movement north to allow Thumm's divisions to narrow their dangerously wide sectors.

For the Americans, especially the veterans of the 3d and 36th Infantry Divisions, this was an opportunity to continue to put to use lessons learned in Italy. However, as the fight for the Vosges wore on, new divisions were committed to the mountain fray. The newly arrived 100th and 103d Infantry Divisions were committed in the VI Corps zone to help crack the German winter lines.

The 100th Infantry Division, known as the "Century Division," was activated at Fort Jackson, South Carolina, in November 1942 and, like most U.S. infantry divisions in World War II, followed the U.S. Mobilization Training Plan. The division was commanded by Maj. Gen. Withers A. Burress, Virginia Military Institute Class of 1914. "Pinky" Burress was a World War I combat veteran who saw service in France with the 23d Infantry Regiment in the 2d Infantry Division. He had commanded the Century Division since its activation. The 100th participated in Second Army maneuvers in the Cumberland Mountains of Tennessee in the winter of 1943–44, during which its soldiers received superb preparation for their eventual commitment to the Vosges winter campaign. Although more than three thousand infantrymen were transferred out of the division during the spring of 1944 as replacements for other units already in combat, the division received nearly six months' supplementary training at Fort Bragg, North Carolina, before departing the New York Port of Embarkation for Marseilles. During that time, new infantrymen and recently redesignated infantrymen who had previously been assigned to the ASTP, antiaircraft units, or Army Air Forces were integrated into the Century Division's three infantry regiments, the 397th, 398th, and 399th.[90]

The 103d Infantry Division, nicknamed the "Cactus Division" after the logo on its shoulder patch, was activated at Camp Claiborne, Louisiana, in November 1942. Like the 100th Division, it was a standard AUS formation, and as such participated in Third Army maneuvers in Louisiana in the autumn of 1943. Unlike the 100th, however, the 103d was commanded by a National Guardsman, Maj. Gen. Charles C. Haffner, Jr., of Chicago. From November 1943 until September 1944, the Cactus Division received supplementary training at Camp Howze, Texas, to integrate the more than four thousand soldiers who joined its ranks as replacements for the mostly junior infantrymen who were levied overseas from the division's 409th, 410th, and 411th Infantry Regiments as fillers for units depleted in combat. As with the 100th Division, many of the replacements joining the 103d were "retreads" from the technical services or antiaircraft and aviation troops, and this period served to retrain and amalgamate these whiz kids and fly-boys into the Cactus Division.[91] The Germans were not the only ones committing retreads to the fray. American outfits had a minority of such soldiers, who were amalgamated into the gaining organization's "family" through extensive prebattle unit training. In German formations, newly designated infantrymen often were in the majority and had little time to develop cohesive bonds or confidence in their officers.

The upcoming battles along the Vosges winter line in the VI Corps sector would pit three understrength German infantry divisions (the *16th* and *716th Volksgrenadiers* and the *198th Infantry*), one up-to-strength but inexperienced infantry division (the *708th Volksgrenadiers*), a separate infantry regiment (the *360th Cossack*), and miscellaneous *Kampfgruppen* against an American attacking force with greater cohesion and superior numbers. The VI Corps, which was still assigned the mission of seizing Strasbourg by attacking through the minor Vosges passes, consisted of two depleted, tired infantry divisions (the 3d and 36th), two full-strength (but totally green) infantry divisions (the 100th and 103d), and, after 19 November, an armored division combat command (CCA of the newly arrived 14th Armored Division). This gave VI Corps an infantry force ratio of just under 2.9 to 1 in its favor.[92]

Given that the Germans were taking advantage of what Clausewitz considered to be the stronger form of warfare (the defensive) in an area almost ideally suited for such operations, given that the foggy weather all but eliminated American close air support,[93] and given that American infantrymen were forced to live and attack in the open whereas the Germans took advantage of the protection of fortifications and buildings, the odds in the battle for the High Vosges and the German winter line were much closer than the force ratios indicated. In fact, the *LXIV Corps* commander, Generalder Infanterie Thumm, believed that a successful defense was possible, based strictly on the tactical situation.[94] The side that could sustain effective, tactically sound operations would win.

Such was not the case in the U.S. XV Corps zone. To the north of Thumm's *LXIV Corps,* von und zu Gilsa's *LXXXIX Corps* of von Knobelsdorff's *First Army* defended the critical Saverne Gap with the *553d Volksgrenadier Division* and part of the *361st Volksgrenadier Division.* In this sector, the Germans possessed some of the strongest fortifications in the entire Vosges region; there were actually three, and in some areas, *four,* lines of defense built across the Saverne Gap by Organisation Todt laborers. However, as in the rest of the Vosges, the lines were often too far apart to facilitate mutual support, and the German forces were too few in number to simultaneously occupy all of them. If the Americans were to frontally assault these positions and allow the units of *LXXXIX Corps* the opportunity to take advantage of their excellent fields of fire, observation, and obstacles, perhaps von und zu Gilsa's men would have a chance to accomplish their defensive mission. If, however, the lines were penetrated, the terrain was sufficiently difficult and the distances between the lines great enough (up to ten kilometers) that the attackers could move as quickly from one to the next as the defenders. Clausewitz's warnings regarding the unsuitability of mountainous areas for absolute defense had once again gone unheeded by the German commanders.

The southern flank of *LXXXIX Corps* was defended by Bruhn's *553d Volksgrenadier Division,* which had been heavily engaged since replacing the *15th Panzergrenadier Division* in the Parroy Forest in mid-October. Although the men of the *553d* had given ground but grudgingly since, the 79th Infantry Division (and, after 22 October, the 44th) had pushed them out of the Parroy Forest by the beginning of November. As a result, in the second week in November, Bruhn could muster between

2,600 and 2,800 tired infantrymen from his three *Volksgrenadier* regiments to defend the rolling, relatively open terrain of their thirteen-kilometer sector between Remoncourt in the north (just north of the line Avricourt-Embermenil, about halfway) to just south of Domèvre-sur-Vesouze in the south.[95] (See Figure 14.)

Generalmajor Philippi's *361st Volksgrenadier Division* defended the sector to the north of the *553d Volksgrenadiers.* This sector also included three lines of prepared defenses but faced mostly U.S. Third Army units. In the Seventh Army's zone, the terrain in the *361st*'s sector was even more conducive to defense, being heavily wooded along the boundary with the *553d* (the Rechicourt Forest and the Forêt Domaniale de Sarrebourg, north of the Héming-Sarrebourg highway) and containing a large, easily defended lake, the Etang de Gondrexange. One battalion of the *361st*'s *951st Volksgrenadier Regiment,* with about 350 infantrymen, defended that portion of the German sector in the XV Corps zone.[96]

Thus, in the XV Corps zone, the odds were very much different from those in the VI Corps zone to the south. About 3,200 German *Volksgrenadiers* faced 12,016 American infantrymen of the veteran—and rested—79th Infantry Division and the recently committed 44th Infantry Division.[97] Additionally, the Free French 2d Armored Division, with four battalions of tanks and four battalions of armored infantry, stood ready to exploit successes made by the attacking American infantry in the one part of the Vosges region in which armor could conceivably play an important role.

Lieutenant General Patch, commanding Seventh Army, had carefully orchestrated this situation. By aggressively placing continuous pressure on the *Nineteenth Army* and southern wing of the *First* with the attacks at Bruyères and through the Parroy Forest, Patch had inflicted considerable losses on the German units occupying the Vosges positions, and not allowed them desperately needed time to train their disorganized units.[98] Those soldiers lost while defending strongpoints in the Vosges foothills were unavailable for the showdown on the winter lines, where their effectiveness would have been undeniably greater. As a result, the vaunted Vosges defenses would be even more precariously held, and an American breakthrough to one or more of the Vosges passes would be more difficult to prevent. Patch issued an order on 5 November, still focusing his main effort on forcing the minor passes that constituted the shortest routes to his geographical objectives of Strasbourg and the Rhine.[99] Soon, his subordinate corps would initiate a coordinated effort to reach them and simultaneously accomplish his main goal of destroying the enemy in Alsace.

Major General Haislip, commanding XV Corps, issued a field order on 8 November prescribing the conduct of his corps' upcoming attack on the German forces in the Saverne Gap.[100] XV Corps would attempt to penetrate the Saverne Gap defenses and subsequently envelop the forces defending them. Wyche's "Cross of Lorraine" Division had made good use of its sixteen-day break from action by amalgamating replacements through an intensive training program. Refreshed and replenished, the 79th was assigned the main attack to the northeast from positions around Hablainville to seize Sarrebourg. In this way, the attacking echelons would penetrate the first two of the four defensive belts in the Saverne Gap in the extreme north of what was, at the time the plan was formulated, the *21st Panzer Division*'s sector, thus avoiding the bulk of the best German division in *Nineteenth Army*. Attacking parallel to and *behind* this line, the 79th would then drive across the Vesouze River east of Blâmont, envelop the *553d Volksgrenadier Division,* and arrive before Sarrebourg from the south. That the *21st Panzer* had been relieved by the *708th Volksgrenadiers* three days before the attack commenced on 13 November only added to the plan's effectiveness.

In the north, Spragins's 44th Infantry Division would conduct a supporting attack along the boundary of the *553d* and *361st Volksgrenadier Divisions* to immobilize Bruhn's and Philippi's defenders during the 79th's envelopment. Such a route would mean an approach to Sarrebourg from the heavily fortified west, but again, this would fix the defenders in place while the other elements of the corps attacked from less strongly defended directions. This route took the 44th through difficult forest and lake country, but it allowed the division to attack the Vosges defensive belts at their intersection near Héming, eliminating the need to penetrate two distinct belts of fortifications. It also assisted the main attack by ensuring that the *361st Volksgrenadiers* would not be able to mount a counterattack directly into the flank of the main attack's drive on Sarrebourg, a doctrinally correct purpose for such an offensive maneuver. (See Chapter 2.)

Haislip assigned Leclerc's 2d French Armored Division the task of exploiting the penetration made by the 79th. After seizing Sarrebourg, the "Deuxième Blindée" (2ème Blindée) would then dash for Phalsbourg and the pass at Saverne itself. Once through the Saverne Gap, mobile elements of XV Corps would envelop the German units remaining in the Vosges and be available to assist in the capture of Strasbourg. Rather than battering rams, then, the XV Corps's units were scalpels, carving holes in the defenses on which the Germans had pinned so much of their hope in the sector. Instead of using their numerical preponderance to bludgeon the Germans with frontal assaults against prepared positions, the Americans hoped to slice through each of the four defensive lines in narrow penetrations and subsequently envelop the defenders.

For VI Corps, Major General Brooks developed a plan that placed similar emphasis on maneuver. The VI Corps attack plan called for the main attack to be made on 16 November by the 103d Infantry Division against the German defenses in the vicinity of St. Dié, the key to the road net to the Vosges passes beyond. The supporting attack, commencing four days earlier, would be carried out by the 100th Infantry Division, which would cross the Meurthe at Baccarat and penetrate the first Vosges line on a narrow, four-kilometer front on 12 November. Depending on how the situation developed, Burress's "Centurymen" would either roll up the German line by attacking to the southeast along the north bank of the river, enveloping the German *716th Volksgrenadier Division,* or drive to the northeast toward Bionville-Allarmont in the event of conspicuous success by the XV Corps's thrust toward Saverne. This would support the Cactus Division's attack by drawing German units northward, away from the focal point of the main attack to come. The 3d Infantry Division was to conduct local security along the Meurthe between St. Dié and just south of Raon l'Etape and train to integrate its recently arrived replacements.[101] After a week and a half of training, the "Rock of the Marne" Division had to be ready to cross the Meurthe and drive with the 103d on the Saales Pass on or about 20 November.[102]

Not only were the two corps' plans complementary, they were superbly synchronized as well. (See Figure 14.) By launching VI Corps's supporting attack (Burress's 100th Infantry Division toward Raon l'Etape) into the southern sector of the German division holding the northern flank of the entire *Nineteenth Army* front on 12 November, the attention of that division's commander and staff would be focused *away* from the site of the following day's XV Corps assault. As a result, Wyche's 79th Infantry Division, with the 2ème Blindée following, would launch the XV Corps's main attack into an enemy formation whose attention had been firmly arrested by the assault of the VI Corps's 100th Infantry Division the day before. In this way, Patch hoped to tear open the seam between the *First* and *Nineteenth Armies* and drive straight into the Saverne Gap.

The German operational situation along the Vosges winter lines had badly deteriorated by the second week in November. Wiese's *Nineteenth Army* had lost its best division, Feuchtinger's *21st Panzer,* and its best infantry formation—the *198th Infantry Division*—was decisively engaged near Gérardmer by the American 36th Division in a protracted and costly slugging match. Furthermore, the organization and disposition of the two field armies making up *Army Group G* contributed to the Germans' operational problems.

Balck, the vaunted *Panzer* commander, placed the boundary of his two field armies just south of the Saverne Gap. At first glance, this seems to have been a sound decision, ensuring that the defense of this key terrain would be under the firm control of von und zu Gilsa's *LXXXIX Corps,* both divisions of which were solidly ensconced in very strong fortifications. However, analysis of the terrain shows a flaw in this arrangement that proved to be disastrous for *Army Group G.*

Balck arrayed his forces from south to north, along essentially east-west axes from Bas Rupt, south of Gérardmer in the *IV Luftwaffe Corps's* sector north as far as Dieuze, on the boundary between *LXXXIX Corps* and *XIII SS Corps.* The High Vosges, however, break to the *northeast* from Baccarat to Phalsbourg (roughly along the Baccarat-Badonviller railway in the *21st Panzer* cum *708th Volksgrenadier* sector), and degenerate into rolling, sparsely vegetated terrain north of this line. As a result, the left (southern) flank of the *First Army* (*LXXXIX Corps's 553d Volksgrenadier Division*'s sector) dangled in open country, rather than being anchored in the mountains. The sector of *Nineteenth Army*'s rightmost division lay partially in this same open country and partially in the High Vosges between Baccarat and Raon L'Etape. This meant that *Nineteenth Army*'s right (northern) flank also dangled in the less-defensible terrain of the western approaches to the Saverne Gap, and that responsibility for the defense of this avenue of approach lay partially with the rightmost division of Wiese's *Nineteenth Army.* What seems then to have been a satisfactory arrangement by which von und zu Gilsa would control the defense of Saverne was actually a precarious one in which he and Wiese shared the defense of this key terrain. Bruhn and Philippi, defending approximately 90 percent of the rolling countryside to the west of Saverne, answered to von und zu Gilsa, who in turn took his orders from von Knobelsdorff. Krieger, defending the southern 10 percent of the Saverne approaches, answered to Thumm, who took his orders from Wiese. Coordination of the defense of the Saverne Gap therefore had to be carried out at the army group level! Had the *708th Volksgrenadiers* been assigned to *LXXXIX Corps,* this situation would have been avoided. Von und zu Gilsa would have directly controlled the battle for Saverne, and the army boundaries would have been anchored in the High Vosges. Instead, precious time would be wasted waiting for orders from Balck's headquarters, and coordinated efforts at defense would be seriously hampered.

The Germans' problems did not end with training deficiencies and a faulty command and control structure. Not only did these shortcomings adversely affect the soldiers' *ability* to fight, but they damaged their *desire* to fight as well. As Thumm admitted, "their psychological and moral strength were submitted to too great a strain."[103] Much more than the tactical situation, the poor state of his men's morale concerned the *LXIV Corps* commander.[104]

Although the Germans were fighting on the doorstep of the *Vaterland,* by the time of the campaign in the High Vosges many German troops believed that the war was lost.[105] Each U.S. division took thousands of prisoners who simply deserted during this portion of the campaign, a sure indicator of declining morale.[106] Still, German units usually fought well at least initially—and no division-sized elements collapsed completely. German records, of course, do not indicate low morale per se; to have done so in writing would surely have been cause for relief—or worse. The small measure of cohesion achieved in these German units simply could not compensate for these feelings of pessimism. Mixing Sudetenlanders and Austrians with German soldiers may have bolstered the numerical strength of *Army Group G,* but such practices also contributed significantly to the weakening of the social bonds between unit members in pressure situations.[107] Similarly, lacking extensive unit training and missing the cohesive bonds born of shared hardships and living experiences with their comrades prior to commitment to combat (what Janowitz and Shils called "community of experience"[108]), many German soldiers felt no particular loyalty to their units or comrades. Recognizing the dangers of this situation and its potential for disaster, German leaders substituted different measures for genuine cohesion. What they finally decided on was ineffective as a long-term solution. According to U.S. estimates, the fighting zeal of German units at this point in the war was motivated to a significant extent by fear of the National Socialist regime: fear of punishment, fear of shame, and even fear of reprisal against family members in Germany. In an estimate written in early November 1944, Seventh Army intelligence officers concluded that although most German officers still followed orders out of a sense of duty, pride, and professionalism, the case of the average soldier was different. German soldiers in the units fighting for their lives in the Vosges were often blatantly intimidated by their superiors into performing well on the battlefield. Executions were routinely carried out pursuant to courts-martial that found soldiers who had been absent from their units for more than three days guilty of "attempted desertion." Obviously, given the difficulty of regaining contact with a parent unit after being cut off in mountainous terrain, German soldiers were often falsely accused of this capital offense. As part of the Wehrmacht's campaign to discourage desertion, the deadly results of sentencing were widely publicized throughout German units by the chain of command. Prisoners reported instances of threats, beatings, and even shootings of German soldiers by SS units located directly behind army defensive positions.[109] Thumm confirmed that the German soldiers' "lack of fighting power was to be replaced by ruthless command" and that commanders who failed in their missions would be summoned before courts-martial.[110]

Clearly, such techniques could be effective as "ersatz morale," as Seventh Army intelligence officers chose to call it, as long as the danger from one's own officers or from the SS was greater than that offered by the enemy. As Janowitz and Shils put it in their landmark analysis of World War II German army combat motivation:

> The dread of destruction of the self, and the demand for physical survival, while breaking up the spontaneous solidarity of the military group in most cases, thus served under certain condi-

tions to coerce the soldier into adherence to his group and to the execution of the orders of his superiors.[111]

Faced with the choice of fighting to the last man or surrendering to a foe known for his humane treatment of prisoners, it is not surprising that so many German troops opted for the latter. Some Russian and Polish prisoners taken by the advancing echelons of the 103d Infantry Division said they murdered their German officers so they could surrender.[112] Like ersatz coffee, ersatz discipline was really no replacement but only an unsatisfactory, temporary substitute. The deleterious effect of such ersatz morale on combat proficiency was clearly significant in the increasingly uncomfortable and deadly environment of warfare in the High Vosges.

The soldiers and commanders in VI Corps faced their own difficulties in preparation for their drive to the Vosges passes. The infantry units of the three original divisions (the 3d, 36th, and 45th Infantry) had been depleted considerably by the enemy and by the weather after the initial battle for Bruyères and the approach to St. Dié. By 30 October, for example, the 3d Infantry Division's 15th Infantry Regiment had an average of 95 soldiers (53 percent of the authorized strength) present for duty in the line companies of its 3d Battalion; the 1st and 2d Battalions were somewhat better off with averages of 129 (70 percent) and 127 (69 percent), respectively.[113] The 36th Infantry Division's 141st Infantry Regiment counted less than a hundred men in some line companies (E and G) by Halloween, and averaged only 121, or 66 percent.[114] The rifle companies of the 442d RCT, which had gone into the assault of Bruyères actually about 15 percent *overstrength,* were at about 60 percent of their authorized strength by 31 October.[115] These units used the brief respite between the capture of the terrain overlooking the Meurthe and the renewal of the drive toward the Vosges passes to train and integrate the large numbers of infantry replacements arriving at the front.

American morale during this period is difficult to judge from archival evidence. The bulk of the periodic operations reports of infantry units submitted at the time describe morale as "excellent," but these assessments are suspect. Because commanders are responsible for maintaining high morale in their respective units, one cannot imagine a company commander listing his unit's morale as anything but "excellent" if he wished to remain in command! An examination of more than eleven thousand morning reports submitted during this campaign by Seventh Army infantry companies revealed only two that listed morale as other than "excellent."[116]

As the history of the 100th Infantry Division's 397th Infantry Regiment points out, these reports' glowing descriptions were not fully accurate for a number of reasons. Unlike the Germans, the Americans were far from home, and the strange surroundings only added to the confusion and frustration endemic to combat under any conditions.[117] The increasingly worse weather also challenged morale in American infantry units. Troops in field artillery, headquarters, and combat support units frequently lived in temporarily requisitioned Alsatian buildings and ate at least one hot meal daily, brought up in insulated cans by field kitchens, but the lot of the machine gunner, mortarman, medic, and, most of all, the combat rifleman was very different. Unlike their German counterparts, who usually lived in prepared defensive positions complete with thick overhead cover, these men were utterly exposed to the elements. They could rarely get dry in the seemingly interminable Vosges fog and drizzle; they were nearly always cold and could never build fires at night for fear of discovery by the Germans; and they became highly susceptible to the immobilizing agony of immersion foot or trench foot. Their caloric requirements were enormous, climbing steep hills and descending equally steep valleys with forty-five to sixty pounds of personal equipment (see Chapter 1), and they were almost always hungry, for their intake never matched their consumption.

Whereas the Germans, stationary in their mountain strongholds, often managed to cook food, the attacking American infantry practically never ate hot meals, being limited instead to cold, slimy meat from cylindrical green C-ration cans, wolfed down with a greasy metal mess kit spoon. They often were limited to the chocolate or tropical fruit bars and chewing gum that came in K rations. Although it is true that they had all done it before on training maneuvers, it was different in combat because there was no "end of exercise" respite assuring a return to warm, dry barracks and hot mess hall chow. This went on seemingly forever, or until the enemy surrendered, or until shell fragments tore their flesh and sent them bleeding and crying to the aid station, or a "bouncing Betty" blew off a leg, or a bullet sent them to eternity. Certainly, the morale of these men was "a little lower than high" during those grim days in the Vosges.[118]

Still, once the initial shock of combat wore off, the value of the relative emphasis the Americans had placed on cohesion became apparent. Although the U.S. Army did indeed use an individual replacement system, in the Seventh Army, at least, it did not allow fighting units to dwindle "down to the nub" as did the Germans. Even in the infantry rifle companies that took the most severe casualties during the campaign in the High Vosges, rarely was total strength allowed to sag below 67 percent.[119] As a result, replacements joined organizations that, although certainly bloodied, retained something of the "family" or team identities developed in precampaign training, either stateside, in Italy, or both. This provided a degree of comfort and a sense of belonging so essential for the maintenance of suitable morale. Compared to the German practice of throwing together amalgams of stragglers or developing units in six-week divisional training cycles, such practices could not fail to produce greater cohesion and resiliency in the face of setbacks and perseverance in pursuit of victory. Little better evidence of this greater cohesion can be found than the missing in action (MIA) total of 424 for the entire Seventh Army for the month of November.[120] Included in this number are the total number of prisoners captured by the Germans, deserters, and dead whose bodies were unaccounted for during the month. During the same period the Germans lost 23,623 prisoners alone to the Seventh Army—clearly an indication of an inferior state of cohesion as well as a tribute to the effectiveness of American maneuver.[121]

Such cohesion was a perishable commodity and could only be maintained, given an influx of replacements, by unit training whenever possible. Recognizing this, after the casualties sustained in the fighting around Bruyères, VI Corps Field Order Number 7, dated 7 November 1944, ordered the 45th Infantry Division into army reserve for rehabilitation and training, and the 3d Infantry Division into a quiet sector for the same activities.[122] Even the 36th Infantry Division, in almost continuous combat at Bruyères and later against the *198th Infantry Division* near Gerardmer, published directives requiring intensive training in expected tasks during lulls in the fighting.[123]

While battered divisions rested and amalgamated replacements, Seventh Army's drive to crack the Vosges winter lines began with the attack by Maj. Gen. Withers A. Burress's fresh 100th Infantry Division. On or about 10 November, the positions of the *21st Panzer Division* from Raon l'Etape in the south to Montigny in the north had been taken over by the newly arrived *708th Volksgrenadier Division;* the *21st Panzer Division* was needed to contain a threatened breakthrough by the Third Army in Lorraine. No sooner did the *708th* arrive than it was attacked by the Century Division.

The engagement of the *708th Volksgrenadier Division* in the vicinity of Raon l'Etape and Moyenmoutier by the 100th Infantry Division is significant not only because it was the VI Corps's supporting attack, but also because it allows the opportunity to study the results of the clash of an inexperienced U.S. infantry division and an equally "green" German division.

Arrayed in positions that had been extensively prepared by Alsatian and German laborers and improved by Feuchtinger's *125th* and *192d Panzergrenadier Regiments* and the engineer company of the *106th Panzer Brigade* during the previous weeks, the *708th Volksgrenadiers* were off to a fair start. The foul weather grounded all Allied aircraft that could have supported the operation; the precipitous slopes and heavily wooded terrain restricted the American armor to the winding, narrow, and extensively blocked and heavily mined roads; and the *708th*'s left flank was securely anchored on the Meurthe River.

The 100th Infantry Division began its first combat operation with two regiments attacking abreast after crossing the Meurthe at Baccarat. (See Figure 15.) The 397th Infantry Regiment attacked to the east with its line of advance just north of and parallel to the Meurthe, and the 399th Infantry Regiment attacked along a parallel axis to the north. Each assault regiment advanced with two battalions forward and one in reserve. The 100th's remaining regiment, the 398th Infantry, conducted a supporting screen and deception operation along the south bank of the Meurthe to hold German units in place along the high ground north of the river in anticipation of river crossings. Major General Burress thus sent approximately 2,572 infantrymen into the Vosges woods in the early morning of 12 November to meet their numerically equal German counterparts, who were also about to get their first taste of combat.[124] The odds were virtually even, although the Germans held the advantages of terrain and position. It was an infantryman's fight and an infantryman's nightmare. Training and the tactical proficiency

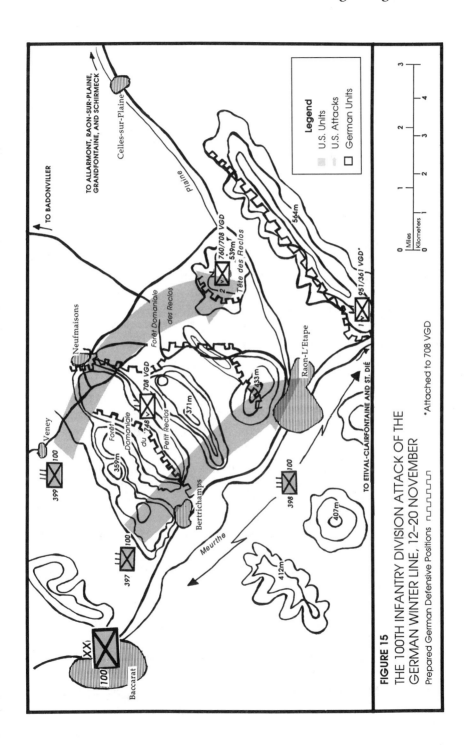

FIGURE 15

THE 100TH INFANTRY DIVISION ATTACK OF THE
GERMAN WINTER LINE, 12–20 NOVEMBER

Prepared German Defensive Positions ⊓⊔⊓⊔⊓⊔

*Attached to 708 VGD

and cohesion borne of "community of experience" would make the difference in the outcome.

Encountering enemy resistance just north of the hamlet of Bertrichamps, the 397th Infantry Regiment attacked through entrenched German positions along 1,200- to 1,500-foot ridges, and ploughed ahead on a narrow, 1,500-meter frontage. In four days of savage fighting in blinding rain and bitter cold, they overran elements of the *748th Volksgrenadier Regiment* to reach the high ground overlooking Raon l'Etape. In the first forty-eight hours alone, the 397th Infantry captured seventy-six disheartened *Volksgrenadiers*.[125]

To the north, the 399th Infantry's thrust along a similarly narrow corridor was no less successful, as these infantrymen of the Century Division slogged forward through elements of the *748th* and *760th Volksgrenadier Regiments* entrenched in the densely forested Forêt Domaniale des Reclos.[126] The defenses in this sector of the Vosges were indeed superb, consisting of two-hundred-meter belts of thoroughly cleared forest covered directly by machine guns in concrete blockhouses and indirectly by preplotted artillery and mortar fire. Here, at least, the engineers of *LXIV Corps* had succeeded in coordinating the efforts of the various labor organizations to construct a doctrinally correct defense, with combat outposts and main lines of resistance within three thousand meters of one another. Although the poorly organized relief of the *21st Panzer Division* had scattered units in a confusing and piecemeal pattern, Krieger's men fought back valiantly against the advancing Americans, mounting frequent platoon and company counterattacks in accordance with the doctrine learned in their brief six-week division training period.[127]

On 15 November, the 3d Battalion, 399th Infantry, blasted through the winter line fortifications along the east side of the Neufmaisons–Raon l'Etape road with bayonets fixed to secure a breach of the first line of defenses. The 1st Battalion then passed through and continued the attack toward the main line of defense along the fifteen-hundred-foot heights overlooking the Plaine River and the Schirmeck–Raon l'Etape road. Coincidentally, it was the second anniversary of the 100th Infantry Division's activation, and the results of two years of training together showed. While the Centurymen pressed the attack into its seventh day, the troops of the *708th Volksgrenadier Division* grew exhausted; Generalmajor Krieger himself attributed this lack of resiliency to inadequate training.[128] By 18 November, Raon l'Etape had been out-flanked and seized by Burress's troops, and the Vosges winter lines in this sector, intended by OKW to hold until April 1945, were ruptured. This spirited and effective attack served both of its purposes: It fixed the *708th Volksgrenadiers* in place, allowing the 103d and 3d Infantry Divisions to attack across the Meurthe against the depleted *716th* and *16th Volksgrenadier Divisions* without fear of interference from the north. It also focused the efforts of the *708th Volksgrenadiers* in the southern portion of their sector, allowing XV Corps to launch its main attack toward Sarrebourg against a distracted and confused foe.[129] (See Figure 14.)

The failure of the *708th Volksgrenadiers* was recognized by Balck, who relieved Generalmajor Krieger on 18 November. The *Nineteenth Army* chief of staff, Oberst Walter Botsch, also criticized Krieger's division's performance, claiming that it had "failed miserably."[130] The corps commander, Thumm, however, understood the *708th*'s problem more acutely, recognizing that its training was insufficient for the demands of winter mountain warfare.[131]

Interestingly, the course and outcome of this battle also impressed the Germans with the abilities of the 100th Infantry Division. The *Army Group G* chief of staff, von Mellenthin, referred to this product of the standard U.S. Army wartime training plan as "a crack assault division with daring and flexible leadership" in testament to its performance in the High Vosges.[132] Later, in the Low Vosges, the Germans would find out that the 100th could defend tenaciously as well.

Haislip's XV Corps attack toward the Saverne Gap jumped off according to plan early in the morning of 13 November. With the 44th Infantry Division fixing the *553d* and *361st Volksgrenadier Divisions* in place, the 79th Infantry Division attacked along a narrow five thousand-meter front from Montigny toward Hattigny (see Figure 14) with two full regimental combat teams, the 314th and 315th. This axis of advance concentrated the strength of 3,824 American infantrymen against approximately 800 men of the *708th Volksgrenadier Division*'s *720th Volksgrenadier Regiment*.[133] Over the next two days, Krieger's troops in this sector also collapsed, with nearly a full company surrendering at Halloville on 15 November alone.[134] As the lead elements of Wyche's 79th Division struck northeast, they entered the sector of Bruhn's *553d Volksgrenadier Division behind* their first two defensive belts, placing, as von Mellenthin put it, "the left wing of the *553d Volksgrenadier Division* in an untenable position."[135] This penetration of the Saverne Gap defenses caused the *553d Volksgrenadiers* to abandon their outstanding forward defensive positions and withdraw eastward toward Sarrebourg.[136]

As XV Corps pressed its attack, the Germans developed serious command and control problems. With two of the three divisions defending the Saverne Gap reeling backward, Krieger attempted to mount a counterattack to restore contact with the *553d Volksgrenadiers* on 15 November. But by the time he marshaled the requisite forces, Wyche's leading elements were attacking them.[137] Recognizing—too late—the difficulty of coordinating the defense of this key terrain between two field armies, on 16 November, *Army Group G* subordinated the *553d Volksgrenadier Division* to *Nineteenth Army*'s *LXIV Corps* to ensure "unified control of the developing battle for Saverne."[138] This decision, intended to unify control of the battle, in fact fragmented it even more. The *LXIV Corps* commanding general could only transmit orders to Bruhn through a tenuous radio link over the Donon heights (elevation 3,350 feet) because wire communications would take too much time to install.[139] The *553d*'s commander, Generalmajor Bruhn, said, "Despite greatest efforts by all branches, we did not manage to establish during the following few days any reliable signal communications with the new, far distant *LXIV Corps*."[140] As a result, orders had to travel by courier or be delivered by Thumm in person, a slow and unwieldy process for a situation described by the *Nineteenth Army* chief of staff as developing "with such speed that the division [the *553d*] could not react quickly enough."[141] As a result, instead of unifying control of the battle for the Saverne Gap, control was practically destroyed by the Germans' own miscalculations. Essentially, no one controlled the corps's battle, and Bruhn's division operated in a command vacuum for three critical days—until it was reassigned to *First Army* on 19 November.[142] By then, the disruption of coordination between the *708th* and *553d Volksgrenadiers* was complete.

Recognizing this, Haislip ordered Leclerc to attack through the hole created by the 79th with the 2ème Blindée on the afternoon of the same day. While the men of the *553d* continued to resist fiercely, all semblance of coherent defense had ceased and the French armor raced toward Saverne, reaching Bouxwiller on the Alsatian Plain on 21 November.[143]

Although the numerical odds in the battle for the Saverne Gap had been tilted in favor of the XV Corps, many more significant factors contributed to the ultimate outcome of the fight. Gross misjudgment of the terrain in the vicinity of the approaches to Saverne by the staff and commander of *Army Group G* resulted in a command arrangement by which responsibility for the defense of this key terrain was divided between two major headquarters. Inferior training and the resultant poor cohesion and tactical ability that plagued a German unit (the *708th Division*) tasked with a key role also contributed to the disastrous outcome.

On the other side, the American plan took maximum advantage of the German errors and was superbly coordinated. Superior training allowed the 100th Infantry Division to succeed in its first combat mission. The Seventh Army's supporting attack had turned into a rout of the German defenders and resulted in a breakthrough to the Alsatian Plain. The attack's objective, facilitating the VI Corps attack through the High Vosges passes, was achieved when mobile elements began the drive toward Strasbourg and threatened to encircle German defenders still fighting in the mountains. (See Figure 16.)

The Seventh Army's main attack, that of Brooks's VI Corps, simultaneously achieved similar, if less spectacular, success. With *Nineteenth Army*'s attention riveted on the XV Corps's attack in the north and the *708th Volksgrenadier Division* rapidly disintegrating in the face of the 100th Infantry Division's assault, attacks by the 3d and 103d Infantry Divisions across the Meurthe toward the Vosges passes at Saales and Ste. Marie-aux-Mines progressed without interference from outside their zones.

VI Corps Operations Instructions Number 9, issued on 19 November, directed O'Daniel and the 3d Infantry Division to attack across the Meurthe at 0645 on 20 November.[144] (See Figure 16.) After five days of training for just this mission, the assault elements (the 7th and 30th Infantry Regiments) of the Rock of the Marne Division slipped across the Meurthe undetected during the hours of darkness on the night of 19–20 November and actually began the attack from positions already established on the east bank near St. Michel-sur-Meurthe[145] (midway between Etival-Clairefontaine and St. Dié).

With the weather finally clear, XII TAC supported the assault with sixty-four P-47 sorties. It was the first time (and nearly the only time) in the campaign that significant close air support was possible. To add

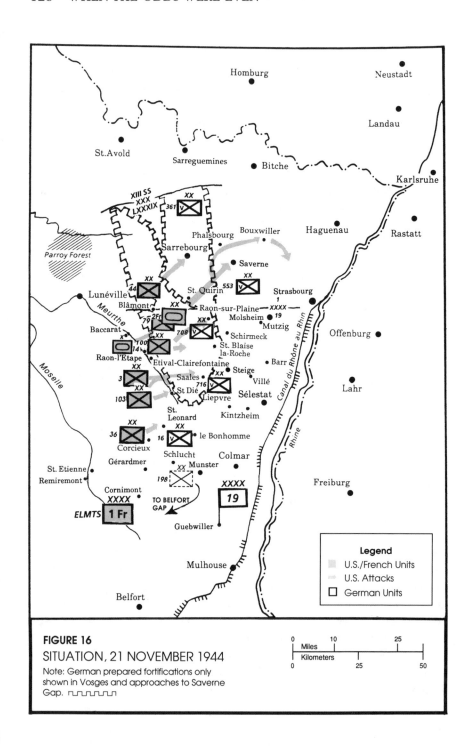

FIGURE 16

SITUATION, 21 NOVEMBER 1944

Note: German prepared fortifications only
shown in Vosges and approaches to Saverne
Gap. ⌐⌐⌐⌐⌐⌐

more weight to the attack, the VI Corps artillery and 3d Division artillery fired a thirty-minute preparation against Richter's *716th Volksgrenadier Division*'s defensive positions. Although the extent to which this support actually destroyed the fortifications of the Vosges lines in the 3d Infantry Division's zone (south of Raon l'Etape to just north of St. Dié) is unclear,[146] it did have serious impact on the morale of the defenders. The 3d Infantry Division's 7th Regiment took forty prisoners from the *716th Division*'s *726th Volksgrenadier Regiment* on the morning of 20 November, all of whom expressed resignation and attributed their defeat to poor leadership and ignorance of the tactical situation.[147] The intense artillery and air attacks probably delivered the coup de grace to their cohesion.

With two regiments of the 3d Infantry Division across the Meurthe and through the first of the Vosges lines, Brooks decided to reinforce success by ordering two regimental combat teams from the Cactus Division across at the same crossing site. While the 3d Infantry Division attacked toward the pass at Saales, Haffner's 409th and 410th RCTs crossed the river on the night of 20–21 November. With the 411th RCT remaining in place to fix the defenders, the 409th and 410th RCTs attacked southeast in an attempt to envelop those elements of the *716th* and *16th Volksgrenadier Divisions* still in their defensive positions overlooking the Meurthe.[148] (See Figure 16.) Brooks, like his counterpart Haislip in XV Corps, chose to penetrate the enemy's formidable positions along narrow frontages and then attempt to envelop the remainder, forcing the defenders to withdraw or face encirclement.

In the area around St. Dié, the enemy chose to withdraw to prepared positions in higher elevations to the east in the second Vosges line. Before the *716th Volksgrenadiers* withdrew, however, they burned the better part of the city of St. Dié. When the Cactus Division's reconnaissance troop and elements of the 409th Infantry Regiment entered the city limits on 22 November, they found the city, which had been home to twenty-three thousand inhabitants, reduced to flaming ruins.[149] Although most of the division's men bypassed the vacated city to push the attack to the east, knowledge of the German atrocity could not fail to arouse resentment among them. Furthermore, since the attack pushed immediately beyond St. Dié (see Figure 17), the destruction of the structures in no way deprived the Americans of shelter. It was pointless, counterproductive savagery.

ORDER OF BATTLE
26 NOVEMBER 1944

U.S. SEVENTH ARMY
*Breakthrough of the
Vosges Passes*

GERMAN ARMY GROUP G
Defense of the Vosges Position

XXXX
7
PATCH

XXXX
19
WIESE

XXXX
1
von KNOBELSDORFF

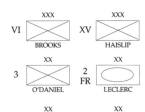

XXX
VI
BROOKS

XXX
XV
HAISLIP

XXX
LXIV
THUMM

XXX
XIII SS
SIMON

XXX
HKV

XX
3
O'DANIEL

XX
2 FR
LECLERC

XX
708 V
KRIEGER

XX
11
von WIETERSHEIM

XX
LEHR
BAYERLEIN

XX
36
DAHLQUIST

XX
79
WYCHE

XX
100
BURRESS

XX
44
SPRAGINS

XX
716 V
RICHTER

XX
17 SS
OSTENDORFF

XX
25
MAASENBACH

XX
103
HAFFNER

X
106
WILSON

XX
16 V
HÄCKEL

XX
256 V
BRUHN

XX
45
EAGLES

X
A   14
KARLSTAD

XX
361 V
PHILIPPI

KEY

X	Combat Command or Group	
XX	Division	
XXX	Corps	
XXXX	Army	

FR	French
LFK	Luftwaffe Feld Korps
HKV	Hoehe Kommando der Vogesen

Infantry

Armor/Panzer

Mechanized Cavalry

Armored Infantry/ Panzergrenadier

Volksgrenadier

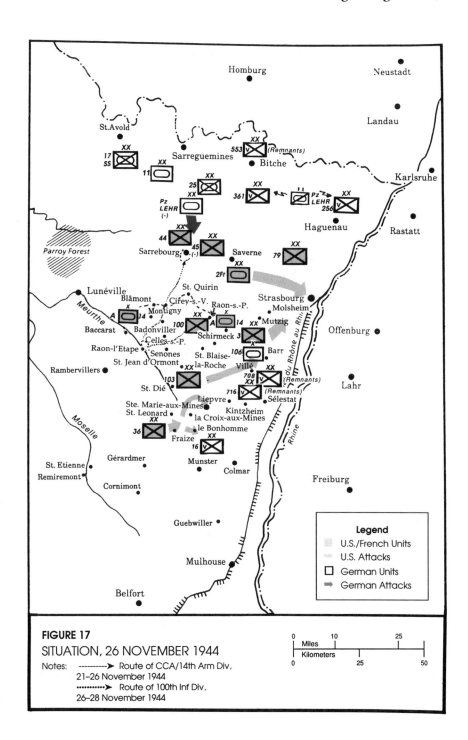

FIGURE 17

SITUATION, 26 NOVEMBER 1944

Notes: ----------▶ Route of CCA/14th Arm Div,
21–26 November 1944
••••••••••▶ Route of 100th Inf Div,
26–28 November 1944

Legend

U.S./French Units
U.S. Attacks
German Units
German Attacks

Recognizing the potential of the successes of the penetration attacks of the 100th, 3d, and 103d Infantry Divisions, and aware of the unexpected breakthrough in the XV Corps zone, Brooks decided to begin the pursuit of his adversaries. Just before midnight on 21 November, he ordered these divisions to form ad hoc task forces to exploit the situation and overtake, encircle, and annihilate the enemy, in accordance with the doctrinal tenets of *FM 100-5*. (See Chapter 3.) Each task force was to be a combined-arms team of reconnaissance, armor, engineer, artillery, and truck-borne infantry units. Their mission was to advance to the Vosges passes in their respective divisions' zones as quickly as possible, bypassing German strongpoints and cutting off their occupiers' routes of retreat. The remaining defenders would then be destroyed by following infantry formations.[150] In this way, the VI Corps commander intended to accomplish his twin missions of capturing Strasbourg and destroying enemy forces in his corps's zone.

In response to the corps commander's directive, Major General O'Daniel formed Task Force Whirlwind, consisting of a heavily reinforced infantry battalion, and sent it forward just before sunrise on 22 November.[151] As soon as the positions of the second Vosges line were penetrated, this unit would race for the Alsatian Plain via the route Saales-Schirmeck-Mutzig to cut off German units trying to reach the pass at Saales.

To facilitate the Century Division's pursuit, Major General Burress formed Task Force Fooks (named for the commander of the 398th Infantry Regiment, who led the task force) and sent it up the road from Raon l'Etape to Senones and St. Blaise-la-Roche. Such a maneuver would eliminate another route of withdrawal for the *708th Volksgrenadier Division* and ensure its destruction before it could gain the freedom of the Alsatian Plain.[152]

Major General Haffner similarly built his encircling element, Task Force Haines, around the 2d Battalion of the 409th Infantry Regiment. He directed it to seize and hold the Steige Pass, thus cutting off the retreat of the *716th Volksgrenadier Division*.[153]

Also intended to take part in the pursuit of *LXIV Corps* units was the first major armored unit to be assigned to Seventh Army. Brigadier General Charles H. Karlstad's Combat Command A (CCA), 14th Armored Division, arrived from southern France and was promptly committed on 20 November. Following in the wake of the 79th Infantry

Division, CCA was initially under XV Corps's control. It jumped off from Baccarat, following the road to Blâmont, Cirey-sur-Vesouze, and St. Quirin (see Figure 17); there, the combined-arms team turned south toward Raon-sur-Plaine and followed the boundary between XV and VI Corps against little resistance. As the Vosges lines collapsed, CCA was to cut off the retreat of elements of the *708th Volksgrenadier Division* and such elements of the *553d Volksgrenadier Division* as had been shouldered into the Vosges by the XV Corps assault farther north.

Generalmajor Richter attempted to halt the attack of O'Daniel's 3d Division toward Saales with the *716th Volksgrenadier Division*'s only remaining reserves, including the recently assigned *360th Ost-Reiter Regiment*. The polyglot assortment of this division's Russian ex-prisoners, Austrians of the *202d Mountain Battalion,* and the German infantrymen of the *716th Volksgrenadiers'* divisional *Füsilier* battalion attempted a desperate defense of the Vosges lines near Nayemont.[154] They defended tenaciously throughout the daylight hours of 22 November, well supported by artillery and mortars, but were encircled and defeated by two battalions of the assaulting 7th RCT by nightfall. With approximately fifty of their comrades dead or wounded, eighty-five more surrendered to the "Cottonbalers'" 1st Battalion alone before the town was secured and the attack continued east.[155] In one engagement, then, about 13 percent of Richter's remaining combat troops became hors de combat at the hands of a single American battalion of 516 infantrymen whose losses amounted to 22 killed, wounded, and missing.[156] Although the Americans in this zone had gained overall numerical superiority, they did not need it; battalion on battalion, company on company, they were outfighting the Germans and overrunning them. Maneuvers such as these, creating such lopsided casualty ratios (greater than six to one) rapidly brought the defenders to the verge of collapse.

On 23 November, the lead elements of the 3d Infantry Division entered Saales after an all-night march through near-freezing temperatures and incessant rain. Nineteen minutes before a tepid sunrise, riflemen of the 3d Battalion, 7th Infantry Regiment, attacked this key town, surprising the German garrison.[157] Although the defenders counterattacked, by midafternoon Saales and the pass leading to routes north and east were in American hands (see Figure 16), closing to retreating German units another route to the Alsatian Plain. Continuing the attack toward

Bourg Bruche, the 7th Infantry ran into a German battalion preparing to counterattack, and broke it up completely, killing seventy-five and capturing approximately two hundred more.[158] Meanwhile, in attempting to force its way up the Saales-Mutzig road, Task Force Whirlwind continually ran into roadblocks and other German resistance that required the assistance of additional, conventionally organized infantry units to breach. With the 30th Infantry Regiment's seizure of Saulxures (between Bourg Bruche and St. Blaise-la-Roche) on the same day, the second Vosges line was penetrated in two important locations. Task Force Whirlwind, however, was consistently stymied in its efforts to cut off the enemy as they sought to avoid entrapment in the Vosges. Assaults by all three regiments of O'Daniel's division were required to battle past roadblocks and other defensive positions into Mutzig by the morning of 25 November, when the task force was dissolved. (See Figure 17.)

Task Force Fooks also achieved only modest success in its pursuit role in the 100th Infantry Division zone. German roadblocks, minefields, abatis, and mortar fire effectively delayed the task force's progress on the narrow, winding mountain road from Moyenmoutier to Senones. Elements of the 397th and 398th Infantry Regiments had to slog forward to reduce these obstacles, and by the time Burress's pursuing task force cleared Le Vermont, it had been outdistanced by infantry units.[159] As a result, elements of the *LXIV Corps* were able to escape to the Alsatian Plain.

Task Force Haines achieved similarly unimpressive results in its attempts to deny German units the use of the Steige Pass. Assaults by all three infantry regiments of Haffner's Cactus Division were required to reduce German defenses around Steige and Villé to seize the Vosges passes, the possession of which would cut off German egress to the vicinity of Sélestat.[160] (See Figure 17.) Although German resistance was inconsistent and unpredictable, the thoroughness of their defensive preparations, linked with the enormous difficulties posed by movement across the cross-compartmented Vosges terrain in the ice, snow, and rain, challenged the progress of the Cactus Division's green troops. By the time the 103d's infantrymen captured these towns, most of the surviving elements of Richter's division had escaped.

Despite the failure of the 103d's pursuit to annihilate the retreating Germans, the combat debut of this division must also be considered a success. In a series of sharp firefights, moving cross-country through some of the most difficult terrain the Vosges had to offer, the 103d Infantry Division broke out on the Alsatian Plain between 29 November and 1 December, having bagged approximately sixteen hundred enemy prisoners.[161]

Outside Villé, a small incident occurred that illustrates the difference between the opposing sides' success in integrating noninfantry replacements into their combat formations. On or about 27 November, Pfc. Will Alpern, a nineteen-year-old automatic rifleman in Company I, 410th Infantry, was speaking with a just-captured German prisoner. The German complained that he was not supposed to be fighting in infantry combat, because he had originally been a ground crewman in the Luftwaffe. He went on to say that he was sure the Americans would never do anything so stupid or desperate as reassign such troops to the infantry. Private Alpern informed the prisoner that *he* had been brought into the army through the ASTP and had been assigned to an Army Air Forces unit before his assignment to the Cactus Division at Camp Howze, Texas, for duty as an infantryman. Alpern's platoon leader then returned the German's rifle and offered him the chance to go back to his own lines; the humbled but the wiser German thanked him, and promptly refused the offer.[162]

Combat Command A of the 14th Armored Division met with frustration in its attempts to pursue and destroy fleeing German units in the High Vosges. Karlstad's unit was slowed as it advanced toward Grandfontaine from St. Quirin by roadblocks, obstacles, and the slick, muddy grades in the road as it winds toward Donon Mountain at the crest of the High Vosges. After arriving at Schirmeck on 26 November, the men of Karlstad's command found that 3d Infantry Division troops were already in the town and well beyond; Mutzig had been reached the day before.

Still, the U.S. operations in this final phase of the battle for the High Vosges earned rare praise from Generalleutnant Thumm, commander of *LXIV Corps*. He remarked that his troops' positions in the Vosges passes were overrun "with surprising speed" and that

> it nevertheless must be admitted that the difficulties with which the enemy had to cope in the mountains, with his artillery and the supply lines, were overcome very quickly.[163]

Actually, despite VI Corps's overall success in seizing and driving through the High Vosges passes, the failures of Task Forces Whirlwind, Fooks, and Haines and CCA of the 14th Armored Division illustrate the validity of Clausewitz's insistence on the suitability of mountains for the conduct of delays, or "relative defense." With high-speed mobility limited to a very few roads (literally two roads in the 100th Infantry Division's zone, namely, Raon l'Etape–Grandfontaine and Moyenmoutier–St. Blaise-la-Roche), it was relatively easy for the Germans of the *708th* and *716th Volksgrenadiers* and other *LXIV Corps* units to foil the VI Corps's attempts at pursuit and annihilation.

This German success, although minor, underscores the irrelevance of the American advantage in quantities of armored forces in the rugged Vosges terrain: Armored forces were ineffective in their efforts to break through the myriad German roadblocks and other obstacles, even though most of them were only tenuously defended. The effectiveness of the *LXIV Corps*'s delay tactics proved that when the Germans used Vosges terrain in consonance with their own doctrine and appropriate Clausewitzian tenets, they could be successful. Attempting to defend the mountain line from fixed, linear positions despite Clausewitz's warnings to the contrary contributed heavily to German failure in the Vosges.

Despite *LXIV Corps*'s success in temporarily holding open mountain escape routes and avoiding annihilation by pursuing VI Corps units, by 27 November all passes in the 3d, 36th, and 103d Infantry Division zones were in American hands. The Rock of the Marne Division had attacked northward toward Schirmeck, linking up with advance elements of Burress's Century Division, and continued the attack to Mutzig on the edge of the Alsatian Plain. (See Figure 17.) With the mission of the latter division accomplished, Patch reassigned the 100th Division to XV Corps on the morning of 27 November and moved it to an assembly area near Sarrebourg in preparation for the thrust to the north, across the Low Vosges.

After Haffner's 103d Infantry Division moved beyond Steige and Villé onto the edge of the Rhenish plain near Barr, the entire division combined with Karlstad's CCA to attack the remains of the *708th Volksgrenadiers* near that town, with the ultimate objective of seizing Sélestat to the south.

The VI Corps's supporting attack in the south, made by Dahlquist's 36th Infantry Division, reached the Alsatian Plain on 29 November after fighting through the rugged, snowbound Vosges terrain around the passes at Ste. Marie-aux-Mines and Liepvre. Their earlier opponents, Generalmajor Schiel's *198th Infantry Division* of Petersen's *IV Luftwaffe Field Corps,* had been withdrawn on 21–22 November to reinforce the southern wing of *Nineteenth Army* against the attacks of the First French Army near Belfort. (See Figure 16.) In this way, it was actually the French who succeeded the Texas Division in its mission of preventing the *198th* from reinforcing the German defenses farther north, in the area of Brooks's main attack. However, Dahlquist's men continued to contribute to the success of the VI Corps's main attack by forcing Petersen to extend Häckel's already badly beaten *16th Volksgrenadier Division*'s sector far to the south in an attempt to cover the vacated *198th*'s zone. (See Figure 17.)

After fighting through the remains of Häckel's *Grenadiers* cross-country from La Croix-aux-Mines, two companies of the 3d Battalion, 142d Infantry Regiment (less than 340 men in all), outflanked and surprised the Germans in Ste. Marie-aux-Mines, routing them and capturing 170 with a loss of only 2 Americans slightly wounded.[164] Soldiers of the 36th Infantry Division (specifically, the 3d Battalion, 142d Infantry Regiment) occupied the medieval fortress of Haut-Koenigsbourg near Kintzheim without resistance on 27 November, and beat back a *16th Volksgrenadier Division* counterattack two days later.[165]

In a way, it was ironic that this historic castle should have been seized undamaged just as VI Corps was breaking out of the Vosges in so many locations. After lying in ruins for 267 years, it had been restored beginning in 1900 at the direction of Kaiser Wilhelm II. As mentioned earlier, it had been a mountain bastion for nobles, clergy, and even robber barons for centuries—until its destruction at the hands of the Swedes during the Thirty Years' War. Haut-Koenigsbourg's gallant defense in that conflict, literally to the last man, contributed to repulsing the invaders from Scandinavia and symbolized the historic impregnability of the Vosges. The fortress's faithfully restored ramparts and towers could have provided significant defenses for the withdrawing Germans, but it was taken intact and undamaged by the victorious Americans.

Even though VI Corps's attempt to encircle and annihilate its adversaries may have failed, the success of XV Corps's supporting attack, which was enveloping the northern wing of *LXIV Corps* and driving through the Saverne Gap toward Strasbourg, contributed not only to the capture of Strasbourg, but also to the destruction of the German forces in the Seventh Army's zone as well. Although the *tactical* envelopment of the erstwhile defenders of the Vosges by VI Corps task forces was largely avoided by effective German delaying actions, the *operational* envelopment was nevertheless effected by Haislip's XV Corps, which burst through the Saverne Gap on 23–24 November. While the 44th and 79th Infantry Divisions assaulted Sarrebourg and parried a *First Army* counterattack from the north (see Chapter 4), Leclerc's 2d French Armored Division raced toward Strasbourg and the Rhine. Thumm later admitted that effective command and control of units under his command began to disintegrate due to

> the fact that enemy forces had reached the Rhine already in the rear of the German positions, [which] had a great influence upon the morale of the German troops. Repeatedly I heard panic stricken troops say, "We won't get out of here any more."[166]

Once on the Alsatian Plain, the highly mobile elements of the Seventh Army had a field day against the disorganized, outnumbered, and relatively immobile German defenders. Once beyond the Vosges, the marauding 2d French Armored Division secured Strasbourg on 25 November after just two days of fighting. Sélestat was seized by the 36th and 103d Infantry Divisions and CCA of the 14th Armored Division by 4 December, and the last vestiges of German resistance in the Seventh Army zone from the High Vosges to the Rhine had been erased. (Serious fighting continued in the First Free French Army zone for months afterward in what became known as the Battle of the Colmar Pocket.) The soldiers of Seventh Army, their mission completed, turned their attention to their next task, part of which required operations in the Low Vosges.

CONCLUSION

A surprised Helmut Thumm, writing more than two years after the campaign, succinctly summarized the battle for the High Vosges in this way: "Here then, contrary to all precedents in history, a force—and a fully motorized force, and in mid-winter at that—had chosen the way across the Vosges."[167] He might have added that they had succeeded, as well.

Lieutenant General Patch and the other leaders of the U.S. Seventh Army committed well-trained, cohesive, and often battle-experienced units to a campaign characterized by shrewd, doctrinally correct maneuver in terrain that made any offensive operations nightmarish. They maintained the combat effectiveness of these units by prompt replacement and prudently timed periods of training for upcoming operations. At higher levels, at least, they maintained a command and staff team that worked together smoothly throughout the campaign, overcoming logistical as well as tactical and leadership challenges. Because of all this, the soldiers of the Seventh Army won where others had lost.

Additional important insight can be gained by viewing the American penetration of the High Vosges from the opponent's perspective. For the first time in history, an army *defending* the Vosges had failed. The Germans' advantages had been manifold. With time and massive labor assets to build multiple-belt fortifications, the leaders of *Army Group G* constructed defenses that did not conform to German defensive or delay doctrine. The far more combat experienced general officer corps of *Army Group G* made gross misjudgments of terrain and tactics. This resulted in their being maneuvered out of territory otherwise ideal for their mission. With little (and usually no) interference from American aircraft, *Army Group G* forces of often comparable— and always adequate—size failed to halt their adversaries. Through poorly conducted operations in the Vosges foothills, the units of *Army Group G* lost so many men and so much equipment to maneuvering U.S. forces that even delay operations in the Vosges defensive lines failed. In the best possible weather for defense, fighting on the doorstep of their homeland against an enemy far from his, the commanders of the German army organized and trained their soldiers so poorly and provided such impoverished leadership that their units could not accomplish a mission in which no army had ever before failed.

Even as VI Corps's units ground their way through the High Vosges passes, the 100th Infantry Division was reassigned to the XV Corps on 27 November.[168] The XV Corps, consisting of the 44th Infantry Division, the 45th Infantry Division (rested, replenished, and recently released from SHAEF reserve), the 12th Armored Division, and the 106th Cavalry Group (Mechanized), as well as the 100th Division, would conduct most of the fight for the Low Vosges, joined by the 103d Infantry Division on the left of VI Corps.

The eighteenth century citadel of Bitche was besieged on numerous occasions but never conquered—until the 100th Infantry Division came along in March 1945.

Heavily laden Japanese Americans of the 442d Regimental Combat Team negotiate a steep slope in the High Vosges outside Bruyères in October 1944.

A heavy machine-gun crew from Company H, 398th Infantry, 100th Division, prepares to go into the line near Reyersviller on 18 December 1944.

Lightly equipped GIs from a mechanized cavalry unit patrol rugged Low Vosges terrain on 17 December 1944.

Infantrymen from the 100th Division advance through a roadblock in the High Vosges after engineers cleared it. The twisting mountain roads were easily blocked, making the rapid mechanized pursuit called for in U.S. tactical doctrine all but impossible.

Soldiers from the 44th Infantry Division pass the body of a dead *SS Panzer-grenadier* as they counterattack through a forest near Achen in an effort to retake ground lost during Operation Nordwind.

The faces of these 79th Division GIs show the effects of prolonged combat. This photo was taken just after they were relieved following the battle for the Parroy Forest in late October 1944.

A machine gunner from the 103d "Cactus" Division's 410th Infantry Regiment overwatches troops advancing past the abandoned Maginot line defenses at Fort Hochwald, near Climbach.

Riflemen from Company K, 398th Infantry Regiment, 100th Division, engage attacking German soldiers from behind the protective cover of a forest berm.

An infantryman from the 398th Regiment keeps a watchful eye on a German prisoner inside Maginot fortifications near Bitche on 16 December 1944.

Mud sloggers of the 44th Division's 71st Infantry Regiment explore the battered face of one of Fort Simserhof's 135mm-gun batteries on 19 December 1944.

Crews of two M8 armored cars and an M3 halftrack from the 12th Armored Division's 92d Cavalry Squadron (Mechanized) laager outside Maginot fortifications in the vicinity of Fort Welschof in December 1944.

Major General Roderick Allen (left), commander of the 12th Armored Division, confers with Maj. Gen. Robert Spragins (center), 44th Infantry Division commander, and Brig. Gen. Riley Ennis, commander of the 12th Armored's Combat Command A.

Soldiers from the 45th "Thunderbird" Division's 157th Infantry Regiment cautiously advance with the aid of an M10 from the 645th Tank Destroyer Battalion in Niederbronn on 13 December 1944.

The presence of armor was limited throughout the campaign. Here, a trio of Thunderbirds go about the tedious task of clearing a farmyard during a sniper hunt in Niederbronn.

The burned-out hulk of a late-model *Pzkw IV* bears mute testimony to the limited usefulness of armor as these 45th Division GIs try on new field jackets with studied indifference around the body of a *Landser*.

Halftracks tow 76mm antitank guns of the 614th Tank Destroyer Battalion (Colored)(Towed) to their next objective. The black troopers were awarded the Presidential Unit Citation for their heroic support of the 103d Division at Climbach in December 1944.

Captain Jack Rothschild examines the shattered remnants of a *Jagdtiger VI* near Gros-Réderching in January 1945. This vehicle was first disabled by a land mine, then later destroyed by M36 Sluggers from the 776th Tank Destroyer Battalion, which supported the 44th Division during Operation Nordwind.

An M4 Sherman from Company B, 25th Tank Battalion, 14th Armored Division, pulls into Wissembourg near the German border on 16 December 1944. The tankers' sluggish pursuit of the Germans through the High Vosges ground to a halt here when Seventh Army encountered the *Westwall* defenses.

Infantrymen from the 103d "Cactus" Division confer with a member of the FFI in the burned-out remains of St. Dié on 21 November 1944.

Soldiers from the 36th "Texas" Division ride to the front on M8 armored cars near Montbronn in early January 1945. The ambulance is carrying casualties from the 45th Division's 179th Infantry Regiment.

GIs of the 3d Infantry Division's 30th Regiment move through slushy snow after crossing a mountain stream in November 1944.

Browning automatic rifleman Pfc. Bill Richards of Company G, 253d Infantry Regiment, 63d Infantry Division, advances in January 1945. Richards is wearing field-expedient foxhole boots designed to keep his feet warm.

A 100th Division GI maintains a frontline vigil in his well-concealed fighting position near Reyersviller in January 1945.

Snow worsened the ordeal for these infantrymen from the 36th "Texas" Division's 141st Infantry Regiment moving forward through the High Vosges on 13 November 1944.

Engineers of the 100th Infantry Division's 325th Engineer Battalion string barbed wire near the frozen corpse of an *SS Panzergrenadier* near Rimling in January 1945. Note the excellent fields of fire this position offers the defenders.

A 70th Infantry Division soldier smashes his way into a building in Wingen in January 1945. The thick walls, intended to insulate buildings against the bitter Vosges winters, made them ideal defensive positions.

Soldiers of the 36th Infantry Division examine the remains of a truck from the 133d Field Artillery Battalion (155mm) destroyed when the Germans shelled Enchenberg in early January 1945.

CHAPTER 4

THE BATTLE FOR THE LOW VOSGES

They used everything they had and they had plenty. . . .
Their job was to take Rimling; our job was to hold it, and
although outnumbered we were never outclassed.
—*History of the U.S. 397th Infantry Regiment*

The last week of November 1944 brought a radical change to the
operational situation in the Vosges Mountains. As the Seventh Army's
supporting attack conducted by XV Corps breached the Saverne Gap
defenses, Patch's main attack with VI Corps pierced the historically
impenetrable shield of the High Vosges. Wiese's *Nineteenth Army*
defenders found themselves enveloped by the XV Corps's 2d French
Armored Division and U.S. 79th Infantry Division. Successful penetrations by VI Corps infantry elements constantly threatened to out-
flank and encircle their prepared positions on local but no less dangerous scales. Any hopes of accomplishing the mission specified in
the early autumn *Führer Befehl* to defend the Vosges until April disappeared in the catastrophe of the last week of November.

Balck, commanding *Army Group G,* found his command split disastrously, with *First Army* forced back in northern Lorraine toward
the Saar and the Palatinate, and *Nineteenth Army* in danger of being
surrounded and destroyed on the Alsatian Plain. To retrieve the situation, he launched a counterattack into the left, or northern, flank of
the XV Corps as it thrust toward Saverne. (See Figure 17.) From his
reserve, he gained the use of the *Panzer Lehr Division,* which had been
resting and refitting in preparation for the upcoming Ardennes offensive. Balck also pulled the *25th Panzergrenadier Division* out of *First
Army*'s *LXXXII Corps* line near Sierck-les-Bains (near the convergence

of the German-French-Luxembourg frontiers) for use in this attack.[1] With these divisions, Balck simultaneously protected the withdrawal of the *361st Volksgrenadier Division* and attempted to abort the XV Corps's lunge toward the critical pass at Saverne. This move constituted the first major action of the 1944 campaign in the Low Vosges Mountains. As the Germans drove south along the limited routes available for armor in this hilly, heavily wooded region, they initially achieved limited success, penetrating the 106th Cavalry Group's screen and recapturing Eywiller, Gungwiller, and Rauwiller.[2] In Rauwiller, a *Kampfgruppe* of the *Panzer Lehr Division* surprised the headquarters company of the 44th's 3d Battalion, 71st Infantry Regiment, and killed or captured almost the entire unit.[3] This attack, however, was repulsed the next day by the remainder of the 44th Infantry Division, assisted by the 45th Infantry Division's 157th Infantry Regiment, which was committed from the reserve after several weeks' replenishment and training, and Third Army's 4th Armored Division.

Although unsuccessful in halting the Americans' attack and penetration of the High Vosges defensive lines, this abortive counterattack did make a lasting impression on Generals Patch and Devers. They recognized that

> a potential threat to the Seventh Army's north flank west of the Vosges would continue as long as the enemy remained in possession of the Siegfried Line along the Franco-German border from Lauterbourg on the Rhine to Saarbruecken on the Sarre.[4]

As a result, even as the counterattack in Lorraine was parried by XV Corps, General Eisenhower issued orders diverting the generally eastward effort.[5] The commanders and men of Seventh Army had succeeded in their mission of capturing Strasbourg and were in the process of accomplishing the other mission assigned by Patch: destroying German forces west of the Rhine in their zone. Furthermore, they had attained an unwritten objective by avoiding a protracted winter mountain campaign against the formidable German Vosges defenses. However, the planned pursuit and strike against the Rhine River defenses were delayed indefinitely as the SHAEF commander ordered elements of Seventh Army to assist in the reduction of the Colmar Pocket on the Alsatian Plain, and the bulk of the XV and VI Corps to turn northward to penetrate the Siegfried line. Operations across the Rhine from the Alsatian Plain, after all, would lead into the maze of the Black Forest, an area as eminently suitable for the defense as the Hürtgen or the Vosges, and nowhere else were the Allies anywhere near the Rhine. Crossing the Rhine could, then, lead to a sort of Colmar Pocket in reverse.

Instead, a Seventh Army offensive to the north would eliminate further danger to the army's northern flank. The events of the autumn battles for Metz and for the Hürtgen forest made it clear to General Eisenhower that sectors had to be narrowed to effect penetrations of the *Westwall.* In keeping with the broad-front strategy, Third Army would drive through the Saarland and the dense Siegfried line fortifications there, while Seventh Army conducted a supporting attack on Patton's right (eastern) flank. A thrust into the Palatinate would allow American armored elements to take advantage of the rolling, relatively open terrain in that area. To prepare for this, the offensive would all but stop as the Allied armies, from the First French on the Swiss border to the Second British and First Canadian in the Low Countries, would gather their strength for the great spring offensive—which was intended to finally crush the Third Reich. The Seventh Army's pursuit of demoralized *First Army* forces would therefore temporarily stop at the edge of the Reich's defenses after securing a suitable line of departure beyond the Siegfried line.

The enemy facing the XV Corps and the leftmost elements of VI Corps in the Low Vosges, known to Germans as the Hardt Mountains, consisted of an amalgam of *First Army* units. These organizations were tasked by *Army Group G* to conduct a delay to a defensive line along mostly revitalized Siegfried line positions, except in the vicinity of Bitche, where they intended to occupy the Maginot fortifications of the so-called Ensemble de Bitche. The delay was to result in the occupation of the *Westwall* defenses no earlier than 15 December 1944, to allow time for adequate refurbishment of the fortifications there.[6] This date was not arbitrarily set; *Army Group B*'s Ardennes counteroffensive was scheduled to begin then, and Feldmarschall Gerd von Rundstedt needed no distractions that would require him to dilute his already marginally adequate attack forces to deal with threats from the south.

The Maginot positions to be occupied were part of the former French Secteur Fortifie de Rohrbach and Secteur Fortifie des Vosges, and constituted some of the strongest positions in the entire Maginot line. It was these *gros ouvrages,* with names such as Schiesseck, Simserhof, and Grand Hohekirkel, and *petit ouvrages* including Oterbiel and Rohrbach, that the Germans themselves failed to take in 1940, preferring to cut them off and await the armistice. It was these fortifications that, thanks to their excellent 360-degree defenses, held out for up to five days beyond the surrender of the rest of the French army in that disastrous spring. Now, ironically, the steel-reinforced concrete emplacements, designed to forever guarantee the security of a French Alsace and Lorraine, would combine with the somewhat less impressive fortifications of the Siegfried line to provide elements of two German corps with their last barrier against the American XV Corps's attempts to penetrate into the German Fatherland.

In the Low Vosges, *First Army* units initially consisted of the *LXXXIX Corps's 361st Volksgrenadier* and *245th Infantry Divisions* and the *XIII SS Corps's 25th Panzergrenadier Division* and *11th Panzer Division;* later, the *257th Volksgrenadier Division* replaced von Wietersheim's "Ghost Division."[7]

Effective control of *First Army* units in the Low Vosges was hampered from the outset by major command structure changes from field army to division level. General der Panzertruppen von Knobelsdorff was replaced as field army commander in the first week of December by General der Infanterie von Obstfelder, a fifty-eight-year-old Prussian World War I veteran who had commanded three different corps since 1940.

After narrowly avoiding annihilation in the Saverne Gap, the battered command structure in *LXXXIX Corps* had required radical restructuring at the beginning of December. General der Infanterie Gustav Höhne replaced General der Infanterie von und zu Gilsa as corps commander, and a new corps chief of staff had to be found to replace the colonel lost near Saverne, when the corps headquarters had been encircled.[8] Like his predecessor, Höhne was also a highly competent commander. The fifty-one-year-old infantryman from Posen was commissioned in 1912, and had served with exceptional distinction in World War I. He rose through the officer ranks of the *Reichswehr,* and commanded the *28th Infantry Regiment* of the *8th Jäger Division* as an *Oberst* in France in 1940. Höhne went on to command the *8th Jägers* in Russia, as well as two corps, and was awarded the Knight's Cross with oak leaves for his valor in the east.[9] His talents would be severely tried in the days to come.

Further complicating an already tenuous situation was the loss of much of the corps headquarters' communication equipment during the rout at Saverne. This deficiency "hampered the command to a large degree" in the ensuing months.[10] Given the extremely rugged nature of the terrain over which the corps would fight, and its exceptionally wide sector (about fifty-six kilometers), this was an especially serious shortcoming, because radio relays and vast amounts of field wire would be essential for responsive control.

Complicating the control aspects of this situation was the introduction, after 6 December, of *XC Corps* headquarters (formerly *IV Luftwaffe Field Corps,* and redesignated as an army formation in late November while in the Colmar Pocket), to control the *11th Panzer Division* and *25th Panzergrenadier Division.* Still under the command of Generalleutnant Erich Petersen, *XC Corps* headquarters arrived at a critical juncture in the fight, which probably only confused an already complicated situation for the Germans.

The *361st Volksgrenadier Division* was commanded by Oberst (after 1 January, Generalmajor) Alfred Philippi, a forty-one-year-old infantryman from Ostmark and recipient of the Knight's Cross for gallantry in action as a regimental commander on the Russian front.[11] The division had been reorganized in Münster in September 1944 from the remnants of the *361st Infantry Division,* which had been destroyed by the Russians the previous July. Its replacement personnel consisted mainly of former Kriegsmarine and Luftwaffe personnel from Westphalia and the Rhineland. Although, in Philippi's opinion, they had "little enthusiasm for commitment in the army," he admitted that

> The combination of men from Westphalia and the Rhineland proved favorable: the tough, persevering character of the Westphalian and the light temperament and verve of the Rhinelander were a good mixture.[12]

In recognition of the need for a considerable period of training to develop this newly formed group into a cohesive, competent combat team, the division commander staved off attempts by higher authorities to commit the unit to action too soon. "Above all," he wrote, "I wished to avoid the fate of having to lead an improvised 'emergency mass' into action, which would break up on its first contact with the enemy."[13] Although he succeeded in delaying deployment to a combat sector for several weeks, the division was nevertheless committed to the battle in Lorraine on 18 October 1944, after only six and a half weeks of training.[14]

Since then, the *361st* had been in nearly continuous action against elements of Patton's Third Army in Lorraine, but had also opposed XV Corps's 44th Infantry Division in its supporting attack toward Sarrebourg during the drive on Saverne. Its subordinate infantry regiments included the *951st, 952d,* and *953d Volksgrenadiers,* but the *951st* had only one battalion, the other having been detached to the *708th Volksgrenadier Division* and destroyed near Raon l'Etape in the combat debut of the 100th Infantry Division. As a result, the *361st Volksgrenadier Division* had only about 1,050 infantrymen at the outset of the delay to the Maginot-Siegfried positions.[15] At the beginning of December, Philippi's division was judged by the *LXXXIX Corps* chief of staff to have "a clear and efficient command as well as able regimental commanders," and a "good combat spirit" that made it "suitable for defensive action."[16] Its strength actually grew during December, and it could count on nearly 2,400 combat infantrymen by 18 December.[17]

The *245th Infantry Division* was commanded by Generalmajor Gerhard Kegler. The division's maneuver elements consisted principally of the *935th, 936th,* and *937th Infantry Regiments,* each of which had two battalions with a significant proportion of retrained Luftwaffe and Kriegsmarine troops, as well as some Russians, Poles, Dutch, and Hungarians, for a total of roughly 2,650 combat infantrymen.[18] Although the Division had recently arrived from retraining in Holland, the *LXXXIX Corps* chief of staff described it this way: "Its training condition was low, [and its] fighting spirit—especially that of the recent replacements—was definitely bad."[19] Furthermore, it was handicapped by poor leadership, and "remained, from the first to the last day of its subordination to *LXXXIX Corps* a special burden."[20]

The *XIII SS Corps* was commanded by SS Obergruppenführer Max Simon, and disposed initially two divisions in the Low Vosges and adjacent rolling hills to the west. Simon had replaced Obergruppenführer Hermann Priess on 16 November, and had been severely pressed by the Third Army and the northernmost elements of XV Corps throughout his brief

tenure in command.[21] Given the antipathy between many of the officers of the army and the Waffen SS, the friction induced by a recent
corps change of command can only have been enhanced by the arrangement by which a Waffen SS corps headquarters directed the two army
divisions in the Low Vosges. Additionally, Simon's background contributed to the problems.

The forty-five-year-old Breslauer had fought in Macedonia and France
in World War I as an enlisted man in the *1st Life Cuirassier Regiment.*
A stint in a *Freikorps* was followed by a nine-year tour in the *Reichswehr's
16th Cavalry Regiment,* after which he joined the *Schutzstaffel* in 1933.
Simon became a protégé of Theodor Eicke, the founder of the
Totenkopfverbände, or "Death's Head" groups, and was actively involved in the organization of concentration camps. Commissioned in
1934, he rocketed to the rank of *SS Standartenführer,* the equivalent
of *Oberst* (colonel) in the army, by 1938. Simon participated in the
Polish, French, and Russian campaigns, and commanded the *3d SS Panzer
"Totenkopf" Division* in the latter theater upon the departure of
Eicke. While on the Russian front, his men committed the usual atrocities
associated with the Waffen SS, including the slaughter of Russian
prisoners. At the time of Nordwind, Simon was anxiously wanted by
the Soviets for war crimes. Before assuming command of the *XIII SS
Corps* in November 1944, he commanded the *16th SS Panzer Grenadier "Reichsführer SS" Division* (named for Heinrich Himmler) in Italy,
where he sanctioned his men's murder of Italian civilians. He was wanted
by the British for that.[22] His army subordinates no doubt squirmed at
taking orders from such a man.

To make matters worse, Simon was an outspoken critic of the army.
Enraged at what he believed was a succession of especially hard missions
near Demyansk in 1942, Simon actually refused an attack order from
the corps commander. The mission subsequently fell to the *8th Jäger
Division,* commanded by then-Generalmajor Gustav Höhne. When the
attack failed, Simon openly rejoiced, and was especially pleased at
the corps commander's threat to court-martial Höhne. Simon also hurled
his vitriolic criticism toward the inability of the army's *X Corps* to
break through the Russian encirclement and relieve his unit in this battle,
a detail surely not lost on the *X Corps* commander, Otto von Knobelsdorff.[23] What happy times must have been had during corps commanders'
meetings at *First Army* headquarters!

The *25th Panzergrenadier Division* was commanded by another veteran of the Russian front, Oberst Burmeister, and consisted at the time of the delay to the Maginot-Siegfried fortifications of a *Kampfgruppe* with about 980 combat infantrymen and thirteen tanks and assault guns.[24] The division had sustained severe casualties in the preceding months, most recently against Third Army elements in the Saar, yet the morale of its men was rated "excellent" by Simon.[25]

Generalleutnant Wend von Wietersheim's *11th Panzer Division* was unquestionably the best of the German units conducting delay operations in the Low Vosges. The "Ghost Division" acquired a fearsome reputation in Russia and fighting against elements of Patton's Third Army. The division had been commanded since September 1943 by Silesian cavalryman von Wietersheim, who had seen brief action at the end of World War I as a junior officer; forty-four years old at the time of the action in the Low Vosges, von Wietersheim was one of the very few army division commanders to remain with his unit until the end of the war.[26] In early December 1944, this division had about 1,675 infantrymen in the *110th* and *111th Panzergrenadier Regiments* and between thirty and forty tanks fit for combat in the *15th Panzer Regiment.*[27]

As the Seventh Army drove into the Alsatian Plain, Lieutenant General Patch reorganized it to maintain contact with Third Army on its left during the latter's drive into Lorraine. The 100th and the 44th Infantry Divisions and, after 5 December, the newly arrived 12th Armored Division were the major maneuver elements of XV Corps, whose mission was to penetrate the German defenses anchored in the old French positions while simultaneously protecting the Third Army flank to the west and north.[28] On the right, VI Corps drew multiple missions, including assisting the First Free French Army in its efforts to reduce the *Nineteenth Army* in the Colmar Pocket, security of the west bank of the Rhine, and breaching the Siegfried line defenses along the Lauter River within its zone.[29]

In the battle for the Low Vosges, this translated into the requirement for XV Corps and elements of the left (western) wing of VI Corps to first pursue the enemy to the border of the Palatinate. Subsequently, the 100th and 44th Infantry Divisions of XV Corps were to penetrate the Maginot positions around Bitche, and VI Corps's 45th and 103d Infantry Divisions were to attack and break through the Siegfried line positions northwest of Wissembourg in their zones. (See Figure 18.)

BATTLES OF MOVEMENT

The commanders in VI Corps learned in the High Vosges that pursuit of a skillfully delaying foe in thickly wooded, mountainous terrain in winter could be a frustrating and tedious task. Avenues of advance facilitating rapid maneuver are few, so even highly mobile forces can be slowed or even temporarily halted by a few well-placed log-crib or abatis roadblocks. If supplemented by mines and then covered by snipers, machine guns, and preregistered artillery fire, the reduction of such obstacles could require the deployment of large infantry formations over significant periods of time, thus allowing the enemy time to regroup, fortify the next position, and rest. Realistic hopes of fulfilling the ultimate doctrinal objective of pursuit—that is, annihilation—disappear rapidly under these circumstances. In such situations, the goal of the pursuing commander is to arrive at the objective with his own forces sufficiently intact to successfully conduct the attack.

This presented a dilemma to the commanders of Seventh Army units in the Low Vosges. In the High Vosges, their assigned mission had been the destruction of the German forces west of the Rhine in their zone and the seizure of Strasbourg. Once forced out of their High Vosges defensive positions, the Germans had nowhere to go except the Alsatian Plain—where American mobility advantages and, to a lesser extent, air power could destroy them. Besides, XV Corps's envelopment would destroy the enemy eventually, even if VI Corps's pursuit had bogged down entirely! After penetrating the Vosges defensive lines, a methodical pursuit, such as was ultimately conducted by VI Corps, was therefore in order to accomplish the mission. Barring unforeseen reinforcement, even a successful delay by the Germans in the High Vosges could only have forestalled, not averted, their destruction.

In the Low Vosges, the parameters of the Americans' mission were considerably different. Time was on *First Army*'s side. Cautiously following the Germans, prudently taking time, and expending resources to reduce each obstacle would certainly preserve the fighting strength of the units involved, but would also give the enemy time to strengthen their Maginot and Siegfried positions to the point that the cost of penetrating them could be unacceptably high. Conducting a hell-for-leather pursuit in which the Germans *might* be largely overwhelmed by American combined-arms spearheads bulling their way up narrow mountain defiles would certainly diminish the time available for

ORDER OF BATTLE
1-20 DECEMBER 1944

U.S. SEVENTH ARMY	**GERMAN ARMY GROUP G**
Pursuit through the Low Vosges	*Delay to the Siegfried/Maginot Lines*

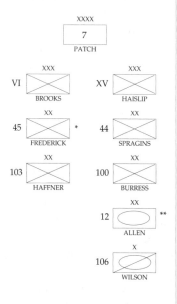

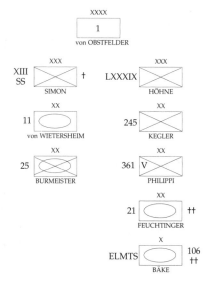

* Reinforced by 47th Tank Battalion, Combat Command B, 14th Armored Division. From 1–5 December, reinforced by 397th Infantry Regiment, 100th Infantry Division.

** After 5 December

† After 6 December, replaced by XC Corps Headquarters (Petersen)

†† 12–18 December and 20–21 December

KEY

X	Combat Command or Group
XX	Division
XXX	Corps
XXXX	Army

Infantry

Armor/Panzer

Mechanized Cavalry

Armored Infantry/ Panzergrenadier

Volksgrenadier

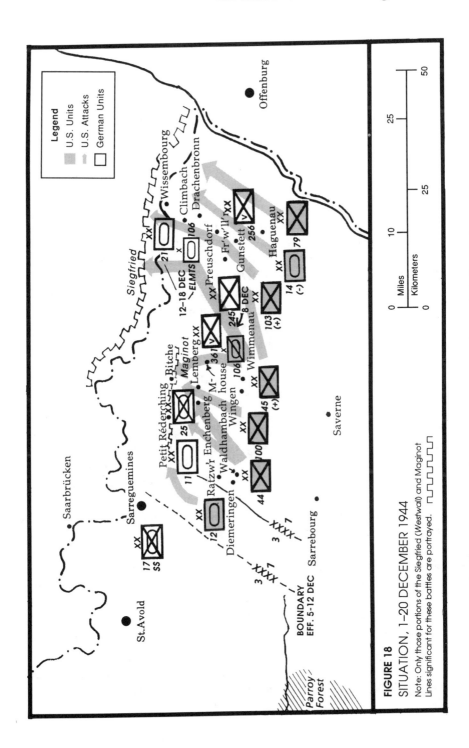

FIGURE 18

SITUATION, 1–20 DECEMBER 1944

Note: Only those portions of the Siegfried (*Westwall*) and Maginot
Lines significant for these battles are portrayed.

preparation of the Palatinate's peripheral defenses, but *could* so reduce the strength of the VI and XV Corps's units that penetration of the Germans' defenses might be impossible. The freshly conjured specters of the Hürtgen debacle bore mute testament to that possibility.

It was incumbent upon Haislip and Brooks and their subordinates to conduct the pursuit to the Maginot and Siegfried lines in a manner that struck a balance between haste and methodicalness. It was up to them to select a course of action that would eliminate the maximum number of would-be defenders of the Siegfried and Maginot lines before they reached those positions' fastness, while preserving as many pursuers as possible for their roles in the critical penetrations that lay inevitably ahead. To accomplish this, they assigned narrow sectors to their divisions in the Vosges, massing numerical strength against weakness. In these constricted zones, each division could advance with two regiments forward and one in reserve. This simultaneously exposed the minimum number of infantrymen to enemy fire and provided a significant force for exploitative maneuver.

From 1 to 15 December, the significantly outnumbered Germans gave ground grudgingly in the Low Vosges as XV Corps (on the western slopes of the Vosges) and VI Corps's 45th and 103d Infantry Divisions (on the eastern slopes) pursued, pressing them back toward the Maginot and Siegfried positions. As an economy of force measure allowing these divisions' zones to remain appropriately narrow on the fifty-kilometer-wide frontage, the 106th Cavalry Group screened the difficult terrain between them.[30] (See Figure 18.) This forced the Germans, principally Philippi's *951st* and elements of the *952d Volksgrenadier Regiments,* to cover the fourteen kilometers between the 100th Infantry Division's 397th Infantry Regiment and the 45th's 157th Infantry Regiment, even though no American infantry were committed against them.

Just as *Nineteenth Army* elements had proven themselves capable of effective delaying actions in the High Vosges, most of the *First Army* units in the Low Vosges displayed similar proficiency. Using the craggy, wooded terrain to their advantage, they were able to prevent a swift American breakthrough to the *Reich*'s frontier by executing correct doctrinal delaying tactics: emplacing extensive minefields, constructing dozens of roadblocks, tenaciously defending natural strongpoints, and vigorously counterattacking on a local scale. Occasionally, they were even able to inflict significant reverses on the pursuing *Amis.*

Such a success was achieved against the Americans advancing through the center of the Low Vosges, Burress's 100th Infantry Division. After the 398th Infantry Regiment seized Wingen-sur-Moder on 4 December, for example, elements of Philippi's *361st Volksgrenadier Division* counterattacked, killing or capturing all of the regiment's Company A.[31] Although not all results were as spectacular as this, German tenacity, such as that displayed by Philippi's *953d Volksgrenadier Regiment* on its next delay line between Lemberg and Mouterhouse, nevertheless provided the Americans a taste of the bitter fighting that lay ahead if the Germans could continue to delay all the way north through the Low Vosges to the *Westwall*.

As the 397th Infantry continued its advance on the right and the 399th passed through the battered 398th Infantry on the division's left, the Centurymen encountered more stiff resistance. Reinforced by the better part of a *LXXXIX Corps* light antiaircraft battalion with self-propelled quad 20mm machine cannons, the *953d Volksgrenadier Regiment* held off Burress's 397th Infantry Regiment at the tiny mountain village of Mouterhouse for two days, and forced his 399th Infantry into a full regimental assault at the town of Lemberg for four days, 7–10 December. (See Figure 19.)

Near Lemberg, Philippi's men had heavily mined the road from Goetzenbrueck to Sarreinsberg and fortified the already stout stone buildings of the typically Vosgian town. Effectively integrating the *flakwagons* 20mm machine cannon and the divisional antitank battalion's 75mm *Panzerabwehrkanonen* with the *Volksgrenadiers'* already-high proportion of automatic infantry weapons and *Panzerfausts,* the defenders also rained artillery fire down on the attackers of the 1st Battalion, 399th Infantry Regiment. Advancing from the valley of the crystal-factory town of St. Louis-les-Bitche, this battalion was pinned down for a full day while the regiment's 3d Battalion vainly attempted to penetrate Lemberg's defenses from the east. When these efforts failed to produce positive results by nightfall on 7 December, the regimental commander, Col. Andrew C. Tychsen (a veteran of the Mexican border campaign and World War I), ordered the 2d Battalion from reserve in Goetzenbrueck to envelop Lemberg from the northeast.

On 8 December, supported by the 399th RCT's Company A, 781st Tank Battalion, the 1st and 2d Battalions conducted a coordinated attack behind an artillery smoke screen and succeeded in penetrating Lemberg's

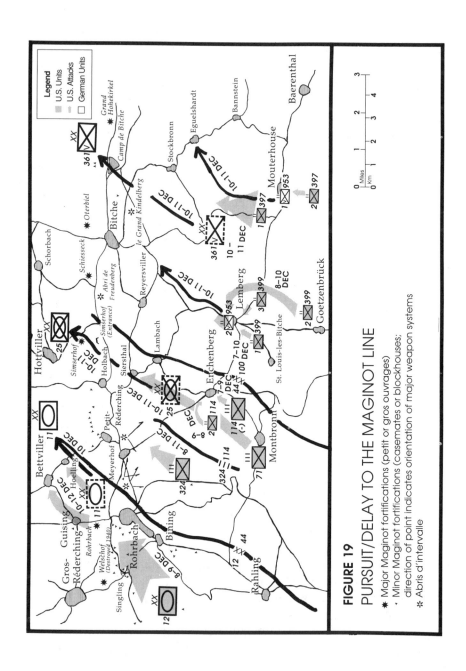

FIGURE 19

PURSUIT/DELAY TO THE MAGINOT LINE

* Major Maginot fortifications (petit or gros ouvrages)
˙ Minor Maginot fortifications (casemates or blockhouses;
  direction of point indicates orientation of major weapon systems
✳ Abris d'intervalle

defenses. The limited utility of armor in Vosges terrain was emphasized by the loss to mines of three of the four tanks in Company A's 1st Platoon, in this its very first action.[32] Throughout the day and night, the Americans fought house to house through the town, but failed to secure the small Vosgian village. On the morning of 9 December, the *2d Battalion, 953d Volksgrenadier Regiment,* counterattacked with self-propelled 20mm machine cannon in support, but could not dislodge Tychsen's men, who finally secured Lemberg on 10 December. Nevertheless, Philippi's troops established a coherent line less than a kilometer north of town, and planned to continue the delay from these commanding thirteen-hundred-foot heights.[33]

Although the 399th had succeeded in seizing Lemberg and opening the way for the 398th Infantry Regiment to pass through and attack toward Reyersviller and Bitche, operations such as these could not be sustained by the Americans for long; casualties in some of the 399th's line companies were staggering. Company C lost 40 men out of 166, Company B lost 44 men out of 164, Company F lost 50 men out of 179, and Company I lost 52 of the 178 men with which it started the struggle to seize this single strongpoint.[34] The German delay was succeeding beyond expectations, causing considerable American casualties and slowing the American advance to a two- or three-kilometer-per-day average.

Like the attacking 100th Infantry Division to its east, the 44th Infantry Division met some stiff resistance during its pursuit along the western Vosges foothills. After repulsing the German armored thrust at Rauwiller on 24–25 November, Spragins's division advanced against sporadically covered minefields and roadblocks for fifteen kilometers until it reached the vicinity of Waldhambach (just east of Diemeringen in Figure 18) and Tieffenbach by 2 December. There it ran into determined German resistance, and the *25th Panzergrenadier Division* counterattacked sharply, delaying the American advance for about twenty-four hours.

From this point north, Burmeister's *Panzergrenadiers* conducted a more effective delay, doggedly contesting each major obstacle and village. As the 44th advanced with the 324th Infantry Regiment on the left, the 114th on the right, and the 71st Infantry in reserve, the *25th Panzergrenadier Division* slowed them down to the same snail's pace as their comrades in the 100th Infantry Division. The *25th*'s *Panther* tanks and *Panzergrenadiers* forced the 324th Infantry to attack for three days just to seize the tiny Vosgian village of Ratzwiller. At Enchenberg, the Germans forced the 114th Infantry to launch a two-battalion attack that took three more days of bitter, seesaw fighting to resolve in favor of the attackers. (See Figure 19.) Here, long-range fire from the 75mm long-barreled main guns of the *Panthers*, as well as hundreds of cleverly concealed antitank mines, so intimidated the crews of the supporting Shermans from the 749th Tank Battalion that, after losing two tanks to mines, no further advances were attempted by them through the highly restrictive mountain terrain. A platoon of supporting M36 Sluggers of the 776th Tank Destroyer Battalion were similarly neutralized. In addition to the mines and accurate gunfire, a freak direct hit by a German mortar round in the open-topped crew compartment of one of the vehicles contributed to their ineffectiveness. From that point on, the tank destroyers also took little part in the action.[35] Enchenberg had to be taken in an all-infantry fight, house to house, with evidently little quarter given or asked by the soldiers of either side.[36]

At the crossroads settlement of Meyerhof, just south of Petit Réderching, the 324th Infantry confronted the Maginot line fortifications for the first time. Defended by elements of the *11th Panzer Division,* these defensive works were put to effective use in halting the 324th's pursuit at the same time that the 114th was assaulting Burmeister's *Panzergrenadiers* at Enchenberg. (See Figure 19.)

It was not even a major fortification of the great Maginot that the Americans encountered on the fourth anniversary of the Japanese attack on Pearl Harbor, yet such was the difficulty they had seizing it that commanders on both sides gained a deep and lasting impression. At Meyerhof was the *abri d'intervalle* constructed in the 1930s for the French 166th Fortress Infantry Regiment, which was to defend the casemates in the terrain between the *petit ouvrage* Rohrbach and the *gros ouvrage* Simserhof. (See Figure 19: The *abri d'intervalle*'s field of observation and fire is indicated by arrows.)[37] Intended mainly as shelter against artillery attack, the above-ground portion of this seven-story-deep subterranean barracks faced south, away from the most likely axis of attack from Germany, and directly toward the advancing Americans.

Like all of the major edifices of the Ensemble de Bitche, however, it was constructed for all-around defense, and its four-foot-thick, steel-reinforced concrete face and steel observation cupolas provided observation over a field of fire that was more than a square kilometer in area, laced with mines, and which provided not one shred of cover. Through this ran the Enchenberg-Gros Réderching road, so this important south-north line of communication could be effectively interdicted by machine-gun fires from this fortification, as well as by indirect fires adjusted from the safety of its steel cupolas. Additionally, on the west side of the road, just east of Rohrbach, was another *abri d'intervalle* and a casemate, also facing south, which covered the approaches to Meyerhof from that side of the sunken railroad embankment.[38] (The arrows in Figure 19 illustrate the interlocking fields of fire achieved by these positions.)

Major General Haislip ordered the 12th Armored Division into its first action to assist with the reduction of these defenses. On 6–7 December, this unit relieved the Third Army's 4th Armored Division between Domfessel and Oermingen, thereby temporarily enlarging the XV Corps zone to include the relatively open terrain between the Sarreguemines-Lorentzen railroad and the Lorentzen-Rohrbach road.[39] (See Figure 18.) This terrain was eminently suitable for armor operations, and the corps commander seized on the opportunity to revitalize the pursuit. The effectiveness of Haislip's envelopment was enhanced by the state of the Maginot fortifications in the 12th Armored Division's zone.

On 15–16 June 1940, elements of the *First Army* under Generaloberst von Witzleben burst through the weak defenses of the Secteur Fortifie de la Sarre near Sarralbe (about ten kilometers south of Sarreguemines), and rapidly swung east to complete the encirclement of the *petit ouvrages* Haut-Poirier and Welschoff and their surrounding casemates. Over the next few days, the Austrians of Generalmajor Edgar Theissen's *262d Infantry Division* utterly wrecked these works, firing their 150mm guns at point-blank ranges (eight hundred meters and less) and overrunning them. As a result, four and a half years later, their unrestored ruins were of no use in halting the American tank-infantry teams penetrating toward the northeast.[40]

On the evening of 8 December, Haislip attempted to invigorate his sluggish and increasingly costly pursuit with the introduction of his newly arrived armored division.[41] The "Hellcats" of Maj. Gen. Roderick Allen's division launched their attack from the extreme left (west) of the Seventh Army and XV Corps sector toward the northeast in an exceptionally narrow five-kilometer frontage. In an attempt to pierce the Maginot line and envelop the German forces to the east, three task forces consisting of elements from all of the division's tank and armored infantry battalions drove elements of von Wietersheim's *11th Panzer Division* from the villages of Singling, Bining, and Rohrbach over the next two days.[42] (See Figure 19.) Attacking obliquely through the battered and useless Maginot positions, the tankers and armored infantrymen of Allen's Hellcats seized Bettviller and Hoelling by 12 December.[43] By advancing so deeply, the 12th Armored Division at once prevented the *11th Panzer Division* from more effectively using the undamaged Maginot fortifications near Rohrbach, and assisted the 44th Infantry Division's efforts to advance against the *11th Panzer Division* near Petit Réderching by threatening them with envelopment. It also forced the *25th Panzergrenadier* and *361st Volksgrenadier Divisions* to the east to abandon their delay line from just north of Lemberg and Mouterhouse to avoid encirclement.[44]

In this way, Major General Haislip employed the 12th Armored Division in a doctrinally sound and effective manner to facilitate the pursuit to the Franco-German frontier. He employed combined-arms teams to envelop and attempt to annihilate the withdrawing foe as soon as he had the assets and maneuver space needed for effective employment of such forces. His success forced all of *XC Corps* and the *361st Volksgrenadier Division* (the westernmost element of *LXXXIX Corps*) to abandon otherwise excellent terrain for the continuation of their delay. By then, however, the Hellcats had clearly run into terrain unsuitable for armor in the heavily wooded western edge of the Low Vosges, so despite their initial accomplishments, Haislip withdrew the division to assembly areas in the vicinity of Rohrbach. The 44th Infantry Division took over its zone on 14–15 December, and began the reduction of the principal obstacle in its zone—the Maginot *gros ouvrage* Simserhof. Simultaneously, the Century Division pursued the outflanked and withdrawing *361st Volksgrenadiers* toward the outskirts of Bitche, where they began the assault on the adjacent *gros ouvrage,* Schiesseck. With his armored division in reserve, Major General Haislip was prepared to exploit the anticipated forthcoming breakthrough of the Maginot line in his corps's zone.

The pursuit in the VI Corps zone to the east achieved more spectacular success. As the 45th Infantry Division ground its way north toward Zinswiller, Niederbronn-les-Bains, and Obersteinbach, the American command structure experienced its first major change. On 3 December, thirty-seven-year-old Maj. Gen. Robert T. Frederick became the second youngest division commander in the U.S. Army when he assumed command of the Thunderbird Division, replacing Major General Eagles, who had been wounded a few days before when his vehicle detonated a land mine.[45]

Although much younger than his peers, the 1928 West Point graduate had considerable experience in command of large units in action. Frederick had organized, then trained and commanded the 1st Special Service Force, the combined Canadian-American commando unit known as the "Devil's Brigade," from 1942 to 1944. An aggressive, "up-front" leader, he and his men saw action in numerous mountain battles in Italy, a mission for which they had been especially trained. As a result of his leadership style, Frederick was wounded on eight occasions by the time he assumed command of the 1st Allied Airborne Task Force, a division-sized Anglo-American parachute and glider unit that assaulted the Mediterranean coast of France during the Dragoon landings in August 1944.[46] It is not surprising, then, that the transition of Eagles to Frederick did not appreciably, if at all, slow the Thunderbird Division's advance as its infantrymen drove northward toward the German frontier.

Resistance on the Alsatian Plain near Mertzwiller, Engwiller, and Mietesheim actually slowed the division's advance more than resistance in the Vosges during the first week of December, for a variety of reasons. Forced to advance in an exceptionally wide zone (fifteen kilometers), the division had advanced with its regiments abreast, with only a small reserve for maneuver. Also, the recently committed *245th Infantry Division* disposed about 2,650 infantrymen against the advance of the 3,380 infantrymen of the 179th and 180th Infantry Regiments, and counterattacked with the attached *Armored Reconnaissance Battalion* of the *Panzer Lehr Division* and an attached tank destroyer battalion in the flatter terrain in that sector.[47] The *361st*

Volksgrenadier Division's *952d Volksgrenadier Regiment,* however, faced 3,891 infantrymen of the 157th and attached 397th Infantry Regiments advancing toward Wimmenau and Zinswiller in the Low Vosges, respectively, with only about 350 *Grenadiers* and no forces with which to counterattack.[48] Nevertheless, the 397th lost most of Company I in the vicinity of Ingwiller on 1 December, before passing back to 100th Infantry Division control and liberating Wimmenau and Reipertswiller on 5 December.[49]

Other aspects of the German situation contributed to the more pronounced success of VI Corps's pursuit as the second week of December began. In addition to the coordination challenges resulting from the introduction of a new headquarters, *XC Corps,* on the western flank of *LXXXIX Corps* after 6 December, Generalleutnant Höhne had unit strength problems as well. Höhne lost the *Panzer Lehr*'s *Armored Reconnaissance Battalion* on 7 December when it was recalled by *OB West* to rejoin its parent division in preparation for the Ardennes counteroffensive less than eight days away.[50] The next day, *LXXXIX Corps* also lost the separate tank destroyer battalion that had reinforced Kegler's otherwise poorly trained and led division, although it received, as partial compensation, two battalions of 88mm dual-purpose towed guns from the *28th Flak Division* in *Army Group G.* As useful as these 88s may have been for point antitank defense, they were of little or no utility in the counterattacks that were an intrinsic part of delay doctrine.

Of even more significant import was the change in the situation of the American opposition. During the night of 7–8 December, elements of the 103d Infantry Division, recently arrived from the Sélestat area, relieved the 180th Infantry Regiment on the Thunderbirds' right flank, thus doubling the number of XV Corps troops committed opposite Kegler's men.[51] This addition also allowed the Thunderbirds the heretofore impractical potential to advance in the doctrinally preferable "two-up, one-back" formation, which protected and rested a third of the division's infantry while providing a significant force for maneuver or reinforcement. As the Cactus Division launched its pursuit against the now-heavily outnumbered *245th Infantry Division* on the Alsatian Plain toward Woerth, the Thunderbird Division drove northwest on a narrower front through the densely wooded eastern slopes of the Low Vosges into the *245th Infantry Division*'s zone toward Lembach. (See Figure 18.) With the 157th Infantry Regiment on the left and the 180th on the right, Major General Frederick chose to use part of his 179th Infantry Regiment to screen the division's left flank. His intent was to protect against a German flank attack through the 106th Cavalry Group.[52] Neither Generalleutnant Höhne nor Generalmajor Kegler, however, had the capability or the intention of doing anything other than holding their delay line together.[53]

The *245th* no longer had armored resources with which to counterattack, and its integral infantry units were unequal to the task in the mountain forests.[54] As a result, on 11 December, according to the *LXXXIX Corps* chief of staff, the VI Corps attacks in the eastern Low Vosges "ripped open the entire [*245th Infantry*] Division front," and drove to a line from Froeschwiller to Gunstett by 12 December. The Americans pursued unstintingly during the next few days, and these round-the-clock operations caused the "complete collapse" of the *245th Infantry Division,*[55] as the pursuers burst into Germany between Schönau and Wissembourg on 15 December.[56]

In a desperate attempt to forestall the VI Corps breakthrough, *Army Group G* committed significant reinforcements: one heavy tank destroyer battalion, three companies of medium tank destroyers from the *106th Panzer Brigade* ("*Hetzers,*" nimble, well-armored, self-propelled 75mm antitank guns),[57] and the experienced and spirited *21st Panzer Division.* The *21st Panzer*'s Generalleutnant Feuchtinger took control of all elements in the *245th Infantry Division*'s zone on 14 December, including the disorganized remnants of the *245th Infantry Division,* the heavy tank destroyer battalion, and the attached *Flak Regiment Köhler,* the 88mm regiment from the *28th Flak Division.*[58] (See Figure 18.) Although these units managed to prevent a catastrophic rupture of the *LXXXIX Corps* line, they, too, were unable to halt the American pursuit to the edge of the *Westwall.*

The 103d Infantry Division entered the Low Vosges just north of Preuschdorf on 13 December with the 409th and 411th Infantry Regiments leading and the 410th Infantry in reserve.[59] At Climbach (see Figure 18), lead elements for the 103d's pursuit encountered the first units of the *21st Panzer Division.* Task Force Blackshear, commanded by the executive officer of the 411th Infantry Regiment, Lt. Col. John P. Blackshear had been created in consonance with American pursuit doctrine, which called for the organization of combined-arms task forces to maintain contact with the enemy, prevent him from establishing a coherent defense, and envelop and annihilate him. The task force consisted of a rifle company of the 411th Infantry reinforced by an engineer platoon mounted in trucks, a platoon of Sherman tanks, and a platoon of 76mm antitank guns towed by half-tracks.[60]

On the morning of 14 December, as the leading elements of Task Force Blackshear rounded the curve in the road leading into Climbach from the south around La Schleife hill, they were taken under fire by 88mm dual-purpose guns and tanks of the *21st Panzer Division* arrayed in the surrounding 1,300- to 1,600-foot heights. For most of the day, the gunners of the 614th Tank Destroyer Battalion (Colored) (Towed) fought from an exposed position south of the town, sustaining 50 percent casualties and losing three of their four 76mm guns. While the Germans focused their attention on the American guns, however, Task Force Blackshear's infantry outflanked the German defenses and seized the town as they moved forward behind a rolling artillery barrage. Despite aggressive counterattacks that night by a battalion of the *192d Panzergrenadier Regiment* supported by more tanks, Task Force Blackshear, reinforced by the 2d and 3d Battalions of the 410th Infantry Regiment (Haffner's reserve), successfully retained Climbach.

The seizure of Climbach simultaneously outflanked the eminently defensible 1,600- to 2,400-foot Hochwald ridge just to the east and the Maginot defenses around Lembach to the southwest. The *LXXXIX Corps* subsequently withdrew across the frontier to the *Westwall* on 16 December to avoid encirclement of its penetrated and compartmented forward units. Even so, that part of its mission that included the requirement to delay south of the Siegfried fortifications until at least 15 December was accomplished, whereas VI Corps had yet to achieve its objective of penetrating the *Westwall*.

By 16 December, all of the American units in the Low Vosges were transitioning from the pursuit to the conduct of penetration attacks. Considering the grueling nature of the terrain, the increasingly severe winter weather, and, most of all, the tenacity of the German delay, the Americans' situation was analogous to that of the long-distance runner who, after a long, arduous, uphill sprint, finds himself confronted with a fifteen-foot-high brick wall. Despite this, American morale remained surprisingly high.

The reaction of the men of the 100th Infantry Division seems to have been typical. Although the 100th's advance northward had achieved the division's first goal of reaching the edge of the Ensemble de Bitche, the tasks of penetrating the vaunted fortresses there, and perhaps the barrier of the *Westwall* beyond, remained to be accomplished. The author of the 397th Infantry Regiment's history observed:

> We were now veterans. We knew the full content of war and we had become more cautious in our association with it. We had seen what it had done and what it could do: we were now more careful to feel our way ahead, rather than advance unknowing toward the enemy. We waited for the support of our artillery. We now instinctively took cover. When replacements, just renamed "reinforcements," took their places among us, we talked with more assurance in answer to their hesitating questions as to what to expect. We were rather proud of our experiences, and appreciated this opportunity to display our hard-won knowledge.[61]

On 14 December, a 398th Infantry Regiment medic summarized more simply his unit's morale at this stage of the campaign when he wrote to his wife: "Incidentally, our division is doing a great job and we're mighty proud of it. There's a sense of unity and good feeling among the men, an 'esprit de corps' which is vital in a set-up such as ours."[62]

Solid morale was evident even in infantry units of the veteran 45th Infantry Division. As it prepared to launch its attack through the *Westwall* and into Germany, the morale of the 157th Infantry Regiment actually rose. "By now," the author of the regimental history wrote, "tired of warfare as they were, everyone was excited with the prospect of being with the first Seventh Army unit into Germany."

Morale was not the only aspect of American combat power that had been preserved; despite the sharp encounters at Waldhambach, Wingen-sur-Moder, Lemberg, Enchenberg, Mouterhouse, and Climbach, the numerical strength of nearly all American infantry units in the Low Vosges had been protected to a significant degree as well. The following table depicts the average strengths of the rifle companies of each American infantry regiment committed to penetrating the German defenses along the border of the Palatinate at the beginning of the pursuit and at the end of it:

TABLE 1. Comparative Average Strengths of American Infantry
Rifle Companies Before and After the Pursuit Through
the Low Vosges[63]

Unit	Present for Duty 1 Dec/16 Dec	% of Authorized 1 Dec/16 Dec
44th Infantry Division		
71st Infantry Regiment	167/146	93/81
114th Infantry Regiment	161/157	89/87
324th Infantry Regiment	155/133	86/74
100th Infantry Division		
397th Infantry Regiment	168/141	93/78
398th Infantry Regiment	179/127	99/71
399th Infantry Regiment	173/142	96/79
45th Infantry Division		
157th Infantry Regiment	140/105	78/58
179th Infantry Regiment	133/124	74/69
180th Infantry Regiment	143/130	79/72
103d Infantry Division		
409th Infantry Regiment	152/153	85/85
410th Infantry Regiment	149/155	83/86
411th Infantry Regiment	167/166	93/92

Not only had the strengths of the rifle companies been largely preserved, but those of the heavy-weapons companies and supporting units
were almost completely intact.[64] The commanders of Seventh Army
units in the Low Vosges had fulfilled their mission's implicit requirement to arrive at the German fortifications without having expended
their assets to the extent that the prosecution of successful penetration attacks would have been unduly jeopardized.

To the commanders of the *First Army* elements in the Low Vosges, preservation of combat power was not nearly as critical for the accomplishment of their mission. Defense of the *Westwall* and Maginot positions would be a far less demanding task than the delay had been; besides, *First Army* could expect a respite from American pressure once *Army Group B*'s counteroffensive began. However, it is useful to examine the impact of the fighting during the third week of December on these units for perspective on future operations.

German combat power did not fare as well as that of the attackers. The slow, brutal mountain delaying actions significantly attrited the defenders' strength and damaged their morale, despite the fulfillment of their stated mission to delay forward of the border fortifications until at least 15 December. Continuous withdrawals under pressure are never conducive to high morale. To halt the Century Division's drive, Oberst Philippi had combed every able-bodied man out of the rear echelon of the *361st Volksgrenadier Division* (signal specialists, supply and transport troops, et cetera); even with this desperate measure, by mid-December, when the lines stabilized, the division was "exhausted," and could count only about 675 men in its infantry battalions, for a loss of 36 percent.[65] Fortunately for this division, its sector after 15 December stretched from about four kilometers east of Bitche to Niedersteinbach. (See Figure 20.) Initially, only the 106th Cavalry Group's screen faced them. Later, the 106th was replaced by Task Force Hudelson, but neither force presented an offensive threat. (See Figure 20.)

The situation of the other German divisions in the Low Vosges was not very different. The *25th Panzergrenadier Division* counted in its ranks only about eight hundred infantrymen and thirteen tanks and assault guns by 18 December, representing a loss of 19 percent in personnel, but a net loss of no armored vehicles.[66] Elements committed to the defense of the Maginot line's Ensemble de Bitche found little more than a temporary respite, for the Americans were soon to assault them there. Fortunately for the battered *25th*, the efforts of their comrades-in-arms in the Ardennes would extend the opportunity for replenishment. Also, on 20 December, a regiment of the newly arrived *257th Volksgrenadier Division* was attached to reinforce this badly mauled unit.[67] The remainder of the *257th* relieved the *11th Panzer Division* at the same time; the latter would no longer play a role in the Vosges. (See Figure 20.)

ORDER OF BATTLE
21–31 DECEMBER 1944

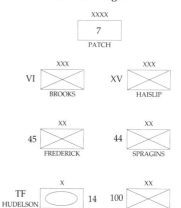

U.S. SEVENTH ARMY
*Adjusting Defensive Positions
in the Low Vosges*

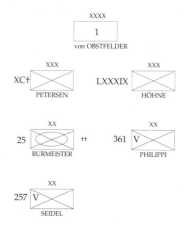

GERMAN ARMY GROUP G
Stabilizing Defensive Positions

Assembling for Attack

† formerly the IV Luftwaffe Feld Korps
†† 25th PGD relieved by 559th VGD 26–28 December

KEY

X	Combat Command or Group	TF	Task Force
XX	Division		
XXX	Corps		
XXXX	Army		

Infantry

Armor/Panzer

Mechanized Cavalry

Armored Infantry/
Panzergrenadier

Volksgrenadier

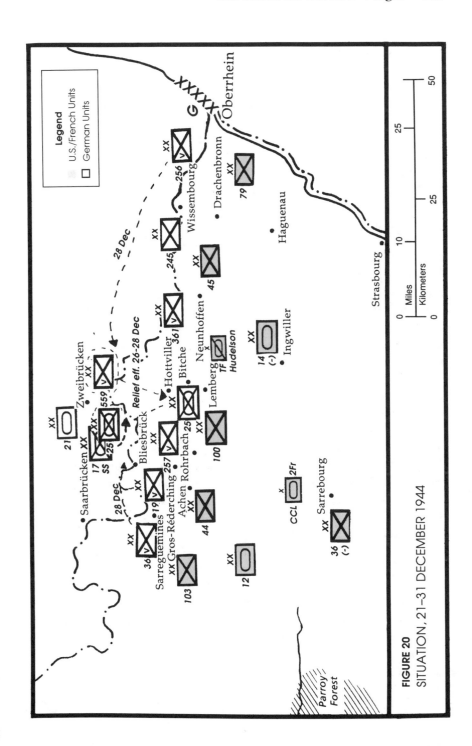

FIGURE 20

SITUATION, 21–31 DECEMBER 1944

The most damaged German unit in the Low Vosges was the *245th Infantry Division,* which had ceased to exist as a coherent formation by 14 December. Remaining combat elements in contact with the enemy had been subordinated to the *21st Panzer Division* on that day and remained so until 18 December. After a massive influx of replacements, bringing the division's three underequipped regiments to nearly full strength (4,952 *Grenadiers* out of an authorized strength of 5,274[68]), and only when these troops were firmly ensconced in the *Westwall,* did the *LXXXIX Corps* commander entrust again the control of the *245th*'s sector to Kegler and his staff.

Upon reaching the new main defensive line in the *Westwall* and Ensemble de Bitche positions, the *First Army* mission changed from delay to defense. *First Army* labor and security organizations had been feverishly preparing these positions for occupation since the beginning of December, although there were again problems coordinating the desires of the field commanders with those of the construction supervisors.[69] Once again, as in the High Vosges, the Americans would try to penetrate a fortified German line from which, by direct order of the Führer, there was to be no retreat.

The American assaults began on 14 December 1944, two days before the twenty-eight divisions of *Army Group B*'s *Fifth Panzer Army, Sixth SS Panzer Army,* and *Seventh Army* unleashed their savage counteroffensive against five U.S. First Army divisions in the Ardennes. Subsequent changes to Seventh Army operations prevented the penetration efforts from taking their full course, so it is impossible to say whether the Americans in the Low Vosges would have accomplished their mission. Nevertheless, it is extremely tempting to analyze the Americans' aborted attempts to penetrate the German defenses, and try to extrapolate from them the results of the battle that might have occurred had Model *not* launched his Ardennes gambit. This, of course, is not based on evidence, but only conjecture. Moreover, so many other factors would have come into play (German mobile reserves, German morale in the absence of the attack, and so forth) that such an attempt would constitute the vaguest kind of conjecture at that. However, an analysis of the inconclusive fighting in the third week of December is important for establishing an accurate perspective on operations commencing 1 January 1945. Such analysis also provides some unique insight into the combat proficiency and effectiveness of the American units assaulting the Maginot line near Bitche.

Recognizing these limitations, some valid conclusions *may* be drawn from operations in the Vosges in the first half of December. First and most indisputable is that the commanders and soldiers of *XIII SS, LXXXIX,* and *XC Corps* accomplished their delay mission. For the most part, they executed a doctrinally correct delay, using the restrictive terrain to optimal advantage, and aggressively counterattacked when appropriate. Although they lost heavily in the process, they prevented a breakthrough into the Palatinate in their sector, and allowed *OB West* to retain its large mobile reserve undiluted for the Ardennes counteroffensive.

For their part, the Americans in VI and XV Corps operating in the Low Vosges executed a pursuit in consonance with their own doctrine to the extent allowed by terrain. They pursued with combined-arms teams and allowed the enemy minimal time to regroup and prepare subsequent delay lines. In testament to this, the *LXXXIX Corps* chief of staff remarked:

> The improvement of rearward positions which had been already ordered in good time by Corps hardly worked out in practice. As everything was in a continuous state of flux a farsighted planning involving the entire Corps sector could not be undertaken. The constant changes in the sector of the *245th Infantry Division* forced the divisions to execute their own planning and reconnoitering in their respective sectors, without Corps being in the position to coordinate the established lines between the divisions. . . . As the divisions, due to the tense situation at the front, were obliged to employ every able bodied man in combat, no forces worth mentioning could be freed for the improvement of rearward positions.[70]

Lieutenant General Patch used Seventh Army's mechanized cavalry group's screen as an effective economy of force measure, allowing the pursuing divisions to advance in sufficiently narrow zones. This ensured that they were able to retain reserves adequate for relentless continuation of the pursuit, while exposing minimum numbers of troops to danger and preserving the force needed for the ultimate mission of penetrating the German frontier defenses. When terrain allowed, the XV Corps commander, Major General Haislip, made advantageous use of his armored division to force a premature German withdrawal from an otherwise eminently defensible line. Rarely in war do both sides accomplish their missions concurrently, but to the extent allowed by strategic circumstances, this is exactly what happened in the Low Vosges during the first two weeks of December 1944.

ATTACK ON THE MAGINOT FORTIFICATIONS AT BITCHE

As the German onslaught rocked American forces in the Ardennes Forest, elements of VI and XV Corps bored into the German defenses in the Low Vosges. In the west, XV Corps's 44th Infantry Division assaulted Fort Simserhof, one of the greatest of all Maginot fortresses, while three kilometers to the east their counterparts in the 100th Infantry Division attacked yet another Maginot *gros ouvrage,* Fort Schiesseck. The artillery and mortar fire from these fortifications, including fire from 75mm and 135mm howitzers and 81mm mortars in steel-reinforced concrete embrasures and disappearing steel turrets, had been inflicting casualties on the Americans even during their attacks on Lemberg, Petit Réderching, and Enchenberg. Although *XC Corps's* Generalleutnant Petersen claimed that, "The use of the Maginot fortifications in reverse [that is to say, against attacks in the direction of Germany] was more than an emergency adaptation," and, "On the whole, however, the situation was unnatural since the fortifications were situated unfavorably," this would have come as a surprise to the American infantrymen and engineers tasked with assaulting them.[71]

It would also have surprised the Germans of Generalleutnant Max von Viebahn's *Berliner Bären* of the *257th Infantry Division* of Witzleben's *First Army* in 1940. By virtue of its breakthrough near Sarralbe on 15 June, the *257th Infantry Division* had the opportunity to attack all of the fortifications of the Ensemble de Bitche from *exactly* the same aspect, that is, *from* France *toward* Germany. Its progress was less than impressive. On 21 June 1940, the division's *457th Infantry Regiment* attacked the *abri d'intervalle* on the Grand Kindelberg near Bitche and failed, losing one officer and four enlisted soldiers killed and twenty-seven men wounded. The next day, the *457th* attacked in vain minor casemates and blockhouses under the control of Fort Grand Hohekirkel near the Biesenberg, nine kilometers east of Bitche, losing ten more killed and thirty-six wounded. Following these failures, attacks were suspended altogether, and the Germans simply waited out the acceptance of the armistice by the garrisons of the Ensemble de Bitche on 30 June.[72] The Germans were unable to penetrate the outer rear defenses of these massive fortifications, and they never progressed against them to the extent necessary for an assault on the fortresses proper.

This was exactly what the 71st and 398th Infantry Regiments had been preparing for while in reserve during the battles of Meyerhof–Petit Réderching, Enchenberg, Lemberg, and Mouterhouse. Unique circumstances called for unique solutions; since both Schiesseck and Simserhof were equipped with long-range indirect-fire weapons, both had to be assaulted simultaneously, lest the armaments of both be concentrated on the force attacking one. Major General Haislip's plan called for each of his infantry divisions to assault one of the fortresses and their outer works. On 14 December, both Spragins's 44th and Burress's 100th Divisions commenced coordinated combined-arms attacks against the outer works of the two fortresses, defended by *First Army* fortress troops and the *25th Panzergrenadier Division.* In keeping with doctrinal requirements for penetrations, Haislip not only attacked in a narrow zone, but he also concentrated massive artillery support against the objective areas. These barrages were fired not only by the divisions' organic 105mm and 155mm howitzers, but from five battalions of XV Corps artillery—including 8-inch howitzers, 4.5-inch and 155mm guns, and giant 240mm howitzers—largely to no avail. On 15 and 16 December, XII TAC launched seventy-eight P-47 fighter-bomber sorties against the fortifications, dropping five-hundred-pound bombs, also with little effect. In fact, observers watched even the heaviest of artillery projectiles and the aerial bombs score direct hits and ricochet off harmlessly![73] Eliminating the Maginot bastions would require infantry and engineer teams to assault them at point-blank range and, with flamethrower, satchel charge, thermite grenade, and bayonet, kill or otherwise neutralize the German defenders.

To isolate the fortresses and attempt to restrict the Germans' ability to counterattack, the remaining regiments of each division executed supporting attacks in the areas adjacent to the fortresses being assaulted. In the 44th's zone, the 324th Infantry attacked to the north of Simserhof toward Hottviller. In the Century Division's zone, the 399th Infantry attacked through the wooded draws near Reyersviller, while the 397th attacked toward the Camp de Bitche, the old French garrison area to the east.

Like the Germans in 1940, the American regiments conducting the main attacks on the fortresses had first to fight past the outer defensive works. The 100th Infantry Division's zone was especially difficult, because it included Fort Freudenberg, a large *abri d'intervalle* dominating the nearly three-hundred-foot-deep draw leading from Reyersviller. (See Figure 21.) Initial attempts to take the place were repelled, but persistence paid off. After three days of crawling, blasting, fighting back counterattacks, and waging subterranean warfare in the tunnels and sublevels of the fort, the Centurymen seized Freudenberg, and penetrated and blocked the personnel and ammunition entrances to Schiesseck. Three more days were needed to fight through the maze of casemates, blockhouses, and other fortifications until Schiesseck's guns were silenced on 20 December. The accompanying engineer company of the 398th Regimental Combat Team, B, 325th Engineers, expended about five thousand pounds of dynamite destroying Schiesseck, sealing defenders inside and wrecking the fort's artillery. A bulldozer employed by the attached 781st Tank Battalion delivered the coup de grace, sealing five of the units by burying them under tons of earth and rock.

One officer and 15 enlisted men were killed and 120 more men were wounded in the assault on Fort Schiesseck. This number is especially significant. At the cost of the same number killed and 57 more wounded, a regiment that was a product of the U.S. Army Mobilization Training Plan, without special training or experience, accomplished what a regiment of the vaunted 1940 German army had utterly failed to do: penetrate the Ensemble de Bitche.[74] Moreover, they accomplished it without the months of training and minute intelligence that had been available to the Germans in 1940.

The assault on Simserhof by the 44th Infantry Division's 71st Infantry Regiment followed much the same pattern. With heavy artillery concentrations and aerially delivered munitions proving all but useless against the fortifications in their zone, the infantrymen and engineers of the 71st RCT attacked Simserhof with pole charges, satchel charges, small arms, and flamethrowers. They seized each of the casemates and other fortifications of the *gros ouvrage* over a six-day period, while

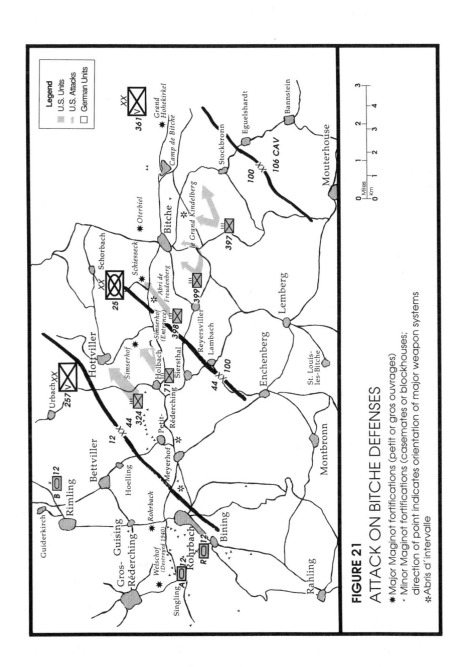

FIGURE 21

ATTACK ON BITCHE DEFENSES

✱ Major Maginot fortifications (petit or gros ouvrages)
▸ Minor Maginot fortifications (casemates or blockhouses;
   direction of point indicates orientation of major weapon systems
✣ Abris d'intervalle

simultaneously beating back numerous *25th Panzergrenadier Division* counterattacks. Upon securing the fortress, they too destroyed the gun turrets and sealed the embrasures of the interconnected emplacements to ensure that they could not be used again in the near future.[75] Their casualties were roughly the same as those suffered by the 398th RCT, again reinforcing the magnitude of their accomplishment.[76]

With Simserhof and Schiesseck neutralized, XV Corps was prepared to seize Bitche and drive northward through the Siegfried line and into the Palatinate. (See Figure 20.) Burress's 397th and 399th Infantry Regiments stood poised to launch an attack on Bitche from the south and west, while the 398th on Schiesseck Hill cut the Bitche-Hottviller road and could adjust artillery on the Bitche-Haspelschiedt route, preventing withdrawal or reinforcement of the German garrison in Bitche.[77] Spragins's 114th Infantry Regiment had relieved the 324th to the left (northwest) of the 71st on the Grosse Vasberg, and thus interdicted the road from Bitche to Nousseviller-les-Bitche; his 324th Infantry Regiment was in reserve. With Combat Commands A and R of Allen's 12th Armored Division in corps reserve as an exploitation force, it appeared that XV Corps was about to accomplish another unprecedented achievement: the conquest of the fortress city of Bitche. As the Germans' Ardennes counteroffensive threatened the 12th Army Group far to the north, the exigencies of the new strategic situation imposed on Seventh Army forced the cancellation of the upcoming attack. Bitche remained unconquered until March 1945, when it fell to the Century Division.

THE BATTLE IN THE SIEGFRIED LINE

While XV Corps was penetrating the Maginot line, VI Corps attempted to do the same to the *Westwall* in its zone. Thirty kilometers to the east, the 45th and 103d Infantry Divisions commenced their assaults into the German fortifications on 16 December.

The French side of the border included numerous Maginot fortifications. Most notable among them were the *petit ouvrage* Lembach and the *gros ouvrage* Four à Chaux, located immediately to the east and west, respectively, of the village of Lembach, and the *gros ouvrage* Hochwald, on both sides of the Hochwald ridge, near Drachenbronn. (See Figure 18.)

The Germans chose not to defend these Maginot works. Unlike those of the Ensemble de Bitche in the XV Corps zone, these truly were situated such that they were unsuitable for defense against an attack from the south; nearly all the casemates, blockhouses, and turrets were on the north side of the area's ridges.[78] Besides, serious damage had been wreaked on part of Fort Hochwald by *Stukas* and heavy artillery in June 1940.[79] About the only useful aspect of the Maginot fortifications in this sector was the cleared fields of fire in the forests, the north sides of which the Germans of the *LXXXIX Corps* would often temporarily defend.[80]

The portion of the Siegfried line into which the westernmost elements of VI Corps slashed on the first day of the Germans' Ardennes counteroffensive was constructed quite differently from the Maginot fortifications on the French side of the border. The *Westwall* contained no massive, fourteen-story-deep behemoths of the military engineer's art. Instead, it consisted of successive belts of mutually supporting concrete pillboxes and observation posts, all protected behind antitank ditches and acres of barbed wire and minefields. According to the Cactus Division's history, "The Germans expected to lose forts, but their theory was that the assault of the hedgehog positions in depth would be so costly to the attacker that eventually he would give up."[81] Indeed, *OB West* ordered the defensive efforts to be made primarily from field fortifications constructed in great depth, with the *Westwall* bunkers to be used only as shelter from American indirect fire.[82]

The possibility was small that the Americans would give up due to excessive casualties, if the U.S. Army's record in the *Hürtgenwald* was any indication. From 16 to 21 December, both the 45th and 103d Infantry Divisions gained ground slowly against the *21st Panzer Division* and the *245th Infantry Division* near Niederschlettenbach and Reisdorf. The Americans found the going exceptionally tough. The 103d Infantry Division history records :

> Small gains were made against the bitterest sort of opposition in the mountainous terrain south of Darrenbach [*sic*] and Reisdorf by use of flamethrowers, Molotov cocktails and satchel charges. . . . The men had things to learn about fighting the Siegfried pillboxes.[83]

The Germans were also distressed by the course of the battle in this sector of the *Westwall*. On 20 December, the performance of the *245th Infantry Division* was again found to be lacking, and control of the division's sector passed once more to Generalleutnant Feuchtinger and his men. The *21st Panzer Division*'s reconnaissance elements found the American penetrations to be "partly larger and more dangerous than was at first expected." Even after the commitment of this armored "fire brigade," the attacks of the 45th Infantry Division's 180th Infantry Regiment near Niederschlettenbach "succeeded in enlarging [their] penetration in width as well as to depth" by 20 December.[84]

Offensive operations were called off by 21 December in response to strategic requirements resulting from the course of the battle in the Ardennes. On 21 December, Lieutenant General Patch issued Seventh Army Field Order 8, requiring his units in the Low Vosges to relieve Third Army units to the west and subsequently defend in sector.[85]

STATIC INTERLUDE

The course of the Ardennes battle completely changed the situation in the Low Vosges. For all of the American divisions there except the 45th, it brought the first requirement for the conduct of a defense. For the commanders of *First Army,* it meant a reversion to the attack for the first time in at least six months; for many of the soldiers, it was their first experience with offensive combat at all.

For both sides, the brief period of relative calm between 21 December and New Year's Eve brought about major adjustments in position. Major General Haislip's XV Corps took over Third Army's XII Corps sector to the west; Haffner's 103d Infantry Division was withdrawn from the VI Corps sector near Reisdorf and relieved the 6th Armored Division in the line from Welferding to the outskirts of Saarbrücken on Christmas Eve.[86] (See Figure 20.) Simultaneously, the 106th Cavalry Group departed the central Low Vosges and relieved Third Army's 6th Cavalry Group near St. Avold.[87] The 44th and 100th Infantry Divisions extended their lines west to cover this new sector as well; each received responsibility for seventeen- to eighteen-kilometer stretches of territory.

The 44th, defending from Welferding to just west of Rimling, covered ground that was mostly open, rolling hills, although the *Grosswald, Lehwald,* and *Bois de Bliesbrücken* in the center of its sector provided shallow patches of dense vegetation. The 100th Infantry Division's sector provided sharply contrasting terrain: Open, undulating farmland in the east gave way to craggy draws and ridges in the center and western part of its assigned area. To assist them in their efforts to defend these large sectors, Major General Haislip assigned an additional infantry regiment from Task Force Harris to each of them effective 31 December 1944.

Task Force Harris consisted of the three infantry regiments of the 63d Infantry Division, under the command of Brig. Gen. Frederick M. Harris, the assistant division commander. Sea-lift constraints prevented the entire division from arriving together in December 1944, so the division's integral 253d, 254th, and 255th Infantry Regiments were brigaded together with a small provisional headquarters and sent north upon arrival in Marseilles. Until the remainder of the 63d Division arrived, the Task Force Harris regiments were parceled out to "veteran" divisions to allow them to retain reserves while covering their extended sectors. The 44th received the 253d Infantry Regiment, and the 100th got the 255th.

Such an organization and commitment of units was obviously uncharacteristic of U.S. Army training and deployment procedures. Further fouling the outlook for these units was the preparatory training they underwent prior to embarking from New York in November 1944. Activated in June 1943, the 63d Infantry Division was used to provide replacements for divisions already in combat to an almost unique degree.[88] Making matters even worse, SHAEF required each regiment to provide 219 junior enlisted men as replacements for losses in the Ardennes shortly before their commitment to the Vosges.[89] The performance of these units in the Low Vosges in the first two weeks of 1945 validates by exception the superiority of normal U.S. Army infantry division organization and training.

Thus reinforced, Major General Spragins deployed the 44th Infantry Division in its sector with the 114th Infantry Regiment on the left, defending Sarreguemines; the 324th in the center, in the *Grosswald* and *Lehwald;* and the 71st on the right, in the *Bois de Bliesbrücken.* Spragins retained the 253d Infantry as a reserve, in the vicinity of Wittring[90] (near Achen in Figure 20). The only high-speed avenues of approach entering his division's zone from the north were the Bliesbrück-Achen road and the road leading from Gersheim to the junction between Rimling and Woelfling, both of which were solidly within the boundaries of the 71st Infantry Regiment, with the 253d

Infantry in depth behind it. Spragins's defense therefore met the doctrinal requirements for defense in depth, to the extent possible given the breadth of the sector, and ensured that responsibility for defense of likely avenues of approach was not split between units.

Major General Burress deployed his division's assets with similar attention to doctrinal correctness. As a former instructor and assistant commandant of the Infantry School at Fort Benning, Georgia, Burress and his G3, Lt. Col. Kenneth Eckland, developed "Plan Tennessee" to ensure that the major armor approach route in the western part of his sector was firmly defended by the 397th Infantry Regiment. Here, from the critical junction of Rimling, roads branched out throughout the Century Division sector to Gros Réderching, Rohrbach (via Guising), and Petit Réderching (via Bettviller). In recognition of the criticality of this sector, Col. John M. King, the regimental commander, established his 3d Battalion in a reverse-slope defense on Schlietzen Hill, just to the west of Rimling; he arrayed the remainder of his regiment in depth with 1st Battalion to the east, near Mehling Farm, and 2d Battalion near Bettviller and Guising.[91]

The remainder of Burress's division was similarly well placed. He emplaced his 398th Infantry Regiment, minus one battalion retained in division reserve, on the Hottviller-Siersthal-Enchenberg road. Astride the Bitche-Lemberg road, Burress deployed the 399th Infantry Regiment also in depth, with the 1st and 2d Battalions forward and the 3d Battalion in reserve. Task Force Harris's 255th Infantry Regiment also remained in reserve, ready to move forward to counterattack or reinforce as needed.[92]

The withdrawal of the 103d Infantry Division and 106th Cavalry Group from the line in the Low Vosges precipitated a complex tactical solution to the challenge of defending the resultant sector. Major General Brooks was now required to defend a sector covering approximately thirty-five kilometers of deeply compartmented, heavily forested terrain, from just southeast of Bitche to Drachenbronn, where the Low Vosges suddenly drop off to the Alsatian Plain. As an economy of force measure, he organized a mechanized task force from elements of the 14th Armored Division and other Seventh Army units, and used them to defend the most easily defensible portion of the Low Vosges in his sector.

Commanded by Col. Daniel Hudelson of Combat Command R, Task Force Hudelson was a confusing amalgam of divisional and nondivisional units, consisting of the 14th Armored Division's 62d Armored Infantry Battalion, most of the 14th's 94th Cavalry Squadron (less one troop and part of another), the separate 117th Cavalry Squadron (a Seventh Army reconnaissance unit), a divisional combat engineer company (A, 125th Armored Engineer Battalion), a nondivisional company of tank destroyers (B, 645th Tank Destroyer Battalion), a company of 4.2-inch heavy mortars (B, 83d Chemical Mortar Battalion, a separate Seventh Army white phosphorous smoke–laying unit), a detachment of the 540th Engineer Combat Regiment (a separate Seventh Army combat engineer unit), and the 14th's 500th Armored Artillery Battalion.[93] This organization represented a marked departure from the American practice of habitual relationships between maneuver and supporting units (see Chapter 2), and its performance in early January would show it. Arrayed more as a screening force than as one for defense, Task Force Hudelson covered a twelve-kilometer sector from just east and south of Bitche to Neunhoffen. (See Figure 20.)

This arrangement still required the 45th Infantry Division to defend in an expanded zone of considerable breadth. The Thunderbird Division extended its line to include the sector recently vacated by the Cactus Division, causing Major General Frederick to commit all three of his infantry regiments to a linear defense over a heavily forested, deeply compartmented, seventeen-kilometer front from Neunhoffen to just west of Drachenbronn. The withdrawal to a coherent line appropriate for defense meant giving up the dearly bought gains in German territory, and moving back to the French side of the frontier.

Not only did this change of mission require a rapid tactical readjustment, but it affected morale as well. The new mission had a profound effect on the men of the 45th, who, after one and a half years of combat against the Wehrmacht in Sicily, Italy, and France, were outraged to be ordered to withdraw from German soil without a fight. According to the 179th Infantry Regiment's history, "The impending necessity of withdrawing broke the hearts of the men who had fought so bitterly to take that ground." As they prepared to fall back, "they prepared defenses to the rear, almost sheepishly awaiting the order which would find the 45th falling back for the first time in its history."[94]

The 157th Infantry Regiment's history described it more fervently:

Morale sunk [*sic*] and the challenging "Win the War in '44" gave way to the grim "Stay Alive in '45. . . ." Withdrawal was nasty medicine to men of the 157th and the bitching was loud and profane. This outfit had held at Salerno and Anzio against every German boast that they would be destroyed; they had left foxholes to break through to Rome; they had chased the Heinie in a mad rout across France; and whipped him badly wherever he made a stand. They had fought long and hard for the feel of German soil under their feet and to leave it without a fight didn't seem right to them. For the first time, their backs were to the enemy.[95]

To add depth and flexibility to the VI Corps defense, on the Alsatian Plain as well as in the Low Vosges, Major General Brooks placed the 14th Armored Division (minus the elements assigned to Task Force Hudelson) in reserve near Ingwiller by 23 December.[96] He also assigned one regiment of Task Force Herren, the 275th Infantry Regiment, to the 45th to add the potential for a defense in depth. Task Force Herren resembled Task Force Harris in almost every respect. Made up of the three infantry regiments of the 70th Infantry Division, it had sailed from the United States without supporting units; the standard Mobilization Training Plan schedule had been butchered by requirements to provide vast numbers of replacements; and more than 650 junior infantrymen had been removed to fill understrength Third Army units in time for their counterattacks into the flank of *Army Group B* in Luxembourg.[97]

Their addition to the 45th Infantry Division was greeted with something less than unrestrained enthusiasm. The history of the 179th Infantry Regiment refers to the members of Task Forces Harris and Herren as "American Volksturm Grenadiers," and relates several anecdotes regarding the incompetence and general lack of battleworthiness of numerous of the 70th's officers.[98] Like that of their counterparts in Task Force Harris, the performance of the units of Task Force Herren in the first two weeks of the new year would prove the decisive importance of effective unit training and corollary cohesion.

The 63d and 70th Infantry Divisions had been among the last to be organized and equipped by the Army Ground Forces (AGF), the command responsible for the creation and training of army ground combat units. Both divisions were scheduled to be trained according to the standard Mobilization Training Plan (see Chapter 2), as the Seventh Army's 79th, 100th, and 103d Infantry Divisions had been. Although the 100th and 103d Infantry Divisions, for example, had also been required to turn over significant quantities of troops during their respective training periods, both units had been filled since December 1942 and had completed all phases of individual and unit training before embarking for Europe in October 1944. The situations of the units destined to enter combat as Task Forces Harris and Herren were quite different from these.

Both the 63d and 70th Infantry Divisions were activated in June 1943, but the 63d possessed only half of its authorized strength as late as September.[99] Both divisions had been heavily stripped of junior enlisted soldiers, nearly all infantrymen, in a series of purges to provide replacements to units already in combat. The 63d lost 3,200 men in February, and an additional 4,185 (3,568 infantrymen) between April and September 1944; the 70th lost 3,000 in February and 3,370 more (2,845 infantrymen) by September. These same purges removed only about half as many men from the 100th (3,675) and one-third as many from the 103d (2,550) during the same period.[100]

Although this attrition clearly played havoc with the effectiveness of the training process, other factors made the situation worse. Neither division ever participated in the twelve-week, large-scale maneuver phase of their training sequence (see Chapter 2), thus losing exceptionally valuable opportunities for all echelons to train together. Their combined-arms training was also cut short. Indeed, whereas the 63d received about the same number of replacements (1,374) as the 100th (1,063) within ninety days of deployment, the 70th Infantry Division was forced to attempt to amalgamate 3,871 men into its combat ranks with a supplemental training phase less than three months before departing for Europe.[101] Due to this chaotic butchery of their training cycles, neither division was scheduled for deployment by the AGF until July 1945, but developments in Europe prompted General Headquarters (GHQ) in Washington to ship them in December 1944.

As 1944 drew to a snowy and bitterly cold conclusion, the commanders of Seventh Army units everywhere began to recognize looming challenges far greater than those posed by their recent sudden and complicated repositioning and reorganization. Aerial photoreconnaissance indicated a buildup of armored forces near Zweibrücken and Saarbrücken; ULTRA, the supersecret decoding operation, had even intercepted orders for a German counterattack in Alsace![102] In a Seventh Army intelligence estimate issued 29 December 1944, units were consequently warned that the most likely German courses of action for the immediate future were to "launch a series of limited objective attacks" or, failing that, "to attack south from Bitche-Sarreguemines area with five to eight divisions with initial objective of seizing Saverne and Ingwiller Passes."[103]

As a result, Seventh Army's defensive preparations increased in vigor, and Lieutenant General Patch issued his second field order in ten days on 30 December. In addition to the implicit requirement for the creation of an outpost line, a main line of resistance (MLR), and a reserve area in consonance with defensive doctrine, Seventh Army Field Order 9 directed units to reconnoiter and organize alternate defensive positions along designated lines to the rear. These would serve as control measures, allowing withdrawal to consecutive, organized, and coordinated positions in the event of a German breakthrough.

Lieutenant General Patch also ordered the creation of an army-level reserve to provide operational depth to his precariously thin forward defenses. The 36th Infantry and 12th Armored Divisions were ordered to be prepared to move on twelve hours' notice to counterattack or reinforce threatened areas of the army front. A new corps headquarters, the XXI, under the command of Maj. Gen. Frank Milburn, was created and ordered to prepare to take control of both of these divisions in future operations. The commanders of VI and XV Corps were further ordered to prepare counterattack plans to restore their lines in the event of a withdrawal or retreat.[104] Throughout these preparations, vigorous patrolling, including reconnaissance patrols and raids, was to be carried out to deny the enemy intelligence regarding American activities and to "dominate No Man's land" between the lines.[105]

In the XV Corps zone, on 31 December, Combat Command L of the 2d French Armored Division arrived from the Colmar region and was immediately placed in reserve near Rauwiller to add depth to Haislip's defense. By New Year's Eve, the Allied forces in the Low Vosges could count on three reinforced infantry divisions (the 44th, 45th, and 100th) and a mechanized task force with a total of 21,002 infantrymen to defend the Seventh Army MLR.[106] In corps and Seventh Army reserve, another infantry division (the 36th), one full armored division (the 12th), and parts of two others (the 14th and 2d French) with about 8,100 more infantrymen were poised to counterattack or otherwise assist in the defense.

New Year's Eve found XV Corps troops in the Low Vosges and the foothills to the west arrayed in doctrinally correct defenses in depth, with coordinated plans for delays and subsequent defensive operations if necessary. Minefields, roadblocks, and barbed-wire obstacles had been emplaced across the front, covered by interlocking fields of fire and registered artillery. Reserves, at the tactical and operational level, were echeloned in depth and ready for forward deployment to counterattack or reinforce hard-pressed sectors. As the New Year approached, work continued on improvement of positions, and the forward units conducted reconnaissance and observation of the seemingly quiet front.

In the VI Corps sector, the men of Task Force Hudelson had extensively mined and blocked the few roads leading into their wide sector. Anticipating relief by elements of Task Force Herren on 1 January, many of its members thought that they were unlikely to be attacked in such rough terrain. Conversing with one of the officers of the 70th Infantry Division who had come forward to coordinate the impending relief, the commanding officer of Company C, 62d Armored Infantry Battalion, remarked, "Sure hate to be relieved in this quiet sector."[107]

THE NORDWIND COUNTEROFFENSIVE

With the Seventh Army stretched dangerously thin by the westward and northward shift necessary to cover vacated Third Army positions, OKW recognized the potential for a second major counteroffensive, not only to gain ground and to inflict damage on American forces in Alsace and Lorraine, but especially to relieve pressure on *Army Group B* forces committed in the Ardennes.[108] According to the *First Army* I.a. (operations officer) Oberst im Generalstab Albert Emmerich, the latter consideration forced the attack to be made as soon as possible.[109]

The objectives of Operation Nordwind, ordered by OKW on 21 December, were ambitious indeed: to regain the Saverne Gap, cut off and destroy American forces in the Low Vosges, and link up with elements of *Nineteenth Army*.[110] *Army Group G*, under the command of General der Infanterie Blaskowitz (who again changed places with Balck on 23 December), would attack southward with strong elements of *First Army*, including six *Volksgrenadier,* one mountain infantry, two *Panzergrenadier,* and one *Panzer* divisions an hour before midnight on 31 December. Elements of *Nineteenth Army* and *Army Group Oberrhein* (on the east bank of the Rhine) were to conduct complementary offensive operations in their zones.[111] Feints and demonstrations would be conducted by *First Army* units in the Saar region to the west on the day before the offensive.

Initially, the operations staff of *Army Group G* intended to conduct the main attack longitudinally *through* the Low Vosges with four *Volksgrenadier* divisions, a mountain division, and a *Panzer* division, starting from a line from Bitche to Neunhoffen and conducting a penetration south to the Wingen-Ingwiller road. (See Figure 22a, Operation Nordwind Plan as of 23 Decembe 1944.) The supporting attack, also a penetration, would be made by one *Panzergrenadier* and one *Volksgrenadier* division, supported by a heavy tank destroyer battalion and several companies of self-propelled armored flamethrowers, attacking south from Gersheim toward Achen, Gros Réderching, and Rohrbach. One *Panzergrenadier* division would be held in reserve to exploit the anticipated breakthrough in the Vosges. The two efforts would then coordinate an encirclement to annihilate the American units in the zone of attack, and seize the Saverne Gap. This concept was mainly based on the *Army Group G* staff's desire to avoid the Maginot fortifications in the hands of the Americans west of Bitche and east of Neunhoffen, and on the correctly perceived weakness of American forces in the zone of the main attack.[112] The planning staff of *First Army* was apprised of the concept in the initial planning memorandum, or warning order, transmitted by *Army Group G* headquarters on 24 December.[113] Interestingly, von Obstfelder and his staff had little or no say in the actual conduct of the attack; this warning order and all subsequent orders specified the exact composition and detailed objectives of each attack group. In marked contrast to American field orders at this level (see Chapter 3, regarding the Seventh Army order for the breaching of the Vosges), such dictation of a subordinate command's internal organization hardly constituted the freedom of action called for by German doctrine for orders. In this way, *Army Group G* withheld the initiative of *First Army* and essentially reduced the role of von Obstfelder's headquarters to one of coordination. (See Chapter 2.)

Besides its stifling influence on *First Army's* doctrinal functions and prerogatives, this plan had two other obvious major flaws: First, it committed a *Panzer* division to the conduct of a penetration in a heavily wooded, mountainous area bound in snow and ice; second, it intended the exploitation to be conducted by a single understrength *Panzergrenadier* division. The first weakness alone probably would have doomed the operation. Only four east-west roads existed to facilitate a breakout into the terrain suitable for armor on either side of the Low Vosges: Neunhoffen-Froeschwiller, Bannstein–Niederbronn-les-Bains, Mouterhouse-Zinswiller, and Wingen-Ingwiller. There are exactly four north-south routes that connect these east-west thoroughfares. The first is a maze of mountain trails, starting from the Bitche-Sturzelbronn road to Bannstein, thence to the Mouterhouse-Baerenthal road (Baerenthal is five hundred meters southeast of Thalhaeuseln), and south either to the tiny hamlets of Melch and Wildengut (both just above Reipertswiller) or directly to Reipertswiller itself; these trails could be easily blocked, and even if they were not, they contained grades so steep that armored vehicles on ice would be unable to advance at more than a crawl, if at all. In the event of clear weather, the nighttime driving necessitated by American air superiority would make these trails all but impassable. The next route is another maze of trails between the Bitche-Bannstein road and the Lemberg-Mouterhouse road, and the same limitations apply.[114]

The other two routes were the Bitche-Lemberg-Goetzenbrueck-Wingen road and, at the eastern end of the Low Vosges massif, the Neunhoffen-Philippsbourg road. Although passable to armored vehicles in winter conditions, this nevertheless left only two roads to be blocked to completely stymie the German exploitation elements.

This plan was presented to Adolf Hitler and the OKW staff on the afternoon of Christmas Eve 1944. According to the *Army Group G* I.a., Oberst im Generalstab Horst Wilutzky, Hitler believed that the attack through the mountains would fail to reach the objective of the Wingen-Ingwiller road. Wilutzky states that Hitler doubted the men's ability to "stand winter conditions." Hitler therefore directed the western attack, south from Gersheim toward Achen and Rohrbach, to be conducted as a main attack also, and that the *21st Panzer Division* be withheld from the initial effort and used as an exploitative reserve, in conjunction with the *25th Panzergrenadier Division*.[115] (See Figure 22b, 25 December Operation Nordwind Plan.)

Although the concept of two main attacks insisted on by Hitler was clearly a violation of German tactical doctrine, the idea of a strong armored exploitation force actually brought the plan closer to German

ORDER OF BATTLE
OPERATION *NORDWIND*

ARMY GROUP G PLAN *23 December 1944*	**PLAN AS ALTERED BY HITLER AND OKW** *Effective 25 December 1944*

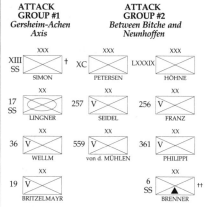

ARMY GROUP G PLAN — 23 December 1944

SUPPORTING ATTACK
Gersheim-Achen Axis

XXX — XIII SS — SIMON †
XX — 17 SS — LINGNER
XX — 257 V — SEIDEL

MAIN ATTACK
Between Bitche and Neunhoffen

XXX — XC — PETERSEN
XX — 36 V — WELLM
XX — 559 V — von d. MÜHLEN

XXX — LXXXIX — HÖHNE
XX — 21 — FEUCHTINGER
XX — 256 V — FRANZ
XX — 361 V — PHILIPPI
XX — 6 SS ▲ — BRENNER ††

First Army Operational Reserve

XX — 25 — BURMEISTER

PLAN AS ALTERED BY HITLER AND OKW — Effective 25 December 1944

ATTACK GROUP #1
Gersheim-Achen Axis

XXX — XIII SS — SIMON †
XX — 17 SS — LINGNER
XX — 36 V — WELLM
XX — 19 V — BRITZELMAYR

ATTACK GROUP #2
Between Bitche and Neunhoffen

XXX — XC — PETERSEN
XX — 257 V — SEIDEL
XX — 559 V — von d. MÜHLEN

XXX — LXXXIX — HÖHNE
XX — 256 V — FRANZ
XX — 361 V — PHILIPPI
XX — 6 SS ▲ — BRENNER ††

First Army Operational Reserve

XX — 25 — BURMEISTER
XX — 21 — FEUCHTINGER

† Reinforced by 653d Heavy Tank Destroyer Battalion and two self-propelled armored flamethrower companies

†† One battlegroup available 1 January; remainder of division available after 2 January

KEY

X	Combat Command or Group	TF	Task Force
XX	Division		
XXX	Corps		
XXXX	Army		

- ⊠ Infantry
- ⬭ Armor/Panzer
- ⊘ Mechanized Cavalry
- ⊠ Armored Infantry/Panzergrenadier
- ⊠ Volksgrenadier
- ◿ Mountain Infantry

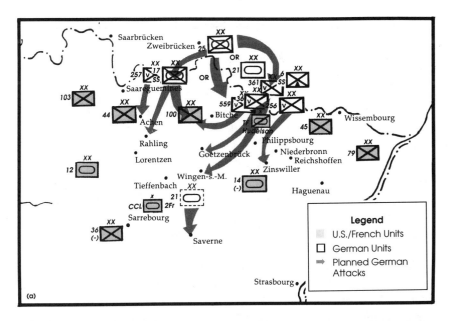

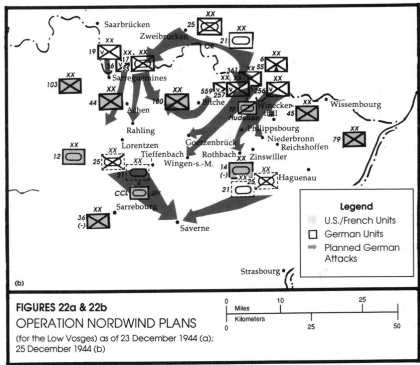

FIGURES 22a & 22b

OPERATION NORDWIND PLANS
(for the Low Vosges) as of 23 December 1944 (a);
25 December 1944 (b)

doctrine in another regard (see Chapter 2); it is unlikely that a single, understrength *Panzergrenadier* division would have had the striking power to exploit a penetration made by the main attack. Furthermore, although Hitler *may* have said that his reservation about the plan sprang from his belief "that the troops would not be able to stand the weather," we have only Wilutzky's word for it; no other record of this briefing survives, because Blaskowitz committed suicide in captivity before writing his account. Given the failure of German armor to successfully penetrate the Ardennes in winter weather, it is *possible* that Hitler (or the OKW planning staff) recognized the unlikelihood of tanks successfully traversing and breaking through the rugged terrain of the Low Vosges Mountains against opposition. His changes to the plan protected the precious armor assets and added a certain flexibility by retaining greater armor reserves.

Thus, the plan ultimately adopted still called for two attacks, neither of which bore the title "main attack," although the weight of the assault east of Bitche indicates it was the main effort. (See Figure 22b.) The only substantial differences involved the order of battle for the attack groups. Under the new plan, the *21st Panzer Division* would be held in reserve with the *25th Panzergrenadiers,* instead of being immediately wedged into icy, winding mountain roads in the face of the enemy. These reserves were to be released only when the attack had progressed as far as the Wingen-Ingwiller road.[116] Also, an additional division, not originally planned for use in the operation at all, would be ordered to attack in the west.

Although the changes made sense, they must have fiercely rankled Blaskowitz. Not only did they come from a *böhmischer Gefreiter* (Bohemian Corporal) to a Prussian who had been an officer when the Führer was in short pants, but worse, they gave more importance and assets to the efforts of the *XIII SS Corps;* in addition, the *Army Group G* commander's antipathy for the Waffen SS has been well documented. It is no wonder that Blaskowitz's subordinates, such as Emmerich, expressed their utter certainty regarding the foreordained failure of the operation, writing that the *First Army* staff believed the success of Nordwind to be "nothing but wishful thinking."[117]

The *1st Attack Group* was simply the *XIII SS Corps,* consisting of the recently reconstituted *17th SS Panzergrenadier Division* and the

36th and *19th Volksgrenadier Divisions,* reinforced by a battalion of heavy tank destroyers and two companies of self-propelled flamethrowers.[118] Obergruppenführer Simon chose to mass two of these divisions, the *36th Volksgrenadier* and *17th SS Panzergrenadier,* on a six-kilometer front to accomplish his mission, specified by Blaskowitz and transmitted through von Obstfelder. With this doctrinally sound massing of forces, the corps commander intended to penetrate the American lines and drive south to facilitate exploitation toward Phalsbourg.[119]

The *17th SS Panzergrenadier Division* was brought to full strength in the days before the initiation of Nordwind.[120] Named the *Götz von Berlichingen Division* in honor of a late medieval German knight, its principal infantry maneuver elements consisted of two *Panzergrenadier* regiments, the *37th* and *38th SS Panzergrenadiers,* with about 4,100 *Panzergrenadiers* total. It also had a heavily reinforced *Panzer* battalion with about seventy assault guns and a company of the *21st Panzer Division*'s *Panther* tanks, and a reconnaissance battalion.[121] Many of the soldiers of this division were *Volksdeutsche,* recently squeezed out of the shrinking borders of the Reich.[122]

The *Götz von Berlichingen Division* was commanded by SS Standartenführer Hans Lingner, a twenty-nine-year-old veteran of ten years in the *Schutzstaffel.* As a junior officer, he had participated in the campaigns in Belgium, the Balkans, and Russia, serving in the latter theater with the *2d SS Panzer Division, "Das Reich."* After his fourth combat wound, while serving in Normandy with the *10th SS Panzer Division, "Frundsberg,"* Lingner was assigned as a regimental commander in the *Götz von Berlichingen Division,* and subsequently replaced SS Brigadeführer Werner Ostendorff as division commander on 30 November.[123] His division's mission (the main attack of *XIII SS Corps*) was to penetrate the American lines between Rimling and Woelfling (near Sarreguemines in Figure 22b), and seize Bining and Rahling, facilitating a potential exploitation by *First Army*'s operational reserve toward the Vosges passes near Tieffenbach and Phalsbourg.[124]

Perhaps out of army-SS rivalry, Lingner's leadership nevertheless was judged "incompetent" by the *First Army* I.a., Oberst Wilutzky.[125] Certainly, there had been considerable command turbulence in the headquarters of the *Götz von Berlichingen Division*: Lingner was the fourth commander since October.

The *36th Volksgrenadier Division* was commanded by Generalmajor August Wellm, a forty-five-year-old infantryman from Niedersachsen. Wellm served as an enlisted man in World War I, and was a police officer between the wars. He returned to the colors in 1934 and commanded an infantry regiment on the eastern front, where he won the coveted *Nahkampfspange* (Close Combat Clasp) in bronze for successful participation in numerous hand-to-hand battles. He assumed command of the *36th Volksgrenadiers* on 1 November 1944.[126]

The *36th Volksgrenadier Division* had been raised from the remnants of the *36th Infantry Division*, destroyed on the eastern front earlier in the year. Its principal maneuver elements consisted of the *118th* and *165th Volksgrenadier Regiments* and the divisional *Füsilier* company, with a total of at least 3,775 infantrymen.[127] This division's mission was to conduct a supporting attack for *XIII SS Corps*, protecting the western flank of the *Götz von Berlichingen Division* and seizing Etting and Kahlhausen (just southwest of Achen).

The *19th Volksgrenadier Division* comprised two three-battalion regiments, the *73d* and *74th Volksgrenadiers,* with a combined strength of about 1,800 infantrymen.[128] It was commanded by Generalmajor Karl Britzelmayr, a Bavarian infantryman with World War I combat experience. A *Reichswehr* veteran, he had commanded infantry units up to regimental size on the Russian front before taking command of the *19th Volksgrenadiers* in October 1944.[129] The *19th Volksgrenadier Division* was clearly the weakest of the units taking part in the western thrust of Nordwind, but its mission was also the least important, comprising a second supporting attack for the weaker of the two attack groups, designed to protect the western flank of the *36th Volksgrenadiers* by seizing the bridge across the Saar at Zetting.

The *2d Attack Group* consisted of the *XC* and *LXXXIX Corps*. The objectives specified for this group by *Army Group G* headquarters included seizing the line Enchenberg-Sarreinsberg (Goetzenbrueck)-Wimmenau and linking up with *XIII SS Corps* to facilitate exploitation toward Phalsbourg and Saverne.[130]

Petersen's *XC Corps* consisted of the *559th* and *257th Volksgrenadier Divisions*. The *559th Volksgrenadier Division* was commanded by Generalmajor Kurt Freiherr von der Mühlen, a thirty-nine-year-old Swabian infantryman. Von der Mühlen entered the *Reichswehr* in 1923, and had served continuously since; his wartime experience included duty on the eastern front as a regimental commander.[131] Withdrawn from *First Army*'s *LXXXII Corps* sector near Saarlouis on 22 December, the division had taken heavy losses in the November and December battles in Lorraine and the *Westwall* at the hands of U.S. Third Army. Massive replacements infused during the last week of December brought two of the *559th*'s three *Volksgrenadier* regiments (the *1126th* and *1127th*) to nearly full strength, although the third regiment (the *1125th*) remained practically nonexistent.[132] Along with the divisional *Füsilier* company, this gave the *559th* an infantry strength of approximately 2,600 men.[133] According to the division commander, "Both officers and men had had little training for attacks in forest areas," and the divisional combat engineers were "poorly trained . . . especially in mine clearance."[134] Despite having only about a week to train together, "its lack of training for an attack could not be considered an obstacle especially as the morale and fighting spirit among the troops, due to the course of events [in the Ardennes] was very good."[135] To fulfill their part in the mission dictated by *Army Group G* and passed through *First Army*, the *559th Volksgrenadiers* were to penetrate the American lines near Reyersviller and seize Lambach and Lemberg. (Near Bitche in Figure 22b.)

Perhaps for a few members of the *257th Volksgrenadier Division,* the coming action near Bitche presented a certain déjà vu. The *257th Volksgrenadier Division* had been formed from the remnants of the *"Berlin Bears"* of the *257th Infantry Division,* which, under Generalleutnant von Viebahn, had penetrated the Maginot near Sarralbe and failed against the outer works of the Ensemble de Bitche in June 1940. After being "battered to unimportant remnants" in Russia earlier in the year, it was resurrected as a *Volksgrenadier* division near Frankfurt-an-der-Oder in late October 1944, and filled to authorized strength with men from a variety of sources. Forty percent of the enlisted men were veterans returning from convalescent leave; the remaining complement were former naval and air force personnel.[136] The new division, led by Generalmajor Erich Seidel, was trained for a little more than five weeks, from late October until the end of November, and ten of these days were used to move the division from its training ground at Frankfurt to the region south of Warsaw, where it was ordered to be prepared to help prevent a feared Soviet breakthrough. In all, the *257th Volksgrenadier Division* went into the attack in December with about four weeks of actual training.[137]

Its component maneuver elements, the *457th, 466th,* and *477th Volksgrenadier Regiments* and the divisional *Füsilier* company possessed "almost completely existing fighting strengths," and could therefore count among their ranks about 3,800 infantrymen.[138] Their part in the *XC Corps* mission was to penetrate the thinly held Forêt Domaniale de Mouterhouse and seize Goetzenbrueck and Sarreinsberg.

Höhne's *LXXXIX Corps* controlled the *361st* and *256th Volksgrenadier Divisions* and the *6th SS Mountain Division.* The *361st Volksgrenadier Division* was still smarting from the losses sustained during the delay conducted in the first two weeks of December. Each of the five remaining infantry battalions received about 250 replacements during the last week of December, to bring the division's infantry strength to about two thousand men by 28 December.[139] Like their comrades in the *559th Volksgrenadiers,* they also lacked training and experience as a team, although their engineer battalion was more competent than that of von der Mühlen's division.[140] Philippi had this to say about the division's morale:

The spirits of the men had, since the beginning of the Ardennes Offensive, shown pleasing improvement. Even though, after the initial successes, it became apparent that the drive had reached a standstill, neither men nor officers considered this a defeat. They were particularly impressed with the fact that, at that stage of the War, the German *Wehrmacht* was still capable of such a concentration of strength. Confidence and faith in the Supreme Command had thus once again been boosted considerably, a fact which was also of importance for the battles ahead. The division valued this very factor as an important prerequisite for the fighting spirits during the upcoming battles.[141]

They would need every bit of the energy imparted by that high morale, too, as the *361st*'s objective was to penetrate the American screen in the Forêt Domaniale de Hanau and seize Wingen-sur-Moder and Wimmenau. This mission entailed a nearly twenty-kilometer cross-country jaunt through dramatically-compartmented, thickly wooded, snowy ravines up to 120 meters deep.

The situation of the *256th Volksgrenadier Division* was worse than that of the *361st.* In the first two weeks of December, steady combat against the VI Corps's 79th Infantry Division and 14th Armored Division had taken a heavy toll. Its *456th*, *476th*, and *481st Volksgrenadier Regiments* and divisional *Füsilier* company included about 1,655 infantrymen, many of whom were former Luftwaffe and Kriegsmarine replacements; the remainder were largely men who had previously been protected from military service due to the technical or economically significant nature of their civilian occupations. Some of the troops, mostly in the support echelons, were original veterans of the *256th Infantry Division,* which had been badly mauled in Russia earlier in the year.[142] While in the process of reorganization in Germany, the division had had only about four weeks of training together before commitment to combat in Holland in early October 1944, and subsequent redeployment to Alsace in November.[143]

The commanding general, Generalmajor Gerhard Franz, a forty-two-year-old Saxon infantryman who had served as the chief of staff of the *Afrika Korps* and had seen combat in Russia, had insisted on intensive training of replacements by cadre already present in the division.[144] The retraining of the former Luftwaffe personnel had gone well; in the words of the division's operations officer, Oberstleutnant im Generalstab Bernhard Kögel, "their inner adaptation was effected with much less tension or friction than had been expected."[145] The land-locked former Kriegsmarine sailors adapted even better. Of them, Kögel insisted,

> Their retraining and incorporation in the Division proved completely successful. They later [by the time of Nordwind] constituted the backbone of the infantry regiments, particularly because of their untapped physical and spiritual resources.[146]

The latest replacements, some 250 recent arrivals of a *Marschbatallion* (replacement unit), however, lacked training and needed time to be brought to standard.[147] Overall, the division was "only fit for defensive operations, due to the fact that it lacked at least two weeks of rest for the purpose of freshening up, training, and reorganizing infantry forces."[148] Despite this, the mission of Generalmajor Franz's men was to penetrate the American positions near Neunhoffen and attack through terrain as difficult as that in the *361st*'s zone to seize Windstein (two thousand meters north of Jaegerthal), Philippsbourg, Untermuehlthal (thirty-five hundred meters southeast of Thalhaeuseln), and Lichtenberg (fifteen hundred meters south of Reipertswiller), and subsequently establish blocking positions along the roads leading to the Alsatian Plain.

The *6th SS Mountain Division* was undoubtedly the best German division in the upcoming fight for the Low Vosges; in fact, it was probably the best German infantry formation on the entire western front in early January 1945. The *Nord Division* was commanded by SS Gruppenführer Karl Brenner, a Bavarian artilleryman and World War I veteran. A police officer during the interbellum years, Brenner became a member of the SS as a matter of course when Himmler took over the German police. Unlike certain of his contemporaries in the *XIII SS Corps,* Brenner was not a fanatical National Socialist. In fact, his pedigree as a moderate was established by his command of the artillery regiment of the *4th SS Panzergrenadier Division, "Polizei,"* made up of former police officers who had volunteered for combat duty. Although he saw only limited action in 1940, Brenner saw extensive combat with the *Polizei Division* near Leningrad. After recovering from a serious bout with rheumatism, he took command of *Nord* in September 1944.[149]

Nord was withdrawn from Finland through Norway and Denmark after the Russo-Finnish armistice of September 1944. Although it had, as a result, lost the services of the *SS-Ski Battalion "Norge"* a group of Norwegian traitors who had volunteered to fight only against the Soviets, it was a full-strength, fully equipped *SS Gebirgs* (mountain) division, perfectly suited for the upcoming attack in the Low Vosges. In the words of the division commander, Karl Brenner:

> Officers and men were, with few exceptions, soldiers of long service, with particular experience in forest and mountain fighting. Morale and fighting spirits were outstanding, caused by the successful battles against the Russians and Finns; till then unbeaten and victorious and as yet not infected like other divisions that had gone through the severe reverses on the Eastern and Western Fronts during 1944.[150]

Its principal component maneuver elements consisted of the *11th SS Mountain Infantry Regiment, "Reinhard Heydrich"* (named after the former head of the SS Security Service, the *Sicherheitsdienst,* who was killed by British-trained Czech commandos in Prague in 1942), the *12th SS*

Mountain Infantry Regiment, "Michael Gaissmair," (named after a medieval Tyrolean German hero), the attached *506th SS Panzer Grenadier Battalion*, and the divisional reconnaissance battalion. In all, there were approximately 6,102 highly motivated, well-trained, superbly equipped infantrymen contributed by this Waffen-SS division.[151] Although scheduled to be present at the outset of the attack, *Nord* did not arrive in full strength by 3 January. This, however, was not inconsistent with its intended use to reinforce and/or exploit the attacks of the *LXXXIX Corps*'s other two divisions.

The *First Army*'s operational reserve, consisting of the *21st Panzer Division* and the *25th Panzergrenadier Division*, also profited by the influx of replacements for Nordwind. The *21st Panzer Division*'s *125th* and *192d Panzergrenadier Regiments* totaled at least 2,000 *Panzergrenadiers;* the *25th Panzergrenadier Division* had about 2,500.

The numerical matchup in the intended zone of attack, then, was as follows: The Americans counted 21,002 infantrymen on the line and about 8,100 in reserve, and the Germans were throwing about 25,832 against them, with reserves of about 4,500 more, for totals of 29,102 for the defenders and 30,332 for the attackers. The initial confrontation, of course, would be between the 25,832 attackers and the 21,002 defenders, with a German advantage (1.23 to 1) startlingly similar to that possessed by the Americans in the High Vosges (1.3 to 1) at the commencement of their attack on Bruyères some three months before.

Like the American attacks of the previous autumn, in Nordwind, overall numerical superiority would be magnified by the concentration of strength against weakness at the point of the main effort. More specifically, the *2d Attack Group* would initially mass about 10,055 infantrymen against Task Force Hudelson's 645 and the 1,716 infantrymen of the 399th Infantry Regiment on the right flank of the 100th Infantry Division. This local superiority of 4.25 to 1 could be increased considerably by the commitment of the 6,102 *SS Gebirgsjäger* and *Panzergrenadiers* of the *6th SS Mountain Division* over the next three days.[153]

There were other similarities between the Seventh Army's attacks in October and November and that of *First Army* in Nordwind. By choosing the center of the Low Vosges as the location of their main effort, the Germans had reduced their need for armor there. Their original plan, changed by Hitler, would have wasted forty invaluable *Panzer IVs* and thirty-four *Panthers* on the easily blocked trails and roads between Bitche and Neunhoffen.[154] Instead, the use of armor would be limited initially to a drive by seventy self-propelled, armored assault guns, about thirty-five armored flamethrowers (*Hetzers* with huge flame cannon), and a battalion of behemoth *Jagdtiger* tank destroyers into the same area where Major General Haislip had employed the 12th Armored Division so effectively at the end of the first week of December. Under the revised plan, the tanks of the *21st Panzer Division*'s *22d Panzer Regiment* and the *25th Panzergrenadier Division*'s tank battalion could reinforce *XIII SS Corps*'s success in the area from Gersheim south to Lorentzen, which Major General Allen's Hellcats had proven to be suitable for armored maneuver when they forced back the *11th Panzer Division* and threatened to envelop the *XC* and *LXXXIX Corps*. Of course, most of the other participating divisions were supported by their divisional assault gun companies.

This attack would have to develop extremely quickly, however, because the Seventh Army's units in the area greatly outnumbered their adversaries in quantities of tanks. The tank and tank destroyer battalions attached to the 44th (749th Tank and 776th Tank Destroyer Battalions) and 100th Infantry Divisions (781st Tank and 824th Tank Destroyer Battalions) alone possessed about 180 M4 Sherman, M36 Slugger, and M18 Hellcat (not to be confused with the 12th Armored Division nickname) armored fighting vehicles. The 12th Armored Division could contribute about 150 more Shermans from its three tank battalions, and the available combat commands of the 2d French and 14th Armored Divisions possessed another 100 or so, if Lieutenant General Patch committed these from reserve.[155] Even the qualitative superiority of the relatively few available *Panthers* and the handful of *Jagdtigers* would be unlikely to successfully challenge these kinds of overwhelming odds (430 Allied vs. about 200 German tanks, tank destroyers, and assault guns). Add to this the expected fair weather in early January, and Allied air superiority would further tip the scales against the Germans in the event of a bogged-down slugging match.

The best (and, by their own doctrine, most correct) use for the Germans' armored assets would be to exploit the penetration made by *XC* and *LXXXIX Corps* in the Low Vosges by rapidly sending the *21st Panzer* and *25th Panzergrenadier Division*s through the area after it was secured and the roads were cleared. If the western attack succeeded—that is, if the Americans reacted to the *XIII SS Corps*'s thrust by sending their armored reserves to meet it—such a maneuver would allow the German operational reserves to effect an encirclement by bursting out of the Low Vosges at Rahling or Diemeringen, cutting the Allied lines of communication, and attacking the Allied armor from the rear. Exactly such a possibility was facilitated by the Führer's alteration of the original Nordwind plan. Although it lacked a clearly identified main attack, the portion of Nordwind to be conducted in the Low Vosges was otherwise doctrinally sound.

Like the Seventh Army's plan of the previous autumn, the German plan intended a penetration of the Vosges to facilitate subsequent maneuver in terrain more suitable for armor. Given the need for rapid success, both to relieve the pressure on *Army Group B* and to take advantage of the anticipated Seventh Army reaction to the *XIII SS Corps's* attack, effective (and doctrinally mandated) tactical reconnaissance of the zone of attack would be essential to ensure timely development of the situation. Similarly, extensive briefings and detailed planning at all echelons would be necessary to facilitate rapid progress, given the generally low level of training and shared combat experience (especially in offensive maneuver) present in most of the assault units. Finally, given the rugged nature of the terrain and the need for especially fast penetration, the troops needed to be well rested for the coming battle.

Those were exactly the things that did *not* happen.

To preserve what they imagined to be secrecy regarding their intentions, the Germans purposely elected to not reconnoiter their zones. In the words of *Army Group G's* operations order to *First Army,* issued at 2345 on 25 December:

> On the entire Army Group front the *impression of a quiet front* is to be simulated immediately. Other than normal reconnaissance, all combat activities are suspended.[156]

In the further interest of security, only division commanders and operations officers were briefed on the attack plan on Christmas Day, 1944; commanders at regimental level and below did not receive word regarding their missions until the night before the attack or, in some cases, on the day of the attack.[157] Obviously, at the platoon and company level, where the fighting would be done, there was practically no time for organization or other essential preparations. Since most of these units had never attacked before, this was disastrous.

As a final, and also calamitous, operational security measure, most units did not move into their attack positions until the night before the attack. As a result, many of the troops went into their first attack ever without having slept for at least twenty-four hours.[158]

These decisions had a momentously negative impact on the course of the battle in the critical initial phase. Oberstleutnant Ernst Linke, operations officer of the *257th Volksgrenadier Division*, later wrote:

> If we to some extent saw clear as to the *strength* of the enemy, the *exact course* of the enemy main combat line was not clear to us whatever. . . . During the short time available until the time of the attack, it was out of the question to obtain the necessary information as to these points: a. because of the lack of time; b. because [of] the secrecy toward the enemy and our own troops. *The Division, therefore, had but insufficient knowledge of the enemy.*[159]

In all but the *361st Volksgrenadier Division*'s zone, where troops and leaders had spent several weeks delaying in the area through which they were about to attack, these shortcomings would cause serious problems with the progress of the offensive.

Thus, Operation Nordwind proceeded without doctrinally mandated reconnaissance or mid- and low-level planning; it also proceeded with tired and inadequately trained troops. On 30 December, as planned, the *347th Infantry Division* initiated deception operations in its sector, across from the 106th Cavalry Group, near Völklingen. During the course of these operations, prisoners taken by Troop C, 106th Cavalry Squadron (of the 106th Cavalry Group), indicated that a major German offensive was due to begin on the following night, around midnight.[160] Evidently, for all their sacrifices regarding operational security, the Germans' efforts were at least partially in vain.

First Army combat operations began as scheduled just before midnight on 31 December. (See Figure 23.) The night was cold, crisp, clear, and bright, with moonlight reflecting off the foot or so of snow that had recently fallen. Without artillery preparation, waves of German infantry, some clad in white camouflage snowsuits, surged toward the

American lines. *Every* known American account of this attack consistently describes the attackers' appallingly primitive tactics in those first hours of 1945. Yelling curses in broken English and German, howling and screaming, the first assaulting SS troops and army infantrymen ran in groups directly into American minefields, barbed wire, and small-arms fire.[161] In most sectors, they were slaughtered.

Despite the purposeful absence of artillery and rocket preparatory fires, little or no surprise was achieved by the *SS Panzergrenadiers* and *Volksgrenadiers* of the *XIII SS Corps.* On the western flank of the attack, the *19th Volksgrenadier Division's 73d Volksgrenadier Regiment* attempted to cross the Blies River in the face of the defenses of the 44th Infantry Division's 324th Infantry Regiment just east of Sarreguemines. It was "smashed by concentrated defensive fire."[162] No further progress was made in this western sector of the 44th Infantry Division's area. Generalmajor Britzelmayr's other regiment, the *74th Volksgrenadiers,* followed Wellm's *36th Volksgrenadier Division* into action.

In the 44th Infantry Division's 71st Infantry Regiment sector on the right of the 44th's line, the 3,775 infantrymen of the *36th Volksgrenadier Division* and the roughly 2,000 men of the *38th SS Panzergrenadier Regiment* ripped through the Americans' combat outposts and slammed into the main line of resistance (MLR) occupied by the 1,188 infantrymen of the 1st and 2d Battalions.[163] Almost immediately, Col. Ercil D. Porter, commander of the 71st, committed his reserve, consisting of the 492 men of the 3d Battalion, to a vigorous counterattack supported by a platoon of tanks from the 749th Tank Battalion.[164] The fighting raged through the long hours of winter darkness, as both sides launched fierce thrusts and counterthrusts. Morainville Farm, overlooking a deep draw just to the west of Rimling, which was the boundary with the 397th Infantry's 3d Battalion, was the scene of blistering, seesaw action in the 2d Battalion's sector. The battle raged there all night, and bullets tore through the snow-covered trees of the Bois de Bliesbrücken in the 1st Battalion's area until well past dawn. Artillery, rocket, tank, and small-arms fire were exchanged throughout New Year's Day; at dusk, elements of the 2d Battalion counterattacked and restored their original lines due west of Rimling.[165]

The two thousand or so SS troops of the *37th SS Panzergrenadier Regiment* of the *"Götz von Berlichingen" Division* stormed into the 654 infantrymen of the Century Division's 3d Battalion, 397th Infantry Regi-

ORDER OF BATTLE
1–15 JANUARY 1945

U.S. SEVENTH ARMY
In the Low Vosges

GERMAN ARMY GROUP G
NORDWIND Counteroffensive

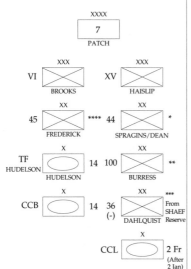

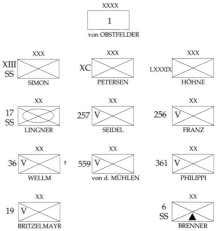

* Reinforced by 253d Inf Rgt, 31 December
** Reinforced by 255th Inf Rgt, 31 December
Reinforced by 141st Inf Rgt 1–4 January
*** Consists 143d Inf Rgt and DIVARTY & Division Troops
**** Reinforced by 274th, 275th, & 276th Inf Rgts after 1 January; reinforced by 313th Inf Rgt (-), 1/314th, and 1/315th Inf Rgts, 2–10 January

First Army Operational Reserve

† Reassigned to LXXXIX Corps 3 January

KEY

X	Combat Command or Group
XX	Division
XXX	Corps
XXXX	Army

TF	Task Force

Infantry	
Armor/Panzer	
Mechanized Cavalry	
Armored Infantry/ Panzergrenadier	
Volksgrenadier	
Mountain Infantry	

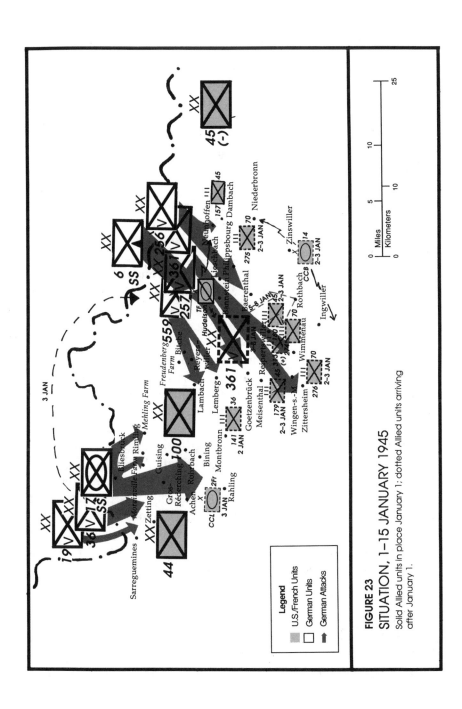

FIGURE 23

SITUATION, 1–15 JANUARY 1945

Solid Allied units in place January 1; dotted Allied units arriving after January 1.

Legend

U.S./French Units

German Units

German Attacks

ment, on Schlietzen Hill on the western outskirts of Rimling just before midnight as well.[166] Attacking in waves, running upright, the attackers' white camouflage parkas did little good as they silhouetted themselves against the moonlight reflecting off the snowfields.[167] As the assaulting Waffen SS men blew through the battalion's combat outposts, they crested the rise of Schlietzen Hill only to face the full fury of the Americans' reverse-slope defense. A single machine gunner, Pvt. Leon Outlaw of Company M, killed more than a hundred attackers with his .30-caliber water-cooled machine gun.[168] Clearly, what the Germans lacked in training or tactical ability they hoped to make up for with élan. Just before dawn, they attacked for the third time since midnight. By assaulting from the north and from the sector temporarily lost by the 71st Infantry to the west, they succeeded in pushing the Americans off Schlietzen Hill. A counterattack at noon by elements of Company K retook the high ground and restored the MLR. Smaller attacks against the 1st Battalion sector near Mehling Farm, two kilometers south-southwest of Epping, were also repulsed.[169]

By nightfall on 1 January, despite heavy numerical superiority in armored vehicles and men, Simon's *XIII SS Corps* was no closer to taking its objectives than it had been before the beginning of the attack.

Generally, the *2d Attack Group* achieved considerably more success on the eastern flank of the *First Army* attack zone. Here, the 2,600 *Landsers* of von der Mühlen's *559th Volksgrenadier Division* hurled themselves at the 1,304 Centurymen of the 1st and 2d Battalions (plus Company L) of the 399th Infantry Regiment near the village of Reyersviller and the College de Bitche, just south of the fortress town.[170] Eight hours later, the attackers had progressed only three kilometers to the southeast, after encountering and clearing minefields that had gone undetected due to the lack of tactical reconnaissance. Even after von der Mühlen's poorly trained engineers breached the American obstacles, the *559th Volksgrenadier Division*'s attackers were halted one kilometer east of Lambach, just north and west of Lemberg, where they ran into the blocking positions of the 399th's 3d Battalion. The decision by the acting regimental commander, thirty-two-year-old Lt. Col. Elery Zehner, to array his regiment in depth clearly paid off. After a seven-hour pause to clear mines and reorganize, the *559th Volksgrenadier Division*'s *1126th* and *1127th Volksgrenadier Regiments* pushed on toward their respective objectives of Lemberg and

Lambach. Neither made appreciable progress, and the members of the 1st and 2d Battalions of the 399th dug in on either side of their 3d Battalion compatriots, roughly on a line from Lemberg to just east of Lambach to Freudenberg Farm (see Figure 23).[171]

The other division of Petersen's *XC Corps,* Seidel's *257th Volks-grenadier Division,* had far more initial success against its much weaker opponents. Sweeping south and west from their assembly areas near the Camp de Bitche, Seidel's thirty-eight hundred infantrymen overran the forward positions of Task Force Hudelson's 117th Cavalry Squadron on the left of the task force sector. The mechanized cavalrymen were no match for the attacking German infantry, and withdrew rapidly to the south. Their precipitous retreat left the 399th Infantry's right flank wide open and vulnerable to envelopment. This threatened not only the 100th Infantry Division but the entire XV Corps! By daybreak, the *477th Volksgrenadier Regiment* had advanced ten kilometers toward its objective of Goetzenbrueck, and added its roughly eighteen hundred infantrymen to the pressure already exerted by the thousand or so surviving members of the *1126th Volksgrenadiers* against the hard-pressed four hundred men of the 3d Battalion, 399th Infantry, near Lemberg.[172] No evidence exists of coordinated efforts by the two *XC Corps* divisions to take this crucial road-junction village, however, and the Americans fought off repeated but piecemeal German attacks. By nightfall, Lemberg was still in American hands, and Major Generals Burress and Haislip prepared to rush reinforcements to the Lemberg area the next day.[173]

To the east, the *457th Volksgrenadier Regiment* of the *257th Volks-grenadier Division* found no obstacles in its path after brushing aside the 117th Cavalry Squadron. By daybreak, the Germans in this sector had also advanced ten kilometers and were on the outskirts of Mouterhouse, which they seized later in the morning. At this point, Seidel requested that Generaloberst Petersen release his *466th Volksgrenadier Regiment* to assist in continuing the attack toward the division's objectives of Goetzenbrueck and Sarreinsberg. His request was granted, and the *466th* marched forward to take part in the attack on the two towns planned for 2 January. Meanwhile, the *457th* reassembled because it had "become disorganized during their night combat" due to the lack of knowledge of the area's terrain, again caused by lack of time for preparation and the absence of reconnaissance.[174] Thus, although the 117th's weak screen failed to halt the *257th Volksgrenadier Division*'s advance, it disorganized this poorly trained unit enough to force the Germans to postpone their attack on Goetzenbrueck and Sarreinsberg for about eighteen critical hours—critical because, on 1 January, the only American combat forces in the towns were part of the 19th Armored Infantry Battalion of the 14th Armored Division, sent forward from VI Corps reserve to help halt the German drive![175] By the time the Germans had reorganized and were prepared to attack on 2 January, Major General Haislip had rushed the Texas Division's 141st RCT into the area to tie in with the 399th's positions to the north near Lemberg and thus establish a coherent defense. The inability of the *457th Volksgrenadiers* to continue the attack probably cost them their objective.

Farther to the east, the *361st Volksgrenadier Division*, whose "leaders and troops benefited greatly by their more thorough knowledge of the terrain," achieved varying degrees of success in the first twenty-five hours of the attack.[176] After penetrating the 117th and 94th Cavalry Squadrons' forward positions, the attacking elements of Philippi's division met their first resistance at Bannstein, on the Bitche-Niederbronn road. Here, the 215 men of Company C, 62d Armored Infantry Battalion (attached to the 117th Cavalry Squadron), held up the roughly 800 men of the attacking *2d Battalion, 953d Volksgrenadier Regiment,* and *1st Battalion, 951st Volksgrenadiers,* until nearly noon on 1 January, after which the attackers advanced to the south.[177] Meanwhile, the *952d Volksgrenadier Regiment,* attacking in the east toward Baerenthal, seized the town after a series of day and night attacks against resistance from an amalgam of Task Force Hudelson elements. By midnight on 1–2 January, the *361st Volksgrenadier Division* had taken Forneau Neuf and the village of Baerenthal on the Lemberg-Zinswiller road, and was preparing to attack to the south and west on the following day to gain its objectives of Wingen-sur-Moder and Wimmenau.[178]

The easternmost element of *First Army*'s *2d Attack Group*, the *256th Volksgrenadier Division,* was not as successful as its neighbor to the west. The *476th Volksgrenadier Regiment* managed to seize only Lieschbach (two thousand meters northwest of Philippsbourg) from elements of the 62d Armored Infantry Battalion by early evening on 1 January, mainly due to terrain misorientation at the outset of the attack. Once again, the lack of tactical reconnaissance hurt the German effort.[179] The *456th Volksgrenadier Regiment* captured Neunhoffen from fragments of the same unit before noon. On the eastern end of the *256th*'s zone, however, serious problems developed when the *481st Volksgrenadiers* attempted to take Dambach (two thousand meters southeast of Neunhoffen) from elements of the 157th Infantry Regiment. According to the *256th*'s operations officer, the moratorium imposed on tactical reconnaissance left them unaware of the much more effective defenses installed there by the veterans of the Thunderbird Division.[180]

By the end of the first twenty-four hours of Operation Nordwind, the *XIII SS Corps* had failed to appreciably dent the American lines in the 44th and 100th Division sectors, much less approach their objectives at Zetting, Rahling, or Bining. As noted in the *Army Group G* war journal, they "gained only insignificant ground" (*"nur geringfügig Boden gewinnen"*).[181] The rapid success necessary to draw *XV Corps* and Seventh Army reserves into the fray, away from the *2d Attack Group* to the east, did not materialize despite numerical advantages of more than three to one against the 71st Infantry Regiment and 3d Battalion, 397th Infantry.

The attacking echelons of *XC Corps* fared somewhat better, but they failed to decisively penetrate the in-depth defenses of the 100th Infantry Division's 399th Infantry Regiment. Furthermore, when an overwhelming numerical preponderance (seven to one) was produced by the arrival before Lemberg of the *559th*'s *1126th* and the *257th*'s *477th Volksgrenadier Regiments,* the coordinated attack necessary to push back the American defenders and clear the way to the corps's objectives never occurred.

General der Infanterie Höhne's *LXXXIX Corps* actually came the closest to achieving some of their objectives, but also failed badly in the seizure of one other, due to ignorance regarding the American defenses near Dambach. With the *Nord Division* arriving in strength shortly, however, the gains made by this corps could rapidly be exploited. Unfortunately for von Obstfelder and his men, the success of the *361st Volksgrenadiers,* in the depths of the Low Vosges in winter, would also be the most difficult to exploit with the armor of *First Army*'s operational reserve.

Despite the lack of initial success, *XIII SS Corps* continued its attacks against the *Bois de Bliesbrücken*–Rimling corridor throughout 2 January. Reinforced by the *74th Volksgrenadier Regiment,* the *36th Volksgrenadier Division* and *17th SS Panzergrenadier Division* continued to hammer at the 71st and 397th Infantry Regiments. Although the 1st and 3d Battalions of the 71st and the attached 3d Battalion, 253d Infantry Regiment, counterattacked several times, armored elements of the *17th SS Panzergrenadier Division* managed to penetrate farther and seize Gros Réderching and even Achen during the morning. Seriously threatened with envelopment from the west and south by this thrust, the 397th Infantry held on doggedly, and the regimental commander, Lt. Col. John M. King, committed his reserve, the 2d Battalion, to reinforce the western approaches. Before the end of the day, Major General Burress committed the bulk of the 100th Division's reserve, namely the 1st and 2d Battalions of the 255th Infantry, to a counterattack at Achen, and they forced the *SS Panzergrenadiers* and tankers of the *Götz von Berlichingen* back to Gros Réderching. The reserve (1st) battalion of the 398th Infantry also reinforced the 397th's open left flank. "By nightfall on the second day [of Nordwind]," wrote the *Army Group G* operations officer, "the attack had lost its momentum."[182]

Although German limited objective attacks against Rimling and Gros Réderching continued until 9 January, using not only the *38th SS Panzergrenadier Regiment,* but dozens of *Sturmgeschütze, Panthers,* thickly armored *Jagdtiger* tank destroyers, and the *Götz von Berlichingen Division*'s reconnaissance battalion as well, no decisive penetration was accomplished; the 3 January commitment of a combat command from the 2d French Armored Division, assured this. To eliminate the "Rimling Salient," formed by the successful retention of this piece of ground by the 100th Infantry Division, the 397th Infantry was withdrawn to positions around Guising (three thousand meters south of Rimling) on 9–10 January.[183] The German attack had certainly not lacked determination: The reconnaissance battalion of the *17th SS Panzergrenadier Division,* for example, lost sixteen platoon leaders and company commanders in the first ten days of 1945.[184]

The *First Army*'s assistant operations officer, Oberst Albert Emmerich, reported on the action as follows:

> The divisions of *XIII SS Corps* very soon met with stubborn enemy resistance and gained only little territory [around Rimling]. . . . The *17th SS Panzer Grenadier Division,* under incompetent leadership, had in the meantime been completely dispersed. . . . Probably because of the insufficient training of the

volks artillery corps, the coordination between the attacking infantry and the supporting artillery was only rarely achieved, so that the artillery support, which was actually strong, did not show its effectiveness either.[185]

The result was that the better-trained, better-led Americans simply defended more effectively than their enemy attacked. Because of the resounding failure of the *1st Attack Group,* Blaskowitz decided to concentrate his army group's efforts on breaking through in the central Low Vosges. The *Army Group G* war journal recorded his decision as follows:

> The other events of the day stress that, due to the developments in the situation of *XIII SS Corps* (strong enemy resistance, only negligible progress of the attack), *Army Group* abandons the further conduct of the plan of 25 December for the intended linkup between both attack groups (*XIII SS Corps* with *XC* and *LXXXIX Corps*) in the vicinity of Rohrbach and the further attacks of the mobile groups *west of the Vosges.* To that end, *Army Group* decides to turn the attack from the southwest to the south and southeast, to make further progress with *Army Group* reserves toward Wimmenau-Ingwiller to reach the [Alsatian] Plain.[186]

In accordance with this decision, the *36th Volksgrenadier Division* discontinued its fruitless attacks against the 44th Infantry Division and began moving to the *LXXXIX Corps* sector, to reinforce the success being achieved there by the *361st* and *256th Volksgrenadier Divisions* and the arriving *6th SS Mountain Division.* From late in the day on 2 January until 5 January, the sole focus of the *First Army* effort was the attack in the Low Vosges. The complementary effect of this, of course, was that it was also the center of attention for the Seventh Army during the same period. By abandoning his supporting attack, Blaskowitz allowed Major Generals Haislip and Brooks to concentrate their efforts on halting the German attack in some of the most eminently defensible terrain in all of western Europe.

Most of the units of the *2d Attack Group* did not make significant progress on 2 January, however. *XC Corps*'s efforts against Lemberg and Goetzenbrueck failed in the face of reinforcements from both the

100th Infantry Division (3d Battalion, 255th Infantry) and VI Corps (141st Infantry RCT) reserves, although elements of the *257th Volksgrenadier Division* managed to seize Meisenthal (fifteen hundred meters southwest of Goetzenbrueck) by late in the day. The *257th*'s operations officer admitted later that the regiment attacking Lemberg "simply had not been equal to the task." When all three regiments' attacks bogged down by 3 January, he ruefully concluded that, "The offensive power of the Division was exhausted," and that without reinforcements, "the Division would be forced to pass over to defensive measures."[187] In this regard, Oberstleutnant Linke's judgment matched that of Generalmajor von der Mühlen, who decided on 3 January that, given the Americans' reinforced posture, "it was not possible to make further headway."[188] For all practical purposes, *XC Corps*'s offensive activities ceased on the third day of the attack. Neither division had accomplished its assigned mission.

The events of 2 January brought similar disappointment in the *LXXXIX Corps* zone, as the attack failed to progress significantly toward its objectives. The exertions of the first day's combat had likewise taken their toll on the *Volksgrenadiers* of Philippi's division. The *Landsers* of the *953d Volksgrenadiers* "appeared greatly worn out, especially the new replacements who were not equal to such strain," in the opinion of the commanding general, as a result of their "exceedingly strenuous night march." The lead battalion of the *952d* was in even worse shape after having "just finished an even more strenuous march on narrow mountain-paths." Accordingly, "Its commitment for the day could no longer be reckoned with."[189] Due to the unsatisfactory condition of the men for the continuation of the attack, "The opportunity which the success of the previous day seemed to have opened up had passed," and the attacks toward the division's objectives had to be postponed until 3 January.[190] The time was well spent by the men of the Texas Division's 141st RCT; they improved their positions around Lemberg, Goetzenbrueck, Meisenthal, and Montbronn.

The second day of the attack also included little action for the *256th Volksgrenadier Division,* as its officers and soldiers attempted to reorganize and prepare to continue the attack. The division's lassitude was propitiously timed for the Americans. By 2 January, Major General Brooks had reinforced the 45th Infantry Division with elements of VI Corps not needed on the Alsatian Plain. Task Force Herren's 274th and 276th Infantry Regiments arrived from the east, as did the 79th Infantry Division's 313th Infantry Regiment (minus the 3d Battalion). The 1st Battalion, 314th Infantry, and 1st Battalion, 315th Infantry, also arrived to help the 45th stem the German tide. Even the 36th Engineer Combat Regiment was attached and assumed defensive positions on the 45th's right flank, releasing the 179th Infantry Regiment for duty on the Thunderbird Division's grossly extended left flank near Wingen. With little effective pressure from the *256th Volksgrenadiers,* Major General Frederick's massively reinforced division took up positions roughly on a line extending south from the 141st Infantry's sector near Goetzenbrueck to Meisenthal-Wingen-Reipertswiller-Baerenthal-Philippsbourg-Dambach. Additionally, Brooks released Combat Command B, 14th Armored Division, from corps reserve to establish positions in depth along the eastern edge of the Vosges from Neuviller-les-Saverne to Niederbronn-les-Bains.[191] The American units so committed not only dug in, but began a series of counterattacks that spoiled nearly every German offensive effort during the next week.

In spite of this defensive reinforcement, 3 January brought the *256th Volksgrenadier Division*'s first significant success. By means of a surprise raid supported by assault guns, the *476th Volksgrenadier Regiment* seized Philippsbourg from the 275th Infantry Regiment and remnants of Task Force Hudelson's 62d Armored Infantry Battalion. One of the divisional objectives had thus been seized. In the process, however, the *476th* so exhausted itself that it became "completely worn out." Furthermore, its battalions had become separated and needed time to consolidate before attempting subsequent operations.[192] Thus the Germans' opportunity evaporated to follow up gains against the incompletely trained combat neophytes of Task Force Herren. The remainder of the *256th Volksgrenadier Division* spent the day in futile attacks on the 157th Infantry's positions near Dambach and fighting back Thunderbird counterattacks on Neunhoffen. Many heavily wooded, snow-covered kilometers lay between their positions and their other objectives of Windstein, Untermuehlthal, and Lichtenberg.

While the *256th* was successfully attacking Philippsbourg, Philippi's division, reinforced by the *"Michael Gaissmair" SS Mountain Regiment,* was attacking toward its objectives at Wingen (with the *12th*

SS), Wimmenau (with the *1st Battalion, 951st Volksgrenadiers* and the *506th SS Panzer Grenadier Battalion*), and Reipertswiller (with the *953d Volksgrenadier Regiment*). The latter attack, against the 1st and 2d Battalions, 313th Infantry Regiment, stalled and ultimately failed when the lead armored vehicle skidded on the icy road toward Reipertswiller, became stuck, and blocked further advances on the road for the rest of the day. (Some idea of what the progress of the attack of the *21st Panzer Division* in this zone would have been like, as envisaged in the original *Army Group G* plan, may be derived from this incident.)

By 4 January, the attack of the *12th SS Mountain Regiment* on the 2d Battalion, 274th Infantry and the 1st Battalion, 276th Infantry north of Wingen was successful in pushing back the American line thirty-five hundred meters to Zittersheim. In Wingen, the SS took approximately 280 enlisted men and eight officers prisoner, mostly from Headquarters and Service Companies, 179th Infantry Regiment." Although one of the *361st*'s objectives had been occupied, none of the other attacks by the *361st* made headway. "Along the entire front to both sides of the Division, the attack had come to a halt," concluded Philippi. He added that,

> With the failure of the attack at Reipertswiller, the heavy losses of the *953d Volksgrenadier Regiment* [down to 150 men present for duty], the call for help by the battalion committed towards Wimmenau [the *1st Battalion, 951st*], the uncertain whereabouts of the *SS-Regiment* committed towards Wingen [there had been no radio contact all day], and the clearly noticeable increase in strength and activity of the enemy, the third day of the attack had clearly been a failure.[194] [Author's comments in brackets.]

The fourth day of Nordwind brought continued grief for *LXXXIX Corps*. In accordance with instructions from *Army Group G,* Höhne's corps shifted its attack toward the southeast, in the direction of Zinswiller.[195] In the opinion of Generalmajor Philippi and Oberstleutnant Reschke, the *LXXXIX Corps* operations officer, the successful prosecution of such an attack was no longer feasible. "Both divisions of the Corps [the *361st* and *256th Volksgrenadiers*] were so battered and weakened," wrote Reschke, "they were no longer capable of launching an attack." Nevertheless, Blaskowitz insisted on continuing the attack toward the Alsatian Plain at Rothbach and Zinswiller. Detaching the

477th Volksgrenadier Regiment from the now-stagnant *257th Volks-grenadier Division* and assigning it to reinforce the *361st,* von Obstfelder forced Philippi to fight in three directions simultaneously, over a fifteen-kilometer front! The *1st Battalion, 952d Volksgrenadier Regiment,* infiltrated south of Baerenthal in an attempt to drive the nine kilometers to Zinswiller; the *12th SS Regiment* continued its seesaw battle with the 2d Battalion, 274th Infantry and 1st and 3d Battalions of the 276th, and the *1st Battalion, 951s Volksgrenadier* grimly held on near Wimmenau. The *361st's* expanded operations to the east—an attempt to compensate for the *256th's* failures—rapidly diluted its dwindling strength. Worse still, other than the capture of Dambach by the *481st Volksgrenadier Regiment,* 4 January saw defensive activity only by the *256th's* other two regiments, in the face of continuous American counterattacks by the 275th Infantry Regiment.[196]

The fifth day of Nordwind brought a series of American counterattacks all along the line. Franz's *456th Volksgrenadier Regiment's* attack toward Niederbronn from Philippsbourg bounced off the 275th Infantry's defenses in the area. While the remainder of the *256th Volksgrenadier Division* remained moribund, the *361st* was just barely holding on as well. The *1st Battalion, 951st Volksgrenadier Regiment,* reported that it had assumed a "hedgehog" perimeter in Wimmenau, and was therefore in mortal danger; the *1st Battalion, 952d Volksgrenadier Regiment,* observed the road from Zinswiller to Baerenthal, and accomplished nothing useful; the *953d* clung to the area north of Reipertswiller in the face of attacks by elements of the 313th Infantry Regiment and attached 1st Battalion, 314th Infantry; and the *"Michael Gaissmair" Regiment* desperately fought off the 179th Infantry's attacks in Wingen.[197]

The dire situation was finally recognized by *Army Group G,* and its war journal entry for the day indicates an almost introspective, melancholy mood:

> The war in the wintry Vosges represented a frightful mission for the inadequately trained troops who had already been overstrained by the incessant battles forward of the Saar. They have up to now won ground in spite of the most difficult weather, terrain, and combat conditions. The combat power of the infantry, however, has decreased considerably. . . . [Author's translation.][198]

Given this estimate of the situation, OKW decided to transfer *First Army's* operational reserve, the *21st Panzer Division* and the *25th Panzergrenadier Division,* from the Bitche area, whence they had been brought in anticipation of a breakthrough, to the area north of Wissembourg. There, the weakened American lines between the Moder and the Lauter would become the target for further *Army Group G* and *Army Group Oberrhein* offensive efforts beginning the following day and continuing for most of the month of January. From this point on, the effort in the Vosges was at best a supporting attack to tie up VI Corps combat power and prevent reinforcement of the American elements to the east. On the Alsatian Plain, of course, the American advantage in quantities of tanks and armored vehicles, as well as their air superiority, could be counted on to assist in the defense. As far as OKW and *Army Group G* were concerned, Nordwind was a failure.

Unfortunately for all concerned, the commanders in the Vosges were unaware of their higher headquarters' intentions. On 7–8 January, one last offensive effort was conducted by *LXXXIX Corps* in an attempt to penetrate to the Alsatian Plain and open the way for the *Panzers* imagined still to be available. Reinforced by a Luftwaffe infantry battalion and the *477th Volksgrenadier Regiment,* the *952d* and *953d Volksgrenadier Regiments* of the *361st Volksgrenadier Division* attacked toward Reipertswiller and Lichtenberg on the seventh. They were halted and thrown back by the 313th Infantry Regiment and the 274th Infantry, reinforced by the 2d Battalion, 276th Infantry. Even worse for the attackers, the *2d Battalion, 952d Volksgrenadiers* was wiped out at the hamlet of Picardie (seven hundred meters east of Reipertswiller) by an American counterattack the next day.[199] Attacks by the 179th and 180th Infantry Regiments on Althorn decimated the *457th Volksgrenadiers*; further counterattacks by elements of the 274th and 276th Regiments at Wingen forced the battered *12th SS Mountain Regiment* to withdraw.[200] All hopes for further progress were abandoned. Over the next few days, that part of the *6th SS Mountain Division* not already committed relieved the *361st* in its zone. After fruitless attacks to the southwest on 10 January by the *256th* in a meaningless attempt to penetrate to Zinswiller, that division, too, was relieved, and the *36th Volksgrenadier Division* took its place.

Casualties on both sides had been considerable. Although exact casualty figures for the Germans are not available, an examination of certain aspects of casualties suffered by American infantry units is illuminating.

Not surprisingly, the casualties suffered by some units of Task Forces Herren and Harris were considerably higher than those of more adequately trained units. During their commitment on the line as part of the 45th Infantry Division, for example, the line companies of the 1st Battalion, 276th Infantry, and 1st Battalion, 275th Infantry, lost an average of 46 percent and 54 percent of their men, respectively. The worst casualties suffered by the line companies of any *integral* infantry battalion of the 45th Infantry Division (all of which were committed to similar, if not more demanding, missions) were the 26 percent sustained by the 3d Battalion, 179th Infantry.[201] Although lack of combat experience may in part account for this disparity, the casualties sustained by fully trained divisions such as the 100th and 103d in their combat debut were much closer to those of the seasoned divisions they fought beside in the High Vosges.

After 10 January, the battle raging east of the Vosges almost split the Americans and French politically, if not tactically. A furor arose over 6th Army Group plans to abandon Strasbourg as early as 3 January, in the event of German success in their offensive, but ultimately this was never necessary. Developments on the Alsatian Plain, however, forced a general realignment of Seventh Army lines on 13 January. Included in the operation was a withdrawal in the Vosges to the line Rothbach-Reipertswiller-Goetzenbrueck to allow the VI Corps on the Alsatian Plain to take advantage of the Moder River–Rothbach Stream defensive line. In no way was this withdrawal related to the desultory and inconclusive, if deadly, fighting that dragged on in the Vosges until the end of January.

CONCLUSION

Operations in the Low Vosges from late November 1944 to mid-January 1945 recapitulated the themes that appeared in the autumn campaign in the High Vosges. The units of *Army Group G* reconfirmed their skill at delaying numerically superior Seventh Army pursuers in terrain eminently suitable for such operations. At the same time, the commanders and men of the Seventh Army conducting the pursuit proved their relentless tenacity and skill at preserving sufficient combat power and morale to penetrate the same fortified positions their opponents had failed to dent four and a half years earlier.

When provided with an opportunity to exert the advantages of numerical superiority themselves, the soldiers of *Army Group G* failed utterly. Flawed in concept from the start, Operation Nordwind was a resounding failure. Poorly trained and organized units conducted attacks in amateurish and wildly wasteful manners, sustaining such heavy casualties that they exhausted themselves in two or three days of combat. Oversupervised by the army group headquarters, the subordinate commands' chances of success with incompletely trained formations almost disappeared with the sacrifice of mid- and low-level planning and doctrinally required reconnaissance in deference to vain hopes for tactical surprise. As a result, the attacks of the *XC* and *LXXXIX Corps* started slowly and never gained momentum. The attackers, their morale raised to a high level by initial *Army Group B* successes in the Ardennes, dashed themselves against doctrinally correct American defenses, which, being arrayed in depth, bent but did not break. Finally, disorganized by constant American counterattacks, the offensive dissipated into a pathetic assortment of poorly coordinated battalion attacks, some of which were launched even after their purpose (clearing the way for armored reserves) had ceased to exist. Only two of the German divisions in the operation reached any of their objectives, and none reached them all.

American units, made up in part of ex–Army Air Forces, antiaircraft artillery, and technical services' troops, led by officers and noncommissioned officers with little combat experience (less than seventy-five days for the 44th Division, forty-seven in the 100th), stonewalled attacks by numerically superior formations of soldiers of similarly mixed background, led by veteran combat leaders. The difference, obviously, was training and the cohesion born of it. Even highly seasoned, previously undefeated SS mountain troops could not defeat like numbers of similarly experienced Americans who had fought in the Apennines and Vosges.

Finally, as exceptions proving the rule, Seventh Army units that were not organized with attention paid to cohesion and extensive training in many cases performed less well. The bastardized Task Force Hudelson barely provided warning to adjacent units of the German attack, let alone effective resistance. Units of the erratically trained 63d and 70th Infantry Divisions sustained the highest casualties and, therefore, came closest to failing of all the Seventh Army infantry units committed in the Low Vosges. Still, even these units, operating without their parent organizations' support echelons, fulfilled their missions and played an important role in halting their adversaries' advances.

The ersatz "American Volksturm Grenadiers" threw back the best that the *Landsers* of the genuine article could offer. Few more telling comparisons could be made.

CHAPTER 5

THE VOSGES CAMPAIGN IN PERSPECTIVE

After the commencement of the great Soviet offensives in East Prussia, Poland, and Czechoslovakia in mid-January 1945, OKW's attention was jerked away to the monumental task of halting this mortally dangerous attack. Four million Soviet troops in sixty-eight field armies, supported by thirteen air armies, crashed into the defenses of *Army Groups Center, A,* and *South* in the fourth, and last, great Russian winter offensive of the war. In response, nearly all remaining quality units were stripped from the western front, including the *21st Panzer* and *25th Panzergrenadier Divisions* from *Army Group G,* as well as most of the replacements for units in the west; nearly all were directed east in a vain attempt to close the gaping holes being enlarged daily in the Germans' lines.

Although combat certainly continued in the Low Vosges, its intensity was not comparable to that of early January or even December. To be sure, any combat is significant for the participants, but for the purposes of this study, the fighting in the area after 13 January is insignificant due to the greatly reduced number of German troops and the growing commitment of *Volksturm* militia to the Siegfried line positions.[1] Additionally, American operations in the area after mid-January were mainly confined to limited objective attacks designed to straighten the MLR and provide a suitable line of departure for the coming final

March offensive. Ultimately, this offensive quickly broke through the Low Vosges and carried rapidly into the Palatinate against mostly token resistance.

With the failure of Nordwind, then, a study of the combat of American and German forces in the Vosges in World War II comes full circle and leaves the historian with some clear conclusions. The great, historically impregnable mountain barrier of the High Vosges had been penetrated by an attacking army for the first time. The bastion of the craggy Low Vosges, also previously impenetrable, had been partially penetrated by one army's attack, but to another had fulfilled its traditional role of impervious obstacle. Exactly how and why these events occurred, both the unprecedented ones and the typical one, has been the focus of this study.

Summary of the Impact of Training

The training afforded the units that fought in the Vosges Mountains varied widely in quantity and quality, and had a major impact on the outcome of the campaign. In the latter stages of World War II, both sides were forced to commit as replacements soldiers whose initial training and military experience suited them primarily for other roles. The American system was far superior in retraining such personnel and welding them into effective fighting forces, however.

Also, due to their nation's far greater experience in the conduct of land warfare over the two previous generations, the Germans possessed a corps of far more experienced field commanders than did the Americans. These commanders, however, were handicapped by the generally poor abilities of their units to execute the plans arranged for them by these capable and seasoned leaders. As a result, the execution of operations by units of *Army Group G* generally was considerably inferior to that of subelements of the Seventh Army.

American units can be basically divided into two major categories for this study: experienced formations and newly introduced ones. Among the experienced formations, the National Guard units drew partially on their traditions and years of peacetime soldiering together and largely on their shared experiences in other theaters of war (both in training and combat) for their cohesion and fighting skills. The introduction to the infantry formations of these divisions of replacements from all parts of the United States seems to have had little effect on the pride and esprit de corps of these units, probably due to the gradual nature of the transition and certainly to the relative universality of the white American culture of the period. The armed forces, reflecting the practice of the larger society, segregated nonwhites. The rationale behind this policy was the potentially negative impact on cohesion that the U.S. Army's leadership feared their presence could introduce in otherwise all-white units. In the Vosges, the superb performance of nonwhite combat units, such as that of the 442d Regimental Combat Team (Nisei) at Bruyères, or the 614th Tank Destroyer Battalion (Towed) (Colored) at Climbach, thus seemed to validate to the leaders of that era the concept of cultural homogeneity's contribution to combat cohesion.[2]

The Regular Army and Organized Reserves units with prior combat experience drew on their long service training together in the United States and their shared combat ventures to maintain and hone the skills necessary for success on the battlefield.

Similarly, the freshly introduced "new" (Army of the United States or Organized Reserves) divisions' effectiveness resulted from long periods together, from activation to deployment, in which the majority of the troops and nearly all of the leaders underwent extensive and comprehensive multiechelon training. Those exceptional units that did not complete the Mobilization Training Plan and/or suffered hemorrhages of trained men and subsequent infusions of ill-trained replacements shortly before commitment to combat suffered much higher casualties and came closer to failure than their better-trained counterparts committed earlier in the campaign. The less impressive results achieved by these exceptions demonstrate the importance of the more complete training and cohesion attained by the majority of the new divisions.

All of the American units in the Vosges took advantage of such opportunities as they received to train and amalgamate replacements. American commanders, although generally having far less combat experience than their German counterparts, recognized the importance of morale; therefore, with the exception of the 442d RCT and some of the battalions in Task Forces Harris and Herren, they did not fight their units down to the point where less than 50 percent of the unit's soldiers remained. This ensured the continuation of the "family" (or perhaps tribal) atmosphere essential for the effective cohesion that bonds men together in the face of extreme adversity.

This maintenance of the elements contributing to unit cohesion forced certain trade-offs in operational techniques. Interestingly, the *LXXXIX Corps* chief of staff, Oberstleutnant Kurt Reschke, believed that the

Americans were far too timid in their pursuit of delaying *First Army* units in the Low Vosges. Following the war's end he wrote:

> After my experiences of 3 1/2 years at the eastern front, I venture to state, that the Russians, in a similar position, would have pierced the area between the Moder and the *Westwall* (about 35 km) in 3-4 days and would have, in one assault, overrun the *Westwall,* which in the beginning of December 1944 was in no way ready for a defense.[3]

Although quite possibly true, what such sentiments do not take into account are the casualties that the Soviets regularly sustained in the conduct of such ventures, and the overall effect such a reckless maneuver would have had on the morale of the soldiers. Far from preserving the American morale that ultimately assisted in throwing back the Nordwind thrusts, it would undoubtedly have wrecked it by ruining the Americans' confidence in their commanders and destroying the core of soldiers whose long standing in the unit ensured its members' continued cohesion. Perhaps the Russians, fighting to liberate their Motherland or to punish the "Hitlerite jackals" who had savaged it, would fight just as hard whether or not they knew their comrades in the same squad and platoon. It could be that unit commissars could arouse passionate hatred of the enemy with a few well-chosen quotations from Lenin or Stalin, but equivalent measures would have been greeted with apathy or derision by the great majority of American soldiers. Although Soviet officers could threaten dire consequences for their soldiers' families for failure on the battlefield, such threats were unheard of (and would have been empty anyway) in the U.S. Army.

As has been pointed out in countless studies and personal memoirs, the American soldiers' motivation to fight derived from affection for their buddies in their squads, sections, crews, and platoons. The destruction of these groups would have been justified only by the most extreme circumstances, and, except for the defense of the central Low Vosges in the first few days of 1945, these circumstances never arose during the campaign. Ironically, then, if U.S. commanders preserved lives and unit identities at the cost of exceptional aggressiveness and impressive gains comparable to those of their Russian allies, it is because victory depended on it.

In addition to the emphasis given the creation and maintenance of cohesion by the Americans in their training practices, the other decisive ingredient in their superior preparation and training was their experience in mountain warfare. All three VI Corps divisions in the battle for the High Vosges had commanders, staffs, cadres, and a large number of rank and file soldiers with extensive experience in mountain fighting in Italy and elsewhere. Furthermore, two of the new divisions that took part in the Vosges battles—the 79th and 100th Infantry Divisions—and both armored divisions that participated in the campaign—the 12th and 14th—had taken part in various of the U.S. Army's two month-long "Tennessee Maneuvers," which closely simulated the terrain they would ultimately fight through in the Vosges. During "Tennessee Maneuvers Number 4," conducted in November-December 1943, the 100th Infantry Division and 14th Armored Division even got a taste of the challenges to be presented by the climate of their future battlefield. Thus, seven of the nine principal combatant U.S. Army divisions in the battle for the Vosges had significant experience in mountain operations.

The training received by most of the German units in the Vosges Mountains campaign was vastly inferior to that of their American counterparts. *Volksgrenadier* divisions, which made up 53 percent of the German divisions committed in the Vosges, typically underwent four to six weeks of collective unit training, although a former commander in the German Reserve Army, in charge of training troops, believed, "For careful activation and training of a division a period of three months was generally considered necessary."[4] Some *Volksgrenadier* units didn't even get *that* much. This inferiority was even more marked in comparison to the minimum of thirty-five weeks of unit training conducted by American new divisions. As Janowitz and Shils noted in their landmark study, "Cohesion and Disintegration in the Wehrmacht," cohesion was worst in "hastily fabricated units" whose soldiers came from diverse backgrounds and "had no time to become used to one another and to develop the type of friendliness which is possible only when loyalties to outside groups have been renounced—or at least put into the background."[5] Not only did the Germans populate these "hastily fabricated units" with men from diverse military backgrounds, but even threw together "*Volksdeutsche*" recruits from Poland, Czechoslovakia, and other areas, who couldn't understand German much less bond with their comrades. The twin deficiencies of inadequate training and pronounced cultural heterogeneity devastated the combat effectiveness of these units.

Although most *Volksgrenadier* divisions possessed at least a cadre of battle-experienced NCOs and officers, by virtue of having been built around surviving members of infantry divisions that had previously been destroyed, the attitudes and morale of these men cannot have been particularly high. Rarely does witnessing the destruction of one's unit promote high spirits. A few of the units of *Army Group G* even had the worst of both worlds, that is, both a cadre that had been soundly beaten in the recent past, and practically no collective training. The *16th Volksgrenadier Division,* for example, was organized around the five hundred or so survivors of the *16th Infantry Division*'s debacle near Épinal in September. Without more than a few days' break in the action, it received wholesale replacements and entire separate battalions, and continued to fight without the benefit of a training period.

The training received by the remaining 47 percent of the *Army Group G* units that fought in the Vosges was superior to that of the *Volksgrenadier* divisions. Most units, such as the *11th* and *21st Panzer Divisions* and *17th SS Panzergrenadier Division,* had had six months to a year together in France to rest and train prior to the invasions in June and August of 1944. After the invasions, however, they were almost constantly in battle. These units fought until they had only a small fraction of their original personnel, and continuously received infusions of replacements, which they had little time to amalgamate due to the constant nature of these units' employment. The decision of *Army Group G*'s leadership to fight these units "down to the nub" was based on the perceived need for constant commitment to prevent Allied breakthroughs. The trade-off between the advantages of badly beaten units' immediate presence at critical points on the line, and fresher, more cohesive units' availability for more effective commitment a few weeks hence, was obviated by the constant Seventh Army pressure throughout the campaign. The *Nineteenth Army* chief of staff, Generalleutnant Walter Botsch, later wrote, "These enemy attacks, which were led in an irregular way in respect to time and place, were a disadvantage to us, since the Army Front was never quiet enough to warrant a period of complete rest."[6] The *Army Group G* chief of staff, von Mellenthin, concurred, stating that in the *Nineteenth Army* sector, "there was always something going on," and that, consequently,

Constant fighting had been detrimental to the recuperation of the troops involved in the withdrawal from southern France. Although it was possible to reinforce the divisions with ammunition and personnel, the continued heavy defensive fighting, especially the combat in the woods near Le Tholy [U.S. 3d Infantry Division zone], resulted in considerable losses on our side. The replacements, inadequately trained, were quickly used up.[7]

In this way, the Americans created a situation in which little cohesion could be maintained in the best-trained German units.

With one exception, none of the German units committed in the Vosges possessed prior training or experience in mountain warfare. Those *Nineteenth Army* units that did gain at least a modicum of experience in the High Vosges were cut off in what became the Colmar Pocket, and never took part in the battle for the Low Vosges, where once again the German troops committed to the fight were unfamiliar with the rigors of mountain combat. The only fully trained German unit to enter the fray fresh and properly trained for mountain warfare was the *6th SS Mountain Division,* and its credible performance in Nordwind proves the wisdom of American commanders in their efforts to deprive the Germans of training opportunities.

Summary of the Impact of Organization

By the time of the Vosges Mountains campaign, the Americans had developed tactical organizations that facilitated the fighting of modern wars to an extent far superior to their adversaries. Each uniformly organized division and regiment was supported by tank and tank destroyer units, and ad hoc task forces of men already familiar with one another could be organized quickly and efficiently. This was especially advantageous during pursuit operations, when highly mobile units were needed to maintain contact with the withdrawing enemy. Such consistent organization and habitual relationships contributed to mutual trust and confidence between the soldiers of adjacent and supporting units, thus furthering cohesion and minimizing the Clausewitzian "friction" accompanying unforeseen changes during battle.

The Americans also retained fairly consistent organization with regard to corps and division command structures throughout the Vosges campaign. From the third week of October onward, both of the principal combatant corps in Seventh Army were commanded by the same men, Brooks and Haislip; only the 45th Infantry Division received a new commander at the height of the fighting.[8] Moreover, the composition of the two corps was relatively stable throughout the campaign, with the 3d, 36th, and 45th Infantry Divisions and 14th Armored Division remaining under VI Corps control, and the 44th Infantry Division and 12th Armored Division serving only in the XV Corps. After the first two weeks of Vosges fighting, the 100th Infantry Division remained under Haislip, and the 103d remained under Brooks until its transfer to XV Corps at the end of December. Consistent organization and command structure contributed to "teambuilding," and thus to continuity of command and reduced friction in the heat of battle. The relative combat inexperience of some of the division commanders magnified the importance of reducing communicative friction.

In contrast to the Americans' stability, German organization during the campaign was chaotic on both the tactical and operational levels. Some infantry divisions had three regiments of two battalions, and some had two regiments of three, but neither type had the important "triangular" organization conducive to the retention of reserves for resting troops, exploiting successes, or conducting counterattacks. Separate regiments of police, Russian turncoats, and Austrian mountaineers found their way into divisional structures throughout the fighting in the High Vosges. Fortress machine-gun battalions of three different varieties were thrust to the front and forced, like square blocks into round holes, into the framework of infantry divisions. Tank and tank destroyer battalions and armored reconnaissance units appeared and disappeared without accomplishing decisive results, and certainly before comfortable working relationships could be developed between commanders and staffs. Divisions were shuffled between corps with frequent irregularity, and rarely did one division remain under the control of a single corps headquarters for more than two weeks. The most telling example of the adverse impact of such practices came when, at the most critical moment in the battle for the Saverne Gap, the *553d Volksgrenadier Division* was switched from the control of one field army with which it *could* communicate, to another, with which it *could not!*

The situation was scarcely better at the operational level. The constant reshuffling of corps and field army assets produced continuous friction. A *Panzer* corps headquarters was removed from the front during the first week of the fighting, and a Luftwaffe corps headquarters fought through the entire High Vosges campaign in control of army divisions. The *Army Group G* commander was relieved just before the fighting in the Vosges, and reinstated when the planning for Nordwind was well under way. The *First Army* commander was relieved during the complicated and critical delay to the German frontier, and the commander of *LXXXIX Corps* was relieved during the XV Corps breakthrough at Saverne. The commanding general of the *708th Volksgrenadier Division* was relieved during the defeat of his unit in the High Vosges. The commander of the *553d Volksgrenadier Division* was captured near Saverne, and the commander of the *17th SS Panzergrenadiers,* who was the fourth to hold that position in as many months, was captured on 10 January, although his division had already been defeated.

Complicating and worsening an already confused situation was the clumsy integration of Waffen SS headquarters and units with army organizations. Officers with very different values, philosophies of war, and military educational backgrounds were forced to attempt coordinated operations, sometimes with acrimonious results. Prussian nobles, such as von Knobelsdorff and von Obstfelder, surely did not savor the requirement of working with former concentration camp guards such as Simon; former objects of Simon's scorn and victims of his obstinacy, such as Höhne, must have despised having to protect his flank. The forces of National Socialism, which resurrected and revitalized the army in the 1930s, ironically imposed the Waffen SS and all of its counterproductive obstacles on army commanders in the last few years of the Third Reich, with significantly negative results.

Summary of the Impact of Doctrine

The significantly different effects of training and organization on the two combatant sides in the Vosges campaign caused otherwise similar tactical and operational doctrines to be executed with decisively different degrees of success.

Both doctrines emphasized the importance of field commanders' flexibility and initiative, particularly in the attack. This doctrine was not fully followed by both sides during this campaign, however. When the Americans attacked, their corps and division commanders were afforded concise and clear missions to be accomplished within appropriately broad parameters. They were also allotted appropriately organized and trained forces. The field order directing the Seventh Army offensive to penetrate the High Vosges (Seventh Army Field Order Number 7, 29 September 1944) specified the twin missions of piercing the Germans' defenses and destroying German forces west of the Rhine, the forces available to corps commanders, their geographical boundaries, and little else. The rest was up to the corps commanders and their staffs to plan and implement; their orders to subordinate divisions likewise reflected this emphasis on flexibility and initiative. The effectiveness of such practices was evident even to the enemy. As the *Nineteenth Army* chief of staff observed, "One had the impression that . . . division commanders themselves had the authority to determine the time of the attacks and could take as much time as they wished to carry out these missions."[9]

The resulting offensive made effective use of creative deception operations devised by the VI Corps and subordinate division commanders to minimize potentially dangerous defensive shifts in alignment. At the corps commander's discretion, it massed most of three divisions to burst through a German division and corps boundary at Bruyères, where the defenders' command and control would be the most difficult, and forced a general German withdrawal to the Meurthe. The offensive forced the Germans to commit, and then consume, considerable numbers of reserves—reserves that subsequently could not be used for the defense of the Vosges defensive lines. The *Nineteenth Army*'s commanding general observed that the defense of the High Vosges, even with all their formidable natural and man-made defenses, was made far more difficult by the absence "of all those forces . . . which had been used up in the foreground battles."[10]

When the "big push" came in mid-November, without operational interference from Seventh Army headquarters, the American spearheads struck weakness with strength and outmaneuvered the defenders with precisely coordinated rapier thrusts that unhinged the Germans' prepared defenses in which they had intended to spend the onrushing winter. Where terrain permitted, rapidly organized armored task forces, raised from habitually supporting units, rampaged through holes created by attacking infantry in the German lines and rapidly enveloped the defenders.

When Lieutenant General Patch directed the pursuit through the Low Vosges, his order (Seventh Army Field Order Number 8, 2 December 1944) similarly directed only the mission (breach the Siegfried line), the forces available, and the unit boundaries. Major Generals Brooks and Haislip and their subordinate division commanders then decided how best to accomplish all tasks inherent in these direct, clear missions. The subsequent American pursuit was prudent but not overly cautious; it drove the Germans back quickly where their resistance was weak, and forced them out of their strongholds where they chose to stand firmly. It massed strength in the terrain most conducive to pursuit, and tied down defenders in more rugged country by using mechanized cavalry screens. Such economy of force measures and the intrinsic "triangular" organization of the units committed allowed the use of "two-up, one-back" formations throughout the pursuit, which preserved the strength of the infantry units for the accomplishment of the ultimate task of penetrating the German defensive lines on the frontiers of the Palatinate. When terrain suitable for armored envelopment was available by change of corps, army, and army group boundaries, the XV Corps commander obtained a rapid and decisive response through his higher headquarters' command channels, rather than dictation of the course of the attack.

Unlike their American counterparts, whose regular adherence to doctrine was supported by training and organization, the German units' preparation and structure contributed to frequent departures from—and violations of—fundamental doctrinal tenets.

The German attack instructions for Nordwind, for example, denied subordinate commanders much flexibility at all. The *Army Group G* orders usurped from von Obstfelder and his *First Army* corps commanders some of the most basic entitlements of their position regarding flexibility and initiative by specifying exact geographical corps objectives and precise corps organizations, including separate battalions to be attached to each attack group. In the name of battlefield deception and security, most of which went for naught anyway, tactical control from army group level also destroyed opportunities for the tactical commanders to exercise initiative by denying them knowledge of the enemy and even the mission until the eve of the attack. Although certain staff officers and commanders, in their postwar reports, attempted to blame such doctrinal violations on the meddling of the Führer, it has been shown by entries in the *Army Group G* war journal that such instructions were issued by Blaskowitz's headquarters *before* Hitler's entrance on the scene.

As a result of this departure from doctrine, in most cases the attackers charged blindly into unknown enemy defenses and attempted to accomplish missions that were impractical after the first or second day of the operation. The attackers' momentum quickly dissipated in a series of assaults conducted with rapidly dwindling strength due to both the defenders' far more flexible response and the atrociously wasteful tactics of the improperly prepared and trained attackers. Masses of howling German infantry charging into minefields swept by American machine-gun, mortar, and artillery fire may have amazed the defenders, but, except in the sector held by a hastily constituted mechanized cavalry task force, it did not dislodge them.

Adherence to doctrinal standards in the defense differed considerably among the two sides as well. The American defense of the French side of the frontier opposite the Palatinate into which Nordwind struck was largely conducted with conspicuous adherence to the tenets of *FM 100-5*. Although established only a few days before the New Year's Eve onslaught, from the regimental level and up, defensive positions were arrayed in depth behind forward obstacles such as minefields, roadblocks, and barbed-wire fences. The defenders launched combined-arms counterattacks vigorously and continuously, not only to restore the MLR, but to disrupt the attackers' plans for continuation of the offensive. Reserves were deftly shuffled into place to plug the yawning gap developing in the central Low Vosges in the aftermath of the collapse of Task Force Hudelson.

Indeed, even this near disaster was mitigated by the unflinching defense of the 100th Infantry Division, which successfully halted simultaneous attacks from three sides and bought the time necessary for reserves to stanch the torrent of German attackers stumbling through the dense terrain vacated by the haphazardly organized mechanized task force. In the end, Patch's gamble to cover the least trafficable portion of his army's sector with this scratch force paid off with the containment of the heaviest of the German blows well shy of their geographical objectives.

The Germans' conduct of the defense was hardly as effective or doctrinally correct. While they proved themselves masters of effective delaying actions, adhering consistently to their doctrine's insistence on strongpoints, coordinated delay lines, and counterattacks, they also conducted their operations in terrain that could scarcely be surpassed for such endeavors. Their attempts to retain ground were another story entirely.

The defense of the High Vosges depended on a series of positions that were rarely constructed in consonance with German doctrinal requirements, being spaced too far apart to facilitate mutual support. German doctrine called for defenses consisting of consecutive belts of increasingly difficult obstacles and formidable positions designed to both weaken the attacker and protect the defender. Due to lack of coordination with the forward fighting elements, the defenses constructed with massive commitment of labor forces in the High Vosges were built too far apart to facilitate the mutual support necessary for the creation of the cumulatively destructive effect intended by German doctrine. Instead of short rearward bounds to sequentially occupy these positions, great leaps of ten kilometers or more, through difficult and exhausting terrain, were required. If the defending units were decisively engaged in their forward positions, as often happened in the High Vosges, few troops would be available for the defense of the main positions. Although the strongpoint defenses of innumerable Vosgian villages and towns effectively stifled most American attempts at rapid advances supported by armored forces, the infantrymen of the Seventh Army rapidly adjusted their tactics to achieve success. "As long as these tactics [attacking up roads supported by armor] were pursued," wrote the *Nineteenth Army*'s commanding general,

> it was possible to create main points of defense and it was comparatively easy to fend off the attacks. When later on the enemy altered these tactics which had been of little success to him and when he made his attacks diagonally through the mountain area, then the lack of forces became alarmingly clear to the defense. Larger and larger losses in terrain resulted from it.[11]

Even the disposition of the forces employed to defend these flawed defensive works was critically faulty. Rather than defending the most important terrain feature in the entire *Army Group G* zone in a unified manner, General der Panzertruppen Balck inexplicably chose to defend the approaches to the Saverne Gap with elements of both the

First and *Nineteenth Armies*. As a result, when the attacks by VI and XV Corps ripped into the southern portion of the sector held by the northernmost *Nineteenth Army* division (the ill-fated *708th Volksgrenadier Division*), the actions of the *First Army*'s southernmost division (the tenacious *553d Volksgrenadier Division*) were coordinated only through circuitous and clumsy communications channels spanning hundreds of kilometers and three echelons of command. Recognizing this in the midst of the fray, Balck attempted to remedy the situation by placing the entire battle under the control of Wiese's *Nineteenth Army* headquarters, which was situated so far to the south as to be incapable of establishing communications with the beleaguered *553d* commander. The battle thus proceeded without effective higher echelon coordination—with predictable consequences for the defenders. If there was a decisive juncture in the battle for the High Vosges, this was it, and the German command bungled it.

The defense of the Maginot and Siegfried fortifications was never carried to its conclusion, so we may never be sure of the outcome of that aborted German defensive mission. Nevertheless, the fact that the Americans managed to penetrate the Ensemble de Bitche with casualties comparable to those suffered by the Germans during their failed effort in 1940 indicates that the Americans possessed the capability of penetrating exceptionally heavy fixed defenses in the face of German resistance.

Overall in the Vosges Mountains campaign, the Americans carried out their defensive and offensive operations in consonance with their doctrine. The Germans, on the other hand, handicapped by inadequate unit training and inappropriate organization, failed to heed their own rules for the conduct of the attack and defense, and consequently suffered defeat. Only in regard to the execution of delays can the elements of *Army Group G* be said to have adhered to their own rules, and in these efforts they were generally successful.

Final Thoughts

This study of the conquest of the Vosges Mountains during the period from mid-October 1944 to mid-January 1945 has shown that the U.S. Seventh Army prevailed even without the vaunted air support available to American units elsewhere in the European theater and without the benefit of significant numerical superiority in the most difficult terrain on the western front. Superior training, organization, and execution of doctrine account for this unprecedented success. A few thoughts regarding the means by which the Americans achieved these necessary advantages are in order.

The Germans began World War II as the acknowledged masters of tactical and operational innovation. Their combined-arms successes in Poland, the Low Countries, France, the Balkans, and even, initially, in Russia stunned conventional military theorists around the world and aroused choruses of "I told you so" from the advocates of combined-arms mobile warfare such as de Gaulle, Fuller, and Patton. Unfortunately for theorists from France and Great Britain, their countries' and armies' situations were such that the immediate demands of survival prevented them from adopting, much less improving on, the German way of war. The Americans, however, had time to watch, listen, and ponder the causes of the overwhelming German successes of 1939–1941.

Even after the disaster at Pearl Harbor jolted the United States into World War II, it was almost a year before American forces sallied forth, and on a small scale at that, to meet the Germans on the desert battlefields of North Africa. The initial results were hardly encouraging. However, because the nation was not being immediately threatened with extinction, the U.S. Army had time to learn from its failures, to adjust, and to fine-tune its training, organization, and doctrine. Despite pressure from the Soviets to open a second front as soon as possible, American political leaders heeded their British Allies' advice and bided their time until the U.S. Army could confront the Germans as equals on the Continent and beat them at their own game.

Hitler, on the other hand, having emasculated his military establishment's advisory capacity with oaths of personal loyalty (which came to mean pure sycophancy), conducted the Reich's campaigns with scant consideration for the impact of strategic exigencies on operations and tactics. As Wilhelm Deist pointed out, by the time of the Polish campaign, and certainly by the French campaign of 1940,

> The Wehrmacht had lost their once so carefully guarded independence in the area of operational planning, and never again fulfilled their task of pointing out planning precautions for potential conflict situations identified by the political leadership.[12]

Rigorous and thorough U.S. Army training, before and during combat, ensured that its soldiers would retain the will to fight under the fast-moving, arduous circumstances that the Germans had orchestrated to deprive most of their adversaries of theirs. The Blitzkrieg, after all, didn't seek the destruction of enemy forces as much as the disintegration of their will to resist, so this training was highly appropriate in its emphasis on the achievement of cohesion. Having badly miscalculated the duration and extent of the war, the Germans, in contrast to the Americans, actually provided worse training to their soldiers as the conflict progressed, due to their need to rapidly field ground formations after the disasters at Falaise and Argentan and in the east.

The U.S. Army's well-trained, integral, combined-arms formations had the potential to prevail in diverse circumstances, against almost any conceivable threat. As the threat to the Third Reich grew in intensity and proximity, the Wehrmacht fielded formations organized without the capability of successfully meeting the enemy threat even on numerically equal terms, in terrain of its own choosing.

A doctrine that encouraged and facilitated initiative and stressed the importance of maneuver down to the lowest levels ensured American units in the Vosges flexibility of response to even the most difficult situations. As German higher-level leaders lost confidence in their poorly performing field elements, they conversely stripped field commanders of their battlefield prerogatives and forced them into disastrously difficult situations. Lieutenant General Lucian Truscott, who commanded Americans in combat against the Germans from the earliest days in North Africa through Sicily, Italy, and the Vosges, summed it up this way:

> When American soldiers first came in contact with the German soldier, the latter was already a veteran with a long military tradition, the product of long and thorough military training, led by experienced and capable officers, and was equipped with the most modern weapons. The German was then better trained especially for operations in small units, and the quality of his leadership was superior. German soldiers displayed an ingenuity and resourcefulness more American than British. The American quickly adapted himself and learned much from the German. Sicily and southern Italy proved that he had mastered his les-

sons well. From Anzio on there was never a question of the superiority of American soldiers.[13]

Oberst Hans von Luck, who commanded units in combat against the French, Russians, and British before leading his *Panzergrenadiers* of the *125th Panzergrenadier Regiment* in the *21st Panzer Division* against Seventh Army soldiers in the Vosges, presented a congruent opinion regarding American forces:

> In one respect, they seemed to have the edge over their British allies: they were extraordinarily flexible; they adapted immediately to a changed situation and fought with great doggedness. . . . We discovered later, in Italy, and I personally in the battles in France in 1944, how quickly the Americans were able to evaluate their experience and, through flexible and unconventional conduct of a battle, convert it into results.[14]

He might have added that those results were obtained when the odds were even.

APPENDIX: EQUIVALENT RANKS

OFFICER

U.S. ARMY	GERMAN ARMY	WAFFEN SS
General of the Army	*Generalfeldmarschall*	*Reichsführer SS*
General	*Generaloberst*	*Oberstgruppenführer*
Lieutenant General	*General der Infanterie, General der Panzertruppen, etc.*	*Obergruppenführer*
Major General	*Generalleutnant*	*Gruppenführer*
Brigadier General	*Generalmajor*	*Brigadeführer*
No equivalent	*No equivalent*	*Oberführer*
Colonel	*Oberst*	*Standartenführer*
Lieutenant Colonel	*Oberstleutnant*	*Obersturmbannführer*
Major	*Major*	*Sturmbannführer*
Captain	*Hauptmann*	*Hauptsturmführer*
First Lieutenant	*Oberleutnant*	*Obersturmführer*
Second Lieutenant	*Leutnant*	*Untersturmführer*

ENLISTED

U.S. ARMY	GERMAN ARMY	WAFFEN SS
Master Sergeant/ First Sergeant	*Stabsfeldwebel*	*Sturmscharführer*
Technical Sergeant	*Oberfeldwebel*	*Hauptscharführer*
Staff Sergeant/ Technician 3d Grade	*Feldwebel*	*Oberscharführer*
Sergeant/ Technician 4th Grade	*Unterfeldwebel*	*Scharführer*
Corporal/ Technician 5th Grade	*Unteroffizier*	*Unterscharführer*
Private First Class	*Gefreiter/Obergefreiter*	*Rottenführer*
Private	*Soldat (Grenadier* in the infantry, *Kanonier* in the field artillery, etc.)	*SS Mann*

NOTES

INTRODUCTION

1. In this work, the term *doctrine* refers strictly to the maneuver aspects of American and German military policy. This differentiates it from the modern military professional's idea of doctrine, which includes an integrated approach combining training, organization, and equipment, as well as maneuver concepts.

The term *combat proficiency* in this work is defined as a combatant side's (or unit's) ability to accomplish combat missions in accordance with its own doctrinal requirements.

Tactical is the term used to describe actions taken to fight a battle, usually at the regimental (sometimes divisional) level and below. *Operational* is the term used in reference to actions taken to conduct a campaign, usually at the corps (sometimes divisional) through army group levels. *Strategic* describes actions at the theater, or warfighting, level.

2. Edward J. Filiberti, "Developing a Theory for Dynamic Campaign Planning" (Fort Leavenworth, Kans.: School of Advanced Military Studies, U.S. Army Command and General Staff College, 1988), 48.

3. Trevor N. Dupuy, *Numbers, Predictions and War* (Indianapolis: Bobbs Merrill, 1979), 37–39.

4. Martin van Creveld, *Fighting Power* (Westport, Conn.: Greenwood, 1982), 46.

5. Allan R. Millett and Williamson Murray, eds., *Military Effectiveness* (Boston: Unwin Hyman, 1988).

6. John F. Turner and Robert Jackson, *Destination Berchtesgaden* (London: Scribners, 1975).

7. Jeffrey J. Clarke and Robert Ross Smith, *Riviera to the Rhine* (Washington, D.C.: Center of Military History, 1993).

8. Russell F. Weigley, *Eisenhower's Lieutenants* (Bloomington: Indiana University Press, 1981), 356.

9. Lise Pommois, *Winter Storm* (Paducah, Ky.: Turner, 1991).

10. They are available there through coordination with the Bundesmilitärgeschichtliches Forschungsamt (Federal Military Historical

Research Bureau), which is in a completely different part of town (in the Old City, on the Grünwälderstrasse), but which has a courier service that makes several trips back and forth each week.

11. Francis Rittgen, *La Bataille de Bitche* (Sarreguemines: Pierron, 1984); *Operation Nordwind* (Sarreguemines: Pierron, 1982).

12. Roger Bruge, *On a Livré La Ligne Maginot* (Paris: Fayard, 1975).

CHAPTER 1

1. Robert D. Heinl, *Dictionary of Military and Naval Quotations* (Annapolis, Md.: Naval Institute, 1966), 198.

2. *Michelin Reiseführer: Elsass-Vogesen-Champagne* (Karlsruhe: Michelinreifenwerke, 1986), 16–18.

3. Ruth Putnam, *Alsace-Lorraine: From Caesar to Kaiser* (New York: Putnam, 1915), 16.

4. Ibid., 13–15.

5. Ibid., 20. Also based on extensive personal experience in the area and on studies of 1:50,000 scale topographic maps of the area, many of which clearly show the trace of various *voie ancienne romaine*.

6. Ibid.

7. Ibid., 33–34.

8. One can still see the remnants of the tide of Reformation as one drives through the Vosges; when villagers are asked why most of their neighbors in the village of Ober so-and-so are Protestant, whereas the majority of the inhabitants of the neighboring settlement of Nieder so-and-so are Catholic, one is likely to receive either a battle anecdote or a lecture on the effects of geography.

9. A short but comprehensive narrative history of this famous fortress may be found in A. Durlewanger, *Haut-Koenigsbourg* (Colmar: Imprimerie S.A.E.P., 1984).

10. Ramsay Weston Phipps, *The Armies of the First French Republic* (London: Oxford University Press, 1929), 89–90. Also see Jean Colin, *Campagne de 1793 en Alsace et dans le Palatinat* (Paris: Librairie Militaire R. Chapelot, 1902), for various notations on the fortunes of the garrison at Bitche, 360–553.

11. J. A. G. von Pflug-Harttung, *The Franco-German War,* trans. J. F. Maurice, C.B. (London: Swan-Sonnenschein, 1899), 102.

12. For one of the best and most detailed graphic depictions of the

Maginot fortifications, see the foldout map included in Bruge's *On a Livré La Ligne Maginot.*

13. Jean-Yves Mary, *La Ligne Maginot* (Cuneo, Italy: L'Instituto Grafico Bertello, 1980), 46–47.

14. Two types of machine guns were generally used in the casemates (and the other types of fortifications) of the Maginot Line: the 7.5mm Model 24/29 light machine gun, which had a maximum effective range of 600 meters and a cyclic rate of fire of 500 rounds per minute, and the MAC 31 medium machine gun, which accurately threw its 7.5mm bullets out to a distance of 1,200 meters at a rate of 750 per minute (ibid., 140). There were also two types of antitank gun in general use, both of them semiautomatic in function: The 47mm AC 47 Model 1934 fired a three-kilogram projectile to an effective range of 1,000 meters, where it had the force to carry through up to 60mm of steel armor, depending on the angle of impact; the less common 37mm AC 37 Model 1934 fired a two-kilogram round to the same range with the correspondingly weaker capability of penetrating up to 40mm of armor (ibid., 143). Both of these antitank weapons clearly had the ability to penetrate even the frontal armor of the most commonly deployed German tanks of 1940, namely the *Panzerkampfwagen* (*Pzkw*) Marks II and III. Only the 47mm gun would have been effective against the American M4 Sherman series of 1944, and even then only against the side or rear plates.

15. Mary, 51–52.

16. Noted during personal exploration of the *abris d'intervalle* of the Secteur Fortifie de Rohrbach in the vicinity of Petit Réderching, France, in March 1988.

17. Mary, 52.

18. Ibid., 55.

19. Bruge, 175–96.

20. The U.S. M4 Sherman series, on which practically all the American fighting vehicles used in the Vosges were based, could successfully negotiate a 60 percent slope; the German *Pzkw* Marks IV and V could manage 57 percent and 70 percent, respectively. See the U.S. Army Aberdeen Proving Grounds' *Tank Data* (Old Greenwich, Conn.: WE, 1969), 1:19, 55, 59.

21. Robert W. Stauffer, "Comparison of Metabolic Responses of Men and Women in Acute Load Bearing Situations" (West Point, N.Y.: Department of Physical Education, 1988), 1–4.

22. From an examination of the G2 weather reports of the U.S. 45th, 36th, and 100th Infantry Divisions during the periods indicated.

23. U.S. Army Infantry School, *Winning in the Cold: Leader's Guide to Winter Combat Readiness. ST 7-175* (Fort Benning, Ga.: U.S. Army Infantry School, 1982), 23.

24. Ascertained by examination of the October G2 journals of the U.S. 3d, 36th, 45th, and 79th Infantry Divisions, the principal combat units engaged during this period.

25. U.S. Army Infantry School, *ST 7-175*, 37.

26. Ibid., 59.

27. Seventh Army, *Report of Operations* (Heidelberg: Aloys Graef, 1946), 2:538–39.

28. Albert Speer, *Inside the Third Reich*, trans. Richard Winston and Clara Winston (New York: Macmillan, 1970), 482.

29. Seventh Army, *Report of Operations*, 2:362.

30. Michael A. Bass, *The Story of the Century* (New York: Century Association, 1946), 97.

CHAPTER 2

1. Heinl, 197.

2. Michael Howard, *Clausewitz* (Guernsey: The Guernsey Press, 1983), 59–61.

3. Michael Howard, "The Influence of Clausewitz," in Carl von Clausewitz's *On War*, trans. and ed. Michael Howard and Peter Paret (Princeton: Princeton University Press, 1984), 41.

4. Russell F. Weigley, *The American Way of War* (New York: Macmillan, 1973), 210.

5. Subsequent versions of the *Field Service Regulations*, beginning with the 1944 revision, were titled *Operations*.

6. Freiherr von Hammerstein-Equord, ed. *Oberkommando des Heeres, Die Truppenführung* (Berlin: Mittler und Sohn, 1936), 11.

7. Ibid., 12.

8. Carl von Clausewitz, *On War*, trans. and ed. Michael Howard and Peter Paret (Princeton: Princeton University Press, 1984), 524.

9. Ibid., 526.

10. Von Hammerstein-Equord, 38.

11. Von Clausewitz, 121.

12. Von Hammerstein-Equord, 47.

13. Ibid., 48.

14. U.S. War Department, *Handbook on German Military Forces* (Washington, D.C.: U.S. Government Printing Office, 1945; reprint, Baton Rouge: Louisiana State University Press, 1990), 211 (page reference is to reprint edition).

15. Von Clausewitz, 302.

16. Von Hammerstein-Equord, 58–61.

17. Von Clausewitz, 84.

18. For a discussion of the critical role of "Intelligence in War," see von Clausewitz, 117.

19. Von Hammerstein-Equord, 11.

20. Ibid., 14 (para. 80).

21. Ibid., 21.

22. "Ein Befehl soll alles das, aber nur das enthalten, was der Untergebene wissen muss, um seinen Auftrag selbständig erfüllen können. Dementsprechend muss der Befehl kurz und klar, bestimmt und vollständig, auch dem Verständnis des Empfängers und unter Umständen seiner Eigenart angepasst sein." (von Hammerstein-Equord, 22.)

23. Ibid., 11.

24. These five types of attacks are discussed in von Hammerstein-Equord, 119–27.

25. Von Clausewitz, 541.

26. Von Hammerstein-Equord, 119–36.

27. Both of these are discussed in U.S. War Department, *Handbook on German Military Forces,* 214–15.

28. Von Clausewitz, 295.

29. U.S. War Department, *Handbook on German Military Forces,* 217–28.

30. Ibid., 228.

31. Von Clausewitz, 264–68.

32. U.S. War Department, *Handbook on German Military Forces,* 217.

33. Ibid., 358.

34. Von Hammerstein-Equord, 186–87.

35. Ibid., 187–88.

36. Ibid., 188–94.

37. U.S War Department, *Handbook on German Military Forces,* 228.

38. Ibid., 255.

39. Von Clausewitz, 420.

40. U.S. War Department, *Handbook on German Military Forces,* 240–42.

41. Ibid., 90–92.

42. W. J. K. Davies, *German Army Handbook* (New York: Arco, 1974), 42–44.

43. John Keegan, *Waffen SS: The Asphalt Soldiers* (New York: Ballantine, 1970), 53.

44. Davies, 36. Also see U.S. War Department, *Handbook on German Military Forces,* 90–133.

45. The disgust registered by German army officers for the SS— and the corollary friction between army commanders and their SS counterparts—was typified by the sentiments of Oberstgeneral Johannes Blaskowitz. Blaskowitz was incensed with the conduct of the SS as early as the Polish campaign of 1939, and made his feelings known in clear terms to the Oberkommando des Heeres (OKH) staff. See Charles W. Sydnor, Jr., *Soldiers of Destruction* (Princeton: Princeton University Press, 1977), 43. Being all but ignored at this level only fanned the fires of this problem. Interestingly, Blaskowitz commanded *Army Group G* in the Low Vosges during Nordwind in January 1945; one of his subordinate corps included the *XIII SS!*

46. Davies, 62.

47. Speer, 467.

48. Ibid., 473–74. The author mentions this and illustrates it with the September 1944 example of a German *Panzer* brigade that had been nearly annihilated because of this problem.

49. Günther Blumentritt, "Ausbildungsmethoden und Manöver im Deutschen Heer," MS. P-200, U.S. Army Europe (USAREUR) Historical Series, 1954, National Archives, Washington, D.C., 33–40.

50. Hellmuth Reinhardt, "Training and Employment of NCO's [sic] and Privates in the German Army," MS. P-012, USAREUR Series, 1947, 12–13. See also Morris Janowitz and Edward Shils, "Cohesion and Disintegration in the Wehrmacht," *Public Opinion Quarterly* 12 (1948): 280–315. In this article, the authors prove, through extensive research conducted among German prisoners of war (PWs) during and after the war, that the cultural ties achieved through such policies was a major factor in the degree of cohesiveness attained by German units. Also, Janowitz and Shils found that the time spent in training together greatly enhanced officer/NCO and soldier confidence, and thus also contrib-

uted in this way to the resilience and cohesion of a given German unit. Those units lacking these recruitment and training-induced bonds were found to suffer higher casualties and to break more easily in combat.

51. Ibid., 21–24.

52. Exceptions to this rule included the *Hermann Göring Panzer Division*, which was generally a well-trained and cohesive unit that saw action in Sicily and Italy.

53. Keegan, 93–107.

54. *FM 100-5, Operations* (Washington, D.C.: U.S. Government Printing Office, 1944), 51. All subsequent citations will be from the 1944 edition, because its 15 June 1944 publication and distribution date make it chronologically appropriate for the Vosges campaign. The commanders and staffs of the combatant American units in the campaign were unquestionably initially trained using the 1941 version of the manual; however, most of the differences between the 1941 *FM 100-5* and the 1944 edition were published earlier as interim changes in September and November 1942 and in April 1943. The commanders and staffs of the units participating in the Vosges in late 1944 would certainly have been trained and schooled under the provisions incorporated in these changes.

55. Ibid., 52.

56. Ibid., 48–50.

57. Ibid., 48.

58. Ibid., 40. Interestingly, these words are identical to those in the 1941 version of the manual, appearing on page 31 of that document.

59. Ibid.

60. Ibid., 27. Again, when the units that ultimately conducted the Vosges campaign were being trained, the 1941 manual was still in effect, so its directions in this regard might be considered critical: The wording found on page 18 of the 1941 version is identical.

61. *FM 101-5, Staff Organization and Operations* (Washington, D.C.: U.S. Government Printing Office, 1941), 21–25.

62. *FM 100-5, Operations,* 110.

63. Ibid., 111.

64. Ibid., 110.

65. Ibid.

66. Ibid., 97 (para. 451).

67. Ibid., 99–103 (paras. 462–73).

68. Ibid., 99 (para. 462).

69. Ibid., 100 (para. 463).

70. Ibid., (para. 465).

71. Ibid., 101 (para. 468).

72. Ibid., 132–33 (paras. 580–86).

73. Ibid., 141-43 (paras. 610–18).

74. Ibid., 143–44 (paras. 616–18).

75. Ibid., 137 (para. 598).

76. Ibid., 145–46 (paras. 627–28).

77. Ibid., 155 (para. 663).

78. Ibid., 145 (para. 625).

79. Technically, there were five types of divisions, if one counts the 10th Mountain Division, a one-of-a-kind alpine unit that saw action late in the war in Italy, and the 1st, 2d, and 3d Armored Divisions, which retained the pre-1943 organization with armored, armored infantry, and armored field artillery regiments vs. combined-arms combat commands. All other U.S. divisions to be deployed to combat zones, including the 1st Cavalry Division, which was organized as an infantry division for overseas deployment, and the 80th Light Division, which was organized as a conventional infantry division by the time that it was deployed overseas, adhered to the standard three patterns. See Shelby Stanton, *Order of Battle: U.S. Army World War II* (Novato, Calif.: Presidio, 1984), 8–12, 17–19.

80. Ibid., 15, 31.

81. Ibid., 9–10.

82. An example of the close working relationship that was developed can be found in the regimental combat history of the 100th Infantry Division's 397th Infantry Regiment. It depicts "The Team" in a two-page cartoon, and represents the Combat Team 397 as a football team, with the infantry representing the linemen, the artillery battalion representing the quarterback ("Our passing star. Beautiful arm."), the supporting tank companies representing the offensive backfield, et cetera. See Samuel Finkelstein, ed., *The Regiment of the Century: The Story of the 397th Infantry Regiment* (Stuttgart: Union Drückerei, 1945), 66–67.

83. This system of creating and training AUS divisions is described in great detail in Robert Palmer, Bell Wiley, and William Keast, *The Procurement and Training of Ground Combat Troops* (Washington, D.C.: U.S. Government Printing Office, 1948), 429–94.

84. Palmer et al., 400–404.

85. Stanton, 4.

86. For example, 36th Infantry Division Training Memorandum 19, 15 October 1944, called for the division's infantry formations to practice prescribed defensive operations during periods of combat lull or while in reserve, in anticipation of defensive operations necessitated by an expected logistical shortfall. Record Group (RG) 407, Entry 427, Box 9847, National Archives, Suitland Reference Branch, Suitland, Md. (Hereafter cited as SRB.)

CHAPTER 3

1. Finkelstein, 72.

2. See Appendix for a table of equivalent U.S. Army, German army, and Waffen SS ranks.

3. Seventh Army, *G-2 History: 7th Army Operations in Europe*, Part II (Headquarters, Seventh Army, 1944), 14. Interestingly, the Germans admitted to far smaller losses. See Friedrich Ruge, *Entscheidungsschlachten des Zweiten Weltkrieges* (Frankfurt am Main: Bernard & Gräfe, 1960), 347. Given the state of *Nineteenth Army* before and after the retreat up the Rhône, the American claim is far more credible.

4. Seventh Army, *G-2 History* (Engineer Section), Part I, 15–31 August 1944, Annex III, 1. Also National Archives Captured German Documents Section (CGDS) file on Johannes Blaskowitz. (Subsequent references to these individual files will be cited as CGDS file.)

5. Seventh Army, *G-2 History*, Part III, 1–31 October 1944, Annex III, 1. Also CGDS file on Hermann Balck.

6. Weigley, *Eisenhower's Lieutenants*, 551, 580, 670.

7. Seventh Army Field Order Number 6, 29 September 1944, 1–2, included in Seventh Army, *Report of Operations*, 936–37.

8. Weigley, *Eisenhower's Lieutenants*, 236.

9. Lucian K. Truscott, Jr., *Command Missions* (New York: Dutton, 1954; Novato, Calif.: Presidio, 1990), 442.

10. Leo V. Bishop et al., eds., *The Fighting Forty-Fifth* (Baton Rouge: Army and Navy, 1946), 6.

11. Casualties in all three divisions during the Italian campaigns had been considerable. The 3d Infantry Division, for example, lost more than 2,200 killed and 9,200 wounded during this period; additionally, some 22,000 nonbattle casualties were sustained. However, more than

67 percent of the injured or sick were returned to their units by the middle of 1944. [See the tables in Donald Taggart, ed., *The History of the Third Infantry Division in World War II* (Washington, D.C.: Infantry Journal, 1947), 102, 150, 188.]

12. *The Cross of Lorraine: A Combat History of the 79th Infantry Division* (Baton Rouge: Army and Navy, 1946), 8–9.

13. Ibid., 74.

14. Stanton, 132.

15. Seventh Army Field Order 6, 1–2.

16. See VI Corps Operations Instructions 1, 11 October 1944, 1–2, included in Seventh Army, *Report of Operations,* 363–64.

17. Maurer Maurer, ed., *Air Force Combat Units of World War II* (Washington, D.C.: Office of Air Force History, 1983), 205, 450.

18. With eight .50-caliber machine guns and a bomb load of up to 1,500 pounds, the well-armored P-47 could both inflict and sustain considerable punishment. Its 428-MPH top speed also allowed it to be successful in dogfighting, although there was little of this to be done in the face of sparse Luftwaffe appearances during the period. However, it was, like nearly all fighters of the period, strictly a fair weather/daylight machine, without instruments allowing effective operations during low-visibility conditions. From John Batchelor and Bryan Cooper, *Fighter: A History of Fighter Aircraft* (New York: Scribners, 1973), 120, 125.

19. Strengths calculated from an examination of the morning reports for the line and heavy-weapons companies of the 3d, 36th, and 45th Infantry Divisions and the 442d Regimental Combat Team for 15 October 1944. Found on microfilm in the National Archives and Records Administration Annex (NARA), St. Louis, Mo., as follows:

3d Infantry Division
    7th Infantry Regiment: 1,805
    15th Infantry Regiment: 1,737
    30th Infantry Regiment: 1,631
36th Infantry Division
    141st Infantry Regiment: 1,580
    142d Infantry Regiment: 1,784
    143d Infantry Regiment: 1,623
45th Infantry Division

157th Infantry Regiment: 1,936
179th Infantry Regiment: 1,570
180th Infantry Regiment: 1,809
442d Regimental Combat Team: 2,220

20. Derived from Seventh Army G2 Estimate of the Enemy Situation 3, 30 September 1944, 2, RG 407, Entry 427, Box 2625, SRB; from Seventh Army, *G-2 History,* Annex I, 9; and from estimates cited in the notes regarding individual unit strengths below.

21. *"Anlagenmappe, Heeresgruppe G am 16.10.1944, abends," Bundesmilitärgeschichtliches Forschungsamt* (Federal Military Historical Research Bureau), Freiburg im Breisgau, Germany (Item 75141/10, Roll 142, Frame 7188134).

22. Gustav Höhne, "Report on the Reconnaissance and Construction of the Vosges Positions, 8 August to 15 October 1944," MS. B-043, USAREUR Series, 1950, 1–6. Also Hans Täglichsbeck, "LXIV Corps Defensive Construction (16 September 1944–25 February 1945)," MS. B-504, USAREUR Series, 1947, 2–5.

23. Täglichsbeck, 5–9.

24. Helmut Thumm, "Report on the Commitment of LXIV Corps in Alsace During the Period 28 September 1944 to 28 January 1945," MS. B-050, USAREUR Series, 1946, 4.

25. Based on the sketches provided by Generalmajor Täglichsbeck in his manuscript, the first and second Vosges defensive positions were about 10,000–20,000 meters apart.

26. Hans von Luck, *Panzer Commander* (New York: Dell, 1989), 167, 227. Feuchtinger was relieved of command of the *21st Panzer Division* on 25 January 1945 and was convicted by court-martial for dereliction of duty; he had been away from his post several times during the campaign in France, including during the fateful days of the Normandy invasion. He was saved from a firing squad by the intervention of Nazi party cronies.

27. Seventh Army, *G-2 History,* 1–31 October 1944, Annex I, 9. Unfortunately, the account of the division commander, Edgar Feuchtinger ("Report of Operations of the 21st Panzer Division Against American Troops in France and Germany, December 1949," MS. A-871, USAREUR Series, 1949, 3–28), is too jumbled to obtain an accurate account of infantry personnel strengths, although the information included does not deny the Seventh Army estimate.

28. Helmut Ritgen, taped interview in *The Great Crusade, Part II* (Grenada Television International, 1985).

29. Feuchtinger, 22.

30. Seventh Army, *G-2 History,* October 1944, Annex III, 3.

31. 3d Infantry Division G2 Periodic Report 79, 3 November 1944, RG 407, Entry 427, Box 3701, SRB, 7.

32. W. Victor Madej, *German Army Order of Battle* (Allentown, Pa.: Game Marketing Co., 1981), 2:25. This work is essentially a reprint of the 1945 edition of the U.S. War Department's *Order of Battle of the German Army.* Strength estimate from Seventh Army, *G-2 History,* 1–31 October 1944, Annex I, 9.

33. Annex C to 45th Infantry Division G2 Periodic Report 64, 18 October 1944, RG 407, Entry 427, Box 3697, SRB, 4.

34. Seventh Army G2 Interrogation Report 80, 15 October 1944, RG 407, Entry 427, Box 3696, SRB, 1.

35. CGDS file.

36. CGDS file.

37. Seventh Army, *G-2 History,* 1–31 October 1944, Annex I, 9.

38. 45th Infantry Division G2 Periodic Report 81, 4 November 1944, RG 407, Entry 427, Box 3701, SRB, 5. Annex I to 100th Infantry Division G2 Periodic Report 3, 12 November 1944, RG 407, Entry 427, Box 3702, SRB.

39. Seventh Army G2 Periodic Report: Interrogation Report 166, 9 November 1944, RG 407, Entry 427, Box 3702, SRB, 1–2.

40. 3d Infantry Division G2 Periodic Report 80, 4 November 1944, RG 407, Entry 427, Box 3701, SRB, 6.

41. CGDS file.

42. Kurt Schuster, "The LXIV Corps from August to November 1944," MS. A-885, USAREUR Series, 1946. Schuster claims that the *198th* was at close to full strength at the outset of the campaign in the Vosges. This number is based on authorized strength figures in *Handbook on German Military Forces,* 114–15.

43. Seventh Army G2 Periodic Report, 9 November 1944, RG 407, Entry 427, Box 3207, SRB, 1.

44. As quoted in Charles Whiting, *The Battle of Hurtgen Forest* (New York: Orion, 1989), 20.

45. Thumm, MS. B-050, 5.

46. CGDS file.

47. Schuster, 19.

48. There are two villages named Le Tholy in this immediate area: The Le Tholy in question is the more southerly of the two.

49. Barry Gregory and John Batchelor, *Airborne Warfare, 1918–1945* (New York: Exeter, 1979), 95.

50. The reason for von Courbiere's relief was indicated as *"wegen körperliche Versagens"* in a 29 November message from *Army Group G* to *OB West*. Included in *Heeresgruppe G Kriegstagebuch (Führungsabteilung) 1.11.–30.11.1944.*

51. The following fortress units were assigned to *IV Luftwaffe Field Corps: 40th, 1432d,* and *1433d Fortress Machine-gun Battalions; 308th* and *310th Superheavy Fortress Machine-gun Battalions;* and the *52d Machine-gun Battalion.* Such units were clearly well suited for defense. Strength figure from Seventh Army, *G-2 History,* 1–31 October 1944, Annex I, 9.

52. VI Corps G2 Periodic Report 70, 24 October 1944, RG 407, Entry 427, Box 3698, SRB.

53. Seventh Army, *G-2 History,* Part III, Annex III, 1.

54. Seventh Army, *Report of Operations,* 531.

55. From an examination of the 3d, 36th, and 45th Infantry Divisions' Division Artillery G3 Journals, 1–6 October 1944 (RG 407, Entry 427, Boxes 6161–6162, 9847–9848, 10945, respectively); also from the 36th and 45th Infantry Divisions' G3 Journals, 1–6 October 1944 (RG 407, Entry 427, Boxes 9847–9848 and 10945, respectively), SRB.

56. VI Corps Operations Memorandum 47, 29 September 1944, RG 407, Entry 427, Box 3792, SRB, 1.

57. Seventh Army, *Report of Operations,* 534.

58. VI Corps G2 Periodic Reports, 15–19 October 1944, RG 407, Entry 427, Boxes 3696 and 3697, SRB.

59. Noted personally while visiting Bruyères in March 1988.

60. 36th Infantry Division Operations Instructions, 12 October 1944, RG 407, Entry 427, Box 9848, SRB, 1–2.

61. 36th Infantry Division G3 Periodic Report, 15 October 1944, RG 407, Entry 427, Box 9847, SRB, 2. The battalions of the 442d Regimental Combat Team followed an unusual organization, consisting of the 2d and 3d Battalions and the formerly separate 100th Battalion.

62. Ibid., 2.

63. VI Corps G2 Periodic Reports, 15–19 October 1944.

64. Seventh Army, *Report of Operations,* 364.

65. Obvious from both a map study and a personal visit in March 1988.

66. VI Corps G2 Periodic Report, 15 October 1944.

67. Ernst Häckel, "The 16th Infantry Division, Part II: The Campaign in the Rhineland," MS. B-452, USAREUR Series, 1947, 11.

68. Chester Tanaka, *Go For Broke* (Richmond, Calif.: Go For Broke, Inc., 1982), 75–76.

69. Seventh Army, *Report of Operations*, 367.

70. Ibid., 369.

71. Ibid., 370–71.

72. Ibid., 371–72.

73. Häckel, 13. Identification of units from Taggart, 253, 256. Strength estimate of penal battalions from examples of those cited in Täglichsbeck, 12.

74. From entries for 26–31 October 1944 in the *Kriegstagebuch* of the *106th Panzer Brigade*, published by Friedrich Bruns, ed., in *Die Panzerbrigade 106 FHH: Eine Dokumentation über den Einsatz im Westen vom Juli 1944–Mai 1945* (published by the *Traditionsverband* of the *106th Panzer Brigade* and the *293d Panzer Battalion* of the Bundeswehr in Celle, 1988), 228–52. The Feldherrnhalle was the building in Munich where Hitler's attempted *putsch* with Ludendorff in 1923 was brought to an end by elements of the army loyal to the government. Ironically, this failure—at the hands of the *Reichswehr*—convinced Hitler that his next grab for power had to be made with the *support* of the army. The *106th Panzer Brigade* was officially named for this Nazi shrine at which Hitler's distrust and courtship of the army was born.

75. From examination of the company morning reports of the 7th and 15th Infantry Regiments for 28 October 1944 (NARA, St. Louis, Mo., Item 10439, Reel 13.90, and Item 10497, Reel 13.93, respectively).

76. Soldiers of the 7th Infantry Regiment were known as "Cottonbalers" in recognition of their regiment's stand behind bales of raw cotton in the face of overwhelming odds at the American victory at New Orleans in 1815.

77. German soldiers convicted of various crimes were sent to *zur besondere Verwendung* (zbV) battalions as a sort of purgatory where they could, through meritorious behavior, earn the right to be reinstated in conventional units. Obviously, the motivation for displaying exceptionally outstanding conduct in battle was high in such units.

78. Taggart, 258.

79. Seventh Army, *Report of Operations,* 387–88.

80. Nathan William White, *From Fedala to Berchtesgaden: A History of the Seventh United States Infantry in World War II* (Brockton, Mass.: Keystone Print, 1947), 177.

81. VI Corps figures from Seventh Army, *Report of Operations,* 373. Seventh Army total from *G-2 History* for the month of November 1944, 9.

82. Ibid., 1030–31. Exact figures include 1,073 killed, 4,782 wounded, and 606 missing.

83. *Oberkommando der Wehrmacht, Kriegstagebuch des Oberkommando der Wehrmacht,* Band IV: 1. Januar 1944–22. Mai 1945 (Frankfurt am Main: Bernard & Gräfe, 1961), 402–403.

84. Helmut Thumm, "Operation in the Central Vosges, 16 Nov–31 Dec 44," MS. B-468, USAREUR Series, 1947, 1.

85. Täglichsbeck, 10–14.

86. Seventh Army, *Report of Operations,* 392.

87. Josef Paul Krieger, "Fighting of the 708th 'VolksGrenadier-Division' in November 1944 at the Vosges Front," MS. B-451, USAREUR Series, 1947, 2.

88. VI Corps G2 Periodic Report 90, 13 November 1944, RG 407, Entry 427, Box 3703, SRB, 1; Seventh Army, *G-2 History,* Part IV, 1.

89. CGDS file.

90. Bass, 15–40.

91. Ralph Mueller and Jerry Turk, *Report After Action: The Story of the 103d Infantry Division* (Innsbrück: Wagnersche Universitäts-Buchdrückerei, 1945), 1–11.

92. Exactly, 23,445 to 8,225. American strength was calculated from an examination of the morning reports for the rifle and heavy-weapons companies of the 100th Infantry Division on 12 November (first day of their attack) and similar documents for the 3d, 36th, and 103d Infantry Divisions and 62d Armored Infantry Battalion for 21 November, the first day of the VI Corps main attack (NARA, St. Louis, Mo.): 397th Infantry, 2,080; 398th Infantry, 2,065; 399th Infantry, 2,038; 7th Infantry, 1,601; 15th Infantry, 1,658; 30th Infantry, 1,602; 141st Infantry, 1,884; 142d Infantry, 1,848; 143d Infantry, 1,862; 409th Infantry, 2,004; 410th Infantry, 2,027; 411th Infantry, 2,058; and the 62d Armored Infantry Battalion, 718. German strength totals from Seventh Army, *G-2 History,* 1–30 November 1944, Annex I, 1.

93. Although XII TAC was augmented in early November by the

320th Bombardment Group, equipped with four squadrons of Martin B-26 "Marauder" medium bombers to relieve the 64th Fighter Wing's P-47s of the interdiction role, there were no flyable days from 5 November to 18 November 1944. The assignment of the 320th Bombardment Group is documented in Maurer, 199–200. The information on the absence of suitable flying weather is gained from an examination of VI Corps G2 Periodic Reports, 5 November 1944 to 19 November 1944, RG 407, Entry 427, Boxes 3701–3704, SRB.

94. Thumm, MS. B-050, 7.

95. Seventh Army, *G-2 History,* 1–30 November 1944, Annex I, 1.

96. Ibid.

97. Calculated from examination of morning reports for the line and heavy-weapons companies of the 44th and 79th Infantry Divisions on 12 November 1944 (NARA, St. Louis, Mo.): 71st Infantry, 2,067; 114th Infantry, 2,089; 324th Infantry, 2,065; 313th Infantry, 1,971; 314th Infantry, 1,973; and the 315th Infantry, 1,851.

98. Confirmed by Walter Botsch, "Nineteenth Army. Combat Operations of Nineteenth Army in the Forward Defense Zone of the Vosges, in the Vosges Mountains, and the Alsace Bridgehead," MS. B-263, USAREUR Series, 1950, 1.

99. Seventh Army, *Report of Operations,* 398.

100. Ibid., 403.

101. VI Corps Field Order 7, 7 November 1944, RG 407, Entry 427, Box 3980, SRB, 1–3.

102. Taggart, 263.

103. Thumm, MS. B-468, 2.

104. Thumm specifically stated that low morale and an absence of "faith in the future" worried him more than the tactical situation. See MS. B-050, 7.

105. Inclosure 2 to VI Corps G2 Periodic Report 89, 12 November 1944, RG 407, Entry 427, Box 3702, SRB, 1.

106. Janowitz and Shils, 282.

107. Janowitz and Shils found this to be true in German units possessing heterogeneity from multiple theaters from 1943 onward (285).

108. Ibid., 288.

109. Inclosure 2 to VI Corps G2 Periodic Report 89, 12 November 1944, 1.

110. Thumm, MS. B-050, 7.

111. Janowitz and Shils, 293.

112. Mueller and Turk, 34.

113. From an examination of the morning reports of the 15th Infantry Regiment, 31 October 1944 (NARA, St. Louis, Mo.).

114. From an examination of the morning reports of the 141st Infantry Regiment, 31 October 1944 (NARA, St. Louis, Mo.).

115. From an examination of the morning reports of the 442d Infantry Regiment, 31 October 1944 (NARA, St. Louis, Mo.). The "Go for Broke" Regiment, which eventually garnered more decorations for individual bravery than any other regiment in the U.S. Army during World War II, was withdrawn and sent to the south of France to refit after this operation. It never returned to the Vosges, being sent instead to reinforce the broken 92d Infantry Division in Italy in the spring of 1945.

116. Exceptions included "Fair" for Company I, 143d Infantry (36th Infantry Division), 12 November 1944, and "Low-Hiked all night" for Company E, 15th Infantry (3d Infantry Division), 25 October 1944 (NARA, St. Louis, Mo.).

117. Finkelstein, 109–10.

118. Ibid., 109.

119. Based on an examination of the morning reports for all Seventh Army infantry companies during the campaign in the High Vosges.

120. Seventh Army, *Report of Operations,* 1029.

121. Seventh Army, *G-2 History,* November 1944, 8.

122. VI Corps Field Order 7, 7 November 1944, 1.

123. 36th Infantry Division Training Memorandum 19 prescribed training to be conducted by battalions in reserve or during rest periods. The stated purposes included the integration of replacements as well as the training of veteran soldiers in neglected skills, such as the establishment of defensive positions.

124. From an examination of the morning reports of the 1st and 2d Battalions of the 397th Infantry and 1st (minus Company B) and 2d Battalions of the 399th Infantry Regiments for 12 November 1944 (NARA, St. Louis, Mo.). German strength for elements of the *708th Volksgrenadier Division*'s organic regiments and attached elements of the *951st* from note 87 and strength of the *1417th Fortress Machinegun Battalion* from Bass, 55.

125. Finkelstein, 80.

126. Technically, this was not the 399th Infantry Regiment's bap-

tism of fire, because it had been briefly attached to the 3d Infantry Division from 3–8 November during the final approach to the Meurthe. It did not, however, take part in the heavy fighting around Le Haut Jacques.

127. Krieger, 5–6, regarding the botched relief of the *21st Panzer Division;* Frank Gurley, ed., *399th in Action* with the 100th Infantry Division (Stuttgart: Stuttgarter Vereinsbuchdrückerei, 1945), 41; Finkelstein, 80; and Bass, 60–61, regarding the German counterattacks.

128. Krieger, 4.

129. Ibid., 8.

130. Botsch, 6.

131. Thumm, MS. B-468, 3. Also recognized in Thumm, MS. B-050, 11.

132. Friedrich-Wilhelm von Mellenthin, "Defensive Battles of the 1st Army in the Bitche Area, Beginning of December 1944," sworn statement while in captivity in Allendorf, July 1946, cited in Bass, 111.

133. American strength calculated from an examination of the 314th and 315th Infantry Regiments' morning reports for 12 November (NARA, St. Louis, Mo.): 314th, 1,973; 315th, 1,851. German strength estimated from Seventh Army, *G-2 History,* November 1944, Annex I, 1.

134. *Cross of Lorraine,* 83.

135. Friedrich-Wilhelm von Mellenthin, "Army Group G (8–16 November 1944)," MS. A-000, USAREUR Series, 1947, 64.

136. Ibid., 70.

137. Krieger, 13.

138. Von Mellenthin, MS. A-000, 70.

139. Thumm, MS. B-468, 3; Botsch, 16.

140. Hans Bruhn, "Engagements of the 553d Volksgrenadier Division in November 1944 on the Vosges Front," MS. B-379, USAREUR Series, 1947, 22.

141. Botsch, 6.

142. Botsch, 16; Bruhn, 22.

143. Seventh Army, *Report of Operations,* 407–11.

144. Ibid., 428.

145. Taggart, 268–69.

146. Gurley, observing the XII TAC efforts in the 100th Infantry Division's zone on the same day, described the close air support as follows, "The Air Corps had bragged that given two days of flying

weather they would knock the Germans out of the war . . . The Infantry [*sic*] watched hopefully, and were unimpressed." (Gurley, 44.)

147. White, 181.

148. Mueller and Turk, 30.

149. Ibid.

150. Seventh Army, *Report of Operations,* 431–32.

151. Task Force Whirlwind consisted of the divisional mechanized cavalry troop (minus one platoon), a platoon of light tanks (M5 Stuarts from the 756th Tank Battalion) and a company (minus one five-tank platoon) of medium tanks (M4 Shermans, also of the 756th), a platoon of tank destroyers (M10 Wolverines of the 601st Tank Destroyer Battalion), a platoon from the divisional engineer battalion (from Company B, 10th Armored Engineers), a battery of six self-propelled 105mm howitzers (M7 Priests of the supporting 93d Armored Field Artillery Battalion) and the 1st Battalion, 15th Infantry Regiment, in twenty-five two-and-a-half-ton trucks (Taggart, 270–71).

152. Task Force Fooks was organized almost identically to Task Force Whirlwind, and consisted of the divisional mechanized cavalry troop, a company of medium tanks (M4s from the 753d Tank Battalion), a platoon of tank destroyers (M10s from the 636th Tank Destroyer Battalion), a platoon from the divisional engineer battalion (from Company B, 325th Engineers), a battery of six self-propelled 105mm howitzers (M7s of the supporting 69th Armored Field Artillery Battalion), and the 2d Battalion, 398th Infantry Regiment, borne in two half-ton trucks (Bass, 68).

153. Seventh Army, *Report of Operations,* 441.

154. White, 182.

155. Ibid., 182–83.

156. Computed from an examination of the 7th Infantry Regiment's morning reports for 21–23 November 1944 (NARA, St. Louis, Mo.).

157. White, 184.

158. Ibid., 186–87.

159. Bass, 68–69.

160. Seventh Army, *Report of Operations,* 442–43; Mueller and Turk, 33–34.

161. Mueller and Turk, 35–36.

162. William Alpern, Greens Farms, Conn., interview with author, 6 October 1992.

163. Thumm, MS. B-050, 12.

164. *The Fighting 36th* (Nashville: Battery, 1979), 47.
165. Häckel, 23–24.
166. Thumm, MS. B-050, 13.
167. Thumm, MS. B-468, 16.
168. VI Corps G3 Periodic Report 105, 28 November 1944, RG 407, Entry 427, Box 4848, SRB, 1.

CHAPTER 4

1. Friedrich-Wilhelm von Mellenthin, "*Army Group G* (16 November to 3 December 1944)," MS. B-078, USAREUR Series, 1946, 97–98.
2. Thomas J. Howard, et al., *The 106th Cavalry Group in Europe 1944–1945* (Augsburg: Himmer, 1945), 74–82.
3. David Bishop et al., *"Mission Accomplished": The Combat History of the 44th Infantry Division* (Atlanta: Albert Love, 1946).
4. Seventh Army, *Report of Operations,* 419–20. Also Weigley, *Eisenhower's Lieutenants,* 407–408. Weigley is in error regarding the disposition of American forces and the composition of German units.
5. Seventh Army Field Order 7, 2 December 1944, in Seventh Army, *Report of Operations,* 938–39.
6. Kurt Reschke, "Defensive Combat of LXXXIX Inf Corps in the Lower Alsace and in the Westwall from 6 to 31 December 1944," MS. C-003, USAREUR Series, 1948, 6–7.
7. During the last week of November, the divisions on the left, or eastern, flank of *First Army* were controlled by a provisional headquarters known as *"Höhe Kommando Vogesen"*; von und zu Gilsa's *LXXXIX Corps* headquarters at Saverne had been nearly overrun during the XV Corps attack. *LXXXIX Corps* headquarters was back in action near Bitche by 1 December. (*Army Group G* situation maps for 26 November and 1 December 1944.)
8. Von Mellenthin, MS. B-078, 101.
9. Seventh Army, *G-2 History,* 1–31 December 1944, Annex III, 2.
10. Reschke, MS. C-003, 5.
11. CGDS file.
12. Alfred Philippi, "361st Volksgrenadier Division (31 August–16 December 1944)," MS. B-626, USAREUR Series, 1947, 4.
13. Ibid., 6.
14. Ibid., 8.

15. Reschke, MS. C-003, 75. This estimate agrees exactly with Seventh Army intelligence estimates in the Seventh Army, *G-2 History,* Part IV, 1–31 December 1944, Annex II, 1.

16. Reschke, MS. C-003, 75.

17. From a chart called "*Übersicht eigener Kräftegliederung, St. 18.12.44.*" in *Heeresgruppe G Kriegstagebuch 3b (Führungsabteilung), 1.12–31.12.1944.* Again, this matches very closely the Seventh Army G2 estimate of 2,300 for 31 December 1944 found in Seventh Army, *G-2 History,* 1–31 December 1944, Annex II, 1.

18. Based on the estimate of 60 percent strength in the *245th Infantry Division*'s infantry units at the outset of the campaign, provided by Reschke, 77. (Authorized total infantry strength for a 1944 Infantry Division would have amounted to 4,417 in the rifle and heavy-weapons companies of its six infantry battalions and divisional *Füsilier* battalion, according to the *Handbook on German Military Forces,* 93, Figure 9, and 114, Figures 33–37.) The nationalities of the prisoners are from an intelligence estimate in Mueller and Turk, 42–43.

19. Reschke, MS. C-003, 77.

20. Ibid., 78.

21. Max Simon, "Report on the Rhineland and Southern Germany Campaign," MS. B-487, USAREUR Series, 1947, 4.

22. Seventh Army, *G-2 History,* 1–31 December 1944, Annex III, 2. Also, numerous details regarding Simon's background from Sydnor, 49–50, 160, 275, 317.

23. Sydnor, 239–41, 244, 247, 252–53.

24. From Petersen's estimate of 35 percent strength in "XC Infantry Corps (18 September 1944 to 23 March 1945)," MS. B-071, USAREUR Series, 1946, 17. Full strength of rifle and heavy-weapons companies from *Handbook on German Military Forces,* Figure 63, 126; Figure 65, 127; Figure 71, 129; and Figure 90, 137.

25. Simon, 6.

26. CGDS file.

27. From Simon's estimate on the number of tanks and an estimate of about 60 percent strength in MS. B-487, 5, in conjunction with tables of organization in *Handbook on German Military Forces* (Figures 63 and 64, 126; Figure 65, 127; Figure 69, 128; Figure 71, 129; and Figure 21, 104), giving a full strength in the two *Panzergrenadier* regiments' rifle and heavy-weapons companies of 2,792.

28. Seventh Army Field Order 7, 2, in Seventh Army, *Report of Operations,* 939.

29. Ibid.

30. Thomas Howard, 84–85.

31. Bernard Boston, ed., *History of the 398th Infantry Regiment in World War II* (Washington, D.C.: Infantry Journal, 1947), 49; Bass, 73–74; Philippi, MS. B-626, 60.

32. Unit identification from *Up from Marseilles: History of the 781st Tank Battalion* (Nashville: Benson, 1945), 9; account of the action at Lemberg in Gurley, 61.

33. Philippi, MS. B626, 63.

34. Bass, 76–80; Gurley, 57–63; and Philippi, MS. B-626, 62–63. Loss figures are derived from an examination of 399th Infantry Regiment morning reports for the period of the battle for Lemberg, 7–10 December 1944 (NARA, St. Louis, Mo.).

35. Joseph S. Hasson, *With the 114th in the ETO: A Combat History* (Baton Rouge: Army and Navy, 1946), 42–46.

36. Ibid., 33–60. The author, who took part in the engagement, provides a particularly intense, graphic description of the battle for Enchenberg in this section of the regimental history.

37. Mary, 267.

38. Noted personally during visits in November 1984 and March 1988. In many ways, time has stood still in this corner of France. All of the fortifications still exist, including the barbed wire, and clear traces of field fortifications are evident. Many houses still bear the scars of the fighting, and, according to the inhabitants of the area, farmers tending the fields in the vicinity were occasionally injured or killed by mines (French, German, and American) well into the 1970s. There are few places in Western Europe where a battle can be reconstructed in the historian's mind without a fair amount of interpretation, but the area bordered by Achen in the west, the Hagenau-Sarreguemines road in the south, Wissembourg in the east, and the French-German frontier in the north is as close to unaltered as one could hope to find.

39. Temporary boundary changes indicated on 44th Infantry Division Situation Overlay, Inclosure to G3 Periodic Report 51, 7 December 1944.

40. Bruge, 175–96. Between 15 and 19 June 1940, the *262d Infantry Division* was one of nine infantry divisions of General Ritter von Leeb's *Army Group C,* which penetrated the Secteur Fortifie de la Sarre.

Theissen's division surrounded the *petit ouvrages* Haut-Poirier and Welschoff and, ironically, destroyed them with concentrated artillery fire *from the south,* the same direction from which Allen's 12th Armored Division attacked four and a half years later!

41. The 12th Armored Division did not close on Le Havre from ports in England until 17 November. It arrived in Lunéville on 2 December after a three-hundred-mile motor march from the coast. See *A History of the United States Twelfth Armored Division* (Baton Rouge: Army and Navy, 1947), 24–25.

42. These task forces, all under the control of Combat Command A, consisted of the 23d Tank Battalion with elements of the 17th Armored Infantry Battalion, 43d Tank Battalion and the entire 66th Armored Infantry Battalion, and the 714th Tank Battalion and Company C, 56th Armored Infantry Battalion. Ibid., 28.

43. Ibid., 27–29.

44. Philippi, MS. B-626, 63–64; Petersen, MS. B-071, 18; Reschke, MS. C-003, 12.

45. Seventh Army, *Report of Operations,* 465. The youngest division commander in the U.S. Army was Maj. Gen. James M. Gavin, commander of the 82d Airborne Division. Gavin was eight days younger than Frederick. See *1990 Register of Graduates* (West Point, N.Y.: USMA Association of Graduates, 1990), 397, 402.

46. Gerard M. Devlin, *Paratrooper!* (New York: St. Martin's, 1979), 439–40.

47. German strength figures from Reschke, MS. C-003, 77. Attachment of armored units in Reschke, 11–12. Method for computing *245th Infantry Division*'s strength from note 18 above. American strength figures for the total soldiers in the rifle and heavy-weapons companies of the 179th and 180th Regiments are from these units' morning reports for 1 December 1944 (NARA, St. Louis, Mo.).

48. German strength derived from Philippi's statement that *952d Volksgrenadier Regiment* in that sector controlled the remaining battalion of the *951st Volksgrenadier Regiment* and its own *2d Battalion* in MS. B-626, 56. Reschke estimates the strengths of these units in MS. C-003, 75.

49. Finkelstein, 113–14.

50. Reschke, MS. C-003, 13.

51. Mueller and Turk, 40; Seventh Army, *Report of Operations,* 466.

52. Warren P. Munsell, Jr., *The Story of a Regiment: A History of the 179th Regimental Combat Team* (San Angelo, Tex.: Newsfoto, 1946), 99.

53. Reschke, MS. C-003, 22–27.

54. Ibid., 29.

55. Ibid., 29, 51.

56. Ibid. 25–30; Seventh Army, *Report of Operations,* 463–67, 474–76; Mueller and Turk, 47–50.

57. *Tank Data,* 1:93.

58. Reschke, MS. C-003, 34–39.

59. Mueller and Turk, map between 56 and 57.

60. Ibid., 48.

61. Finkelstein, 115.

62. Keith Winston, *V-Mail: Letters of a World War II Combat Medic* (Chapel Hill, N.C.: Algonquin, 1985), 140. Winston's letters are striking for their candor; other than downplaying his wounds for his family's peace of mind, at no time in his letters from March 1944 to November 1945 does this thirty-two-year-old private first class attempt to conceal his feelings or those of his comrades. Whether positive or negative regarding the war, the army, individuals in the unit, et cetera, his letters are extremely frank.

63. From December 1944 company morning reports of the following infantry regiments' line and heavy-weapons companies (NARA, St. Louis, Mo.): 71st, 114th, 324th, 397th, 398th, 399th, 157th, 179th, 180th, 409th, 410th, and 411th.

64. Examination of the morning reports for the battalion heavy-weapons companies and regimental cannon and antitank companies of all American units committed in the Vosges reveals not one to be below 90 percent strength on 16 December.

65. For a description of the efforts to strengthen the infantry battalions by stripping rear echelon units, see Philippi, MS. B-626, 60–62. Strength estimate from Philippi, "Attack by 361 Volksgrenadier Division in Northern Alsace," MS. B-428, USAREUR Series, 1947, 5.

66. "*Übersicht eigener Kräeftgliederung (Statt von 18.12.44)*" in *Heeresgruppe G kriegstagebuch 3b 1.12.-31.12.44.*

67. Petersen, MS. B-071, 19.

68. Actual strength from "*Übersicht eigener Kräftegliederung (Statt von 18.12.44)*." Authorized strength from *Handbook on German Military Forces,* derived from the same figures as in note 66 above.

69. Reschke, MS. C-003, 60–63.

70. Ibid., 52.

71. Petersen, MS. B-071, 16.

72. Bruge, 205–11.

73. As hard as this may be to believe, it is documented in Bass, 82; Boston, 61; and Bishop, 194. Additionally, the author visited both fortresses in March 1988, through the courtesy of Lt. Col. Daniel Lierville, then the French army exchange officer to the USMA, West Point, and verified the absence of penetrations on the battered outer faces of Simserhof and Schiesseck.

74. Bass, 82–94; and Boston, 55–62. Also, from a September 1986 interview with Lt. Col. (Ret.) John J. Upchurch, who commanded Company B, 325th Engineer Battalion, in this battle.

75. David Bishop, 194–95.

76. By comparing the 71st Infantry Regiment's morning reports from 14–20 December with those of the 398th Infantry Regiment of the same period and allowing for comparable casualties among the supporting engineers, the 71st lost at most ten more men than the 398th.

77. Ironically, in the zone occupied by the men of the 398th Infantry Regiment, just across a dirt road to the east of Schiesseck, was a blue and white monument to the Bavarians who died in the failed German attempt on Bitche in 1870. (Noted during a visit to the area in March 1988.)

78. Noted during a visit to the area in March 1988.

79. Bruge, 109–11.

80. Mueller and Turk, 48.

81. Ibid., 54.

82. Reschke, MS. C-003, 57–58.

83. Mueller and Turk, 54.

84. Reschke, MS. C-003, 71.

85. Seventh Army, *Report of Operations,* 940.

86. Mueller and Turk, 57.

87. Thomas Howard, 86.

88. Bell I. Wiley, "The Building and Training of Infantry Divisions," in Palmer et al., *Procurement and Training of Ground Combat Troops,* 472–73.

89. Seventh Army, *Report of Operations,* 496.

90. David Bishop, 202, 270.

91. Bass, situation overlay, 106.

92. Ibid., 97.

93. Joseph Carter, *The History of the 14th Armored Division* (Atlanta: Albert Love, 1946), 88. Interestingly, the only major motion picture ever made about the Nordwind counteroffensive, *Armored Command,* centered on a slightly fictionalized version of the role of Task Force Hudelson.

94. Munsell, 103.

95. *History of the 157th Infantry Regiment (Rifle) (4 June 43 to 8 May 45)* (Baton Rouge: Army and Navy, 1946), 129.

96. Carter, 92.

97. Seventh Army, *Report of Operations,* 495–96.

98. Munsell, 103.

99. Wiley, 466.

100. Ibid., 472–73.

101. Ibid., Table 4, between pages 480 and 481.

102. Photoreconnaissance results in Seventh Army, *Report of Operations,* 498. ULTRA intelligence in F. W. Winterbotham, *The ULTRA Secret* (New York: Harper and Row, 1974), 180–81.

103. Seventh Army G2 Estimate of the Enemy Situation 6, 29 December 1944, RG 407, Entry 427, Box 4761, SRB, 1.

104. Ibid., 1–3.

105. XV Corps Operating Instructions 77, 28 December 1944, RG 407, Entry 427, Box 4761, SRB.

106. From the 31 December 1944 or 1 January 1945 company morning reports of the line and heavy-weapons companies of the following units (NARA, St. Louis, Mo.): 71st Infantry Regiment, 114th Infantry Regiment, 324th Infantry Regiment, 253d Infantry Regiment, 397th Infantry Regiment, 398th Infantry Regiment, 399th Infantry Regiment, 255th Infantry Regiment, 157th Infantry Regiment, 179th Infantry Regiment, 180th Infantry Regiment, 275th Infantry Regiment, 141st Infantry Regiment, 142d Infantry Regiment, 143d Infantry Regiment, 19th Armored Infantry Battalion, 62d Armored Infantry Battalion, 17th Armored Infantry Battalion, 56th Armored Infantry Battalion, and the 66th Armored Infantry Battalion.

107. Captain Howard Trammell, as quoted in Carter (first page of Chapter VIII).

108. Albert Emmerich, "First Army (20 December 1944–10 February 1945)," MS. B-786, USAREUR Series, 1947, 1.

109. Ibid.

110. Memorandum from the chief of staff, *Army Group G*, "*Gedachter Verlauf der Angriffsoperation der H.Gr. G gegen das Unterelsass,*" 24 December 1944, 3, in *Heeresgruppe G Kriegstagebuch 3b, 1.12.44–31.12.1944.*

111. Horst Wilutzsky, "The Offensive of Army Group G in Northern Alsace in January 1945," MS. B-095, USAREUR Series, 1947, 11–19. (The author was the *Army Group G* operations officer at the time of Nordwind.)

112. Ibid., 14.

113. In MS. B-095, Wilutzsky insists that the tank destroyers, flamethrowers, and *five* infantry divisions were originally allotted to the main attack, but the *Army Group G* warning order (*Gedachter Verlauf*) of 24 December 1944, retained in *Heeresgruppe G Kriegstagebuch 3b* proves him wrong; so does the entry in the *Kriegstagebuch* at 2340 on 23 December 1944. The figures cited in the text of the present work reflect the order of battle specified in the warning order and the *Kriegstagebuch.*

114. These routes were driven by the author in a Range Rover with four-wheel drive during the snow and sleet storm that hit the area in March 1988. In daylight, with no one shooting at him, it was an extremely difficult, tedious, and slow journey.

115. Wilutzsky states that this decision forced *Army Group G* to allot to the supporting attack the assault guns and heavy tank destroyers which they had planned to use to weight the main attack through the Vosges, thus diluting the main effort. Again, the *Army Group G* warning order of 24 December proves him wrong, since these assets were already allocated to the supporting attack. Wilutzsky is attempting to blame the Führer's changes for the failure of Nordwind, but the original plan actually already included the flaws attributed to Hitler.

116. Wilutzsky, 18.

117. Emmerich, 5.

118. Emmerich, 7, states the *653d Heavy Tank Destroyer Battalion* possessed *Jagdtigers,* the tank destroyer version of the famed *Königstiger* tank. The photo on page 568 in Seventh Army, *Report of Operations,*

confirms this. The *Jagdtiger* was the heaviest armored vehicle employed in combat in World War II (seventy-nine tons) and possessed the thickest frontal armor as well (250mm). Only with the 90mm guns carried by the 776th Tank Destroyer Battalion's M36 Sluggers could American tankers hope to engage it successfully from the front, and even then from perilously close range. This, however, presented another dilemma, as the *Jagdtiger* carried a 128mm main gun capable of destroying any armored vehicle in the Seventh Army's inventory at ranges from five hundred to a thousand meters greater than they could engage it. Fortunately for the Americans, antitank mines were effective against its tracks, and because the *Jagdtiger* had no revolving turret, once it was immobilized by a mine, it could be safely—and effectively—engaged from the side or rear. (See *Tank Data,* 1:107.) The self-propelled flamethrowers were modified *Hetzers,* based on a photo in Hasson, 83.

119. *XIII SS Corps* mission specified in the *Army Group G* Operation Order to *First Army* of 25 December 1944, 2345 hours, included in *Heeresgruppe G Kriegstagebuch 3b.*

120. Wilutzsky, 15.

121. Strength of the line and heavy-weapons companies of an *SS Panzergrenadier Regiment* from *Handbook on German Military Forces,* Figure 76, page 130, Figure 65, page 127, and Figure 71, page 129. Other organizational details in Figure 18, page 100. Unusual organization and strength of *Panzer* battalion in Emmerich, 7, and confirmed in Wilutzsky, 18.

122. Simon, 3; Kurt Hold, "The Winter Battles in the Vosges," MS. B-767, USAREUR Series, 1948, 16.

123. Seventh Army, *G-2 History,* 1–31 December 1944, Annex III, 4.

124. All objectives for the divisions in Nordwind are taken from *"Anlagenmappe Karten Nr. 30, Planung Heeresgruppe G Unternehmen Nordwind, 28.12.44"* in *Heeresgruppe G Kriegstagebuch 3b.*

125. Emmerich, 8.

126. CGDS file.

127. From *"Übersicht eigener Kräftegliederung,"* 18 December 1944, and assuming few, if any, casualties between then and the commencement of Nordwind thirteen days later, due to the light nature of combat during the period.

128. The Seventh Army, *G-2 History,* indicates this strength, and it is probably about right, because the *"Übersicht eigener Kräftegliederung"*

as of 18 December indicates about 1,300 before the pre-Nordwind reinforcement by replacements.

129. Ibid., 1–31 December 1944, Annex III, 4.

130. *Army Group G* Operation Order, 25 December 1944.

131. CGDS file.

132. Freiherr Kurt von der Mühlen, "Report Concerning the Participation of the 559th Volksgrenadier Division in Operation 'Nordwind'," MS. B-429, USAREUR Series, 1947, 2–6.

133. Assumes von der Mühlen's "nearly full strength" estimate to mean 95 percent. Total troops from the authorized strengths of the infantry line and heavy-weapons companies of a *Volksgrenadier* division with only two double-battalion regiments provided in tables in *Handbook on German Military Forces,* 117–18. Authorized strength of the divisional *Füsilier* company from same source, 97.

134. Von der Mühlen, 6.

135. Ibid., 4.

136. Ernst Linke, "Participation by the 257th Volksgrenadier Division in the Offensive Operation 'Nordwind'," MS. B-520, USAREUR Series, 1947, 4–5.

137. Ibid., 3–6.

138. Estimate of fighting strength from Linke, 8. Interpreting this as 95 percent, and using the authorized strength as compiled in note 18.

139. Philippi, MS. B-428, 5–12.

140. Ibid., 5.

141. Ibid., 6.

142. Estimate of 40 percent of authorized strength and addition of one 250-man *Marschbattalion* in Bernhard Kögel, "Offensive Operations of the 256th Volksgrenadier Division in Northern Alsace, during January 1945 (Operation 'Nordwind')," MS. B-537, USAREUR Series, 1947, 5, 6, 12. Authorized strength from same source and method in note 18, but computed for a division with all six infantry battalions.

143. Ibid., 4.

144. Personal data on Franz from his CGDS file. Training technique from Kögel, 10.

145. Kögel, 12.

146. Ibid., 11.

147. Ibid., 12.

148. Ibid., 9.

149. Seventh Army, *G-2 History*, 1–31 January 1945, Annex VII, 3.

150. Karl Brenner, "The 6th SS-Mountain Division 'Nord' and Its Part in Operation 'Nordwind,' Northern Alsace, 1 January to 25 January 1945," MS. B-476, USAREUR Series, 1947, 2–5.

151. Brenner says that *Nord* was at full strength for Nordwind. (Brenner, 5) Full infantry strength meant 6,781 (6,130 in the combat companies of the *two infantry regiments and division recon battalion, and 651 in the combat companies 506th SS Panzer Grenadier Battalion*), based on *Handbook on German Military Forces*, 98, 123, and 127. In January, 1996 correspondence to the author, Wolf Zoepf, adjutant of the *3d Battalion, 12th SS Mountain Regiment* in Nordwind, insists that *Nord* was actually at about 90% strength at the outset of Nordwind; hence 6, 102.

152. *21st Panzer Division*'s total from Feuchtinger, 48, although Seventh Army, *G-2 History*, places the figure 50 percent higher. *25th Panzergrenadier Division*'s total from Seventh Army, *G-2 History*, 1–31 January 1944, Annex I, 1.

153. Taken from the 1 January 1945 morning reports for the line and heavy-weapons companies (as appropriate) of the 62d Armored Infantry Battalion, the infantry component of Task Force Hudelson (NARA, St. Louis, Mo., Item 10815, Reel 16.341) and the 399th Infantry Regiment (Item 17494, Reel 20.211).

154. Figures from Feuchtinger, 48. Twenty more *Panzer* IVs arrived by 8 January.

155. Based on Stanton's charts of the authorized strengths of U.S. Army tank and tank destroyer battalions (chart 10, page 19 and chart 13, page 26) and armored divisions (chart 9, page 18). This assumes units were at 90 percent strength, which seems to be the average from unit daily operations summaries.

156. "*In der gesamten Front der Heeresgruppe ist ab sofort der Eindruck einer ruhigen Front vorzutäuschen* (emphasis in the original). *Ausser der normalen Aufklärung sind alle Kampfhandlungen einzustellen.*" Contained in *Heeresgruppe G Kriegstagebuch 3b, 1.12.–31.12.1944*, 3. (Translation by the author.)

157. Emmerich, 7. Kögel indicates briefings on the day of the attack on page 22.

158. Kögel, 21; Linke, 16; Philippi, 28.

159. Linke, 13.

160. 106th Cavalry Group S2 Periodic Report for 30 December 1944, quoted in XV Corps G2 Summary for 3 January 1945, RG 407, Entry 427, Box 4761, SRB. This incident is also cited in Thomas Howard, 87.

161. Gurley, 76; Thomas Howard, 89; David Bishop, 204; Carter, Chapter VIII, 2; Bass, 103; Finkelstein, 175.

162. Karl Britzelmayr, "19th Volksgrenadier Division during the Period 1 September 1944 to 27 April 1945," MS. B-527, USAREUR Series, 1946, 30.

163. American strengths of the line and heavy-weapons companies of the 71st Infantry Regiment's 1st and 2d Battalions from company morning reports for 1 January 1945 (NARA, St. Louis, Mo.). German strengths previously documented in notes 121 and 127.

164. Ibid., for companies I, K, L, and M.

165. David Bishop, 204–205.

166. From the 1 January 1945 company morning reports of companies I, K, L, and M, 397th Infantry Regiment (NARA, St. Louis, Mo., Item 06493, Reel 5.266).

167. Finkelstein, 107–108; David Bishop, 52–53.

168. Bass, 107.

169. Ibid., 108–109; Finkelstein, 170–71.

170. American strength from company morning reports of line and heavy-weapons companies of 1st and 2d Battalions (plus Company L), 399th Infantry Regiment, 1 January 1945 (NARA, St. Louis, Mo.). German strength as determined in note 133.

171. Gurley, 76–83; von der Mühlen, 7–8.

172. Strength of the *477th* from note 31, and assuming minimal casualties from the light resistance offered by the 117th Cavalry; strength of the *1126th* from note 133, assuming two hundred men lost in the initial assault. Third Battalion, 399th Infantry, strength from company morning reports of companies I, K, L, and M for 1 January 1945 (NARA, St. Louis, Mo.).

173. Neither von der Mühlen nor Linke mention combined or coordinated attacks by their respective units against Lemberg, and Petersen merely mentions that both units attacked it and failed. (Petersen, 24.)

174. Linke, 22.

175. Carter, Chapter VIII, 4.

176. Philippi, MS. B-428, 10.
177. Carter, Chapter VIII, 2. American strength figure from company morning report for C, 62d Armored Infantry Battalion (NARA, St. Louis, Mo.); German strength estimate from Philippi, MS. B-428, 12. Description of course of the battle from Philippi, MS. B-428, 24–25; Carter, Chapter VIII, 2–5.
178. Philippi, MS. B-428, 24–26.
179. Kögel, 28.
180. Ibid., 27.
181. *Heeresgruppe G Kriegstagebuch 4, 1.1.1945–28.2.1945*, 1.
182. Wilutzsky, 26.
183. Bass, 105–120; Finkelstein, 169–82; David Bishop, 204–205; Emmerich, 8–9.
184. Helmut Günther, *Das Auge der Division: Die Aufklärungsabteilung der SS-Panzer-Grenadier-Division "Götz von Berlichingen"* (Preussisch Oldendorf: Verlag K. W. Schütz, KG, 1985), 334.
185. Emmerich, 8.
186. *"Aus dem übrigen Tagesgeschehen ist hervorzuheben, dass die H.Gr. auf Grund der Lageentwicklung bei XIII. SS Korps (starker Feindwiderstand, nur geringfügiges Fortschreiten des Angriffs) von der Weiterverfolgung der in der Planung vom 25.12. vorgesehenen Vereinigung der beiden Angriffsgruppen (XIII. SS-Korps sowie XC. und LXXXIX. AK) im Raum Rohrbach und des weiteren Vorstosses unter Einsatz der schnellen Verbände westlich der Vogesen absieht. H.Gr. entschliesst sich dazu, den zunächst nach SW gerichteten Stoss nach S und nach SO abzudrehen, um im weiteren Verlauf mit den H.Gr.-Reserven über Wimmenau-Ingweiler in die Ebene zu gelangen."* Heeresgruppe G *Kriegstagebuch 4, 1.1.1945–28.2.1945*, 5. (Translation by the author.)
187. Linke, 22–24.
188. Von der Mühlen, 9.
189. Philippi, MS. B-428, 29–30.
190. Ibid., 31.
191. Seventh Army, *Report of Operations*, 572.
192. Kögel, 32.
193. Prisoner statistics from the personal records of Wolf Zoepf, January 1996. As adjutant of the *3d Battalion, 12th SS Mountain Regiment* at Wingen, he was responsible for prisoner accounting, and his numbers further define, rather than contradict the accounts of Brenner

(who claimed 400 prisoners taken) and Munsell, who admitted to a total of 103.

194. Philippi, MS. B-428, 38.

195. *Heeresgruppe G Kriegstagebuch 4*, 11–13.

196. Kögel, 40–42.

197. Philippi, MS. B-476, 44–48; Reschke, 57–59.

198. *"Der Krieg in den winterlichen Vogesen stellt die dafür völlig unausgebildete und durch die andauernden Kämpfe vorwärts der Saar schon vorher überanstrengte Truppe vor eine ungeheure Aufgabe. Sie hat bisher trotz schwierigster Wetter-, Gelände-, und Kampfbedingungen Raum nach vorwärts gewonnen. Die Kampstärken der Infanterie sind jedoch stark abgesunken."* *Heeresgruppe G Kriegstagebuch 4*, 23.

199. Philippi, MS. B-428, 53.

200. Interestingly, the enlisted prisoners taken by the *12th SS* were released unharmed upon the German withdrawal from Wingen; the six officers of 1st Battalion, 179th Infantry, staff escaped shortly later and returned to rejoin their attacking regiment.

201. From an examination of the company morning reports at NARA, St. Louis, Mo., of the line companies of the following units for the period 1–12 January 1945: 157th Infantry Regiment, 179th Infantry Regiment, 180th Infantry Regiment, 274th Infantry Regiment, 275th Infantry Regiment, and the 276th Infantry Regiment.

CHAPTER 5

1. There was still some sporadically ferocious fighting left to be done in the Vosges, the most significant of which occurred from 16 to 20 January. Two kilometers north of Reipertswiller, the *256th Volksgrenadier Division* and the attached *11th SS Mountain Regiment* "Reinhard Heydrich" of the *6th SS Mountain Division* encircled, overwhelmed, and destroyed the 3d Battalion, 157th Infantry Regiment, of Frederick's 45th Infantry Division. This battle, from which bodies of the defenders were found as recently as 1988, has been intensely analyzed by Lt. Col. Hugh Foster, U.S. Army (Ret.), in ongoing research.

2. The problems encountered with the combat performance of the 92d Infantry Division in Italy would seem to dispute this assertion, but the differing circumstances of theater of operations, leadership,

and sheer size of the unit introduce factors not present in the Vosges. American culture of the 1940s differed greatly from that of the 1990s, and the author is by no means inferring a need for segregation in the modern U.S. Army.

3. Reschke, MS. C-003, 17.

4. Hellmuth Reinhardt, "Commentary to Supplementary Study on Volksgrenadier Divisions and Volkssturm," MS. P-065B, USAREUR Series, 1950, 10.

5. Janowitz and Shils, 185.

6. Botsch, 1.

7. Von Mellenthin, MS. A-000, 38.

8. The 44th Infantry Division commander, Major General Spragins, was replaced by the assistant division commander, Brig. Gen. William Dean, but only after the *XIII SS Corps* thrust near Gros Réderching had been contained. Major General Haffner of the Cactus Division turned over command to Maj. Gen. Anthony McAuliffe on 10 January, but the 103d had not been committed in the Vosges since late December.

9. Botsch, 1.

10. Friedrich Wiese, "19th Army in the Belfort Gap, in the Vosges, and in Alsace from the middle of September until 18 December 1944," MS. B-781, USAREUR Series, 1948.

11. Ibid.

12. *"Die Wehrmacht hatte ihre einst so sorgsam gehütete Eigenständigkeit auch auf dem Gebiet der operativen Planung verloren und kam nicht einmal mehr ihrer Aufgabe nach, planerische Vorsorge für die von der politische Führung als möglich bezeichneten Konfliktälle treffen."* Wilhelm Deist, "Die Aufrüstung der Wehrmacht," in *Das Deutsche Reich in Zweiten Weltkrieg,* Band I (Stuttgart: Deutsche Verlags-Anstalt, 1979), 528. (Translation by the author.)

13. Truscott, 555–56.

14. Von Luck, 142.

SELECTED BIBLIOGRAPHY

BOOKS AND JOURNAL ARTICLES

Batchelor, John, and Bryan Cooper. *Fighter: A History of Fighter Aircraft.* New York: Scribners, 1973.

Bruge, Roger. *On a Livré La Ligne Maginot.* Paris: Fayard, 1975.

Clarke, Jeffrey J., and Robert Ross Smith. *Riviera to the Rhine.* Washington, D.C.: Center of Military History, 1993.

Clausewitz, Carl von. *On War.* Trans. and ed. by Michael Howard and Peter Paret. Princeton: Princeton University Press, 1984.

Colin, Jean. *Campagne de 1793 en Alsace et dans le Palatinat.* Paris: Librairie Militaire R. Chapelot, 1902.

Creveld, Martin van. *Fighting Power.* Westport, Conn.: Greenwood, 1982.

Davies, W. J. K. *German Army Handbook.* New York: Arco, 1974.

Deist, Wilhelm. "Die Aufrüstung der Wehrmacht." In *Das Deutsche Reich in Zweiten Weltkrieg,* Band I. Stuttgart: Deutsche Verlags-Anstalt, 1979, 528.

Devlin, Gerard M. *Paratrooper!* New York: St. Martin's, 1979.

Dupuy, Trevor N. *Numbers, Predictions and War.* Indianapolis: Bobbs Merrill, 1979.

Durlewanger, A. *Haut-Koenigsbourg.* Colmar: Imprimerie S.A.E.P., 1984.

Gregory, Barry, and John Batchelor. *Airborne Warfare, 1918–1945.* New York: Exeter, 1979.

Hammerstein-Equord, Freiherr von, ed. *Oberkommando des Heeres, Die Truppenführung.* Berlin: Mittler und Sohn, 1936.

Heinl, Robert D. *Dictionary of Military and Naval Quotations.* Annapolis, Md.: Naval Institute, 1966.

Howard, Michael. *Clausewitz.* Guernsey: The Guernsey Press, 1983.

Janowitz, Morris, and Edward Shils. "Cohesion and Disintegration in the Wehrmacht." *Public Opinion Quarterly* 12 (1948): 280–315.

Keegan, John. *Waffen SS: The Asphalt Soldiers.* New York: Ballantine, 1970.

Luck, Hans von. *Panzer Commander.* New York: Dell, 1989.

Madej, W. Victor. *German Army Order of Battle,* vol. II. Allentown, Pa.: Game Marketing Co., 1981.

Mary, Jean-Yves. *La Ligne Maginot.* Cuneo, Italy: L'Instituto Grafico Bertello, 1980.

Maurer, Maurer, ed. *Air Force Combat Units of World War II*. Washington, D.C.: Office of Air Force History, 1983.

Michelin Reiseführer: Elsass-Volgesen-Champagne. Karlsruhe: Michelinreifenwerke, 1986.

Millett, Allan R., and Williamson Murray, eds. *Military Effectiveness*. 3 vols. Boston: Unwin Hyman, 1988.

Oberkommando der Wehrmacht. Kriegstagebuch des Oberkommando der Wehrmacht, Band IV: *1. Januar 1944–22. Mai 1945*. Frankfurt am Main: Bernard & Gräfe, 1961.

Palmer, Robert, Bell Wiley, and William Keast. *The Procurement and Training of Ground Combat Troops*. Washington, D.C.: U.S. Government Printing Office, 1948.

Pflugk-Harttung, J. A. G. von. *The Franco-German War*. Trans. J. F. Maurice, C.B. London: Swan-Sonnenschein, 1899.

Phipps, Ramsay Weston. *The Armies of the First French Republic*. London: Oxford University Press, 1929.

Pommois, Lise. *Winter Storm*. Paducah, Ky.: Turner, 1991.

Putnam, Ruth. *Alsace-Lorraine: From Caesar to Kaiser*. New York: Putnam, 1915.

Rittgen, Francis. *La Bataille de Bitche*. Sarreguemines: Pierron, 1984.

———. *Operation Nordwind*. Sarreguemines: Pierron, 1982.

Ruge, Friedrich. *Entscheidungsschlachten des Zweiten Weltkrieges*. Frankfurt am Main: Bernard & Gräfe, 1960.

Seventh Army. *Report of Operations*, vol. II. Heidelberg: Aloys Graef, 1946.

Speer, Albert. *Inside the Third Reich*. Trans. Richard Winston and Clara Winston. New York: Macmillan, 1970.

Stanton, Shelby. *Order of Battle: U.S. Army World War II*. Novato, Calif.: Presidio, 1984.

Sydnor, Charles W., Jr. *Soldiers of Destruction*. Princeton: Princeton University Press, 1977.

Truscott, Lucian K., Jr. *Command Missions*. New York: Dutton, 1954; Novato, Calif.: Presidio, 1990.

Turner, John F., and Robert Jackson. *Destination Berchtesgaden*. London: Scribners, 1975.

U.S. Army. *Aberdeen Proving Grounds Series*, vol. 1, *Tank Data*. Old Greenwich, Conn.: WE, 1969.

USMA Association of Graduates. *1990 Register of Graduates*. West Point, N.Y.: USMA Association of Graduates, 1990.

Weigley, Russell F. *The American Way of War.* New York: Macmillan, 1973.
————. *Eisenhower's Lieutenants.* Bloomington: Indiana University Press, 1981.
Whiting, Charles. *The Battle of Hurtgen Forest.* New York: Orion, 1989.
Winston, Keith. *V-Mail: Letters of a World War II Combat Medic.* Chapel Hill, N.C.: Algonquin, 1985.
Winterbotham, F. W. *The ULTRA Secret.* New York: Harper and Row, 1974.

GOVERNMENT REPORTS

U.S. Army Infantry School. *Winning in the Cold: Leader's Guide to Winter Combat Readiness. ST 7-175.* Fort Benning, Ga.: U.S. Army Infantry School, 1982.
U.S. War Department. *Handbook on German Military Forces.* Washington, D.C.: U.S. Government Printing Office, 1945; Baton Rouge: Louisiana State University Press, 1990.

UNPUBLISHED MANUSCRIPTS

Filiberti, Edward J. "Developing a Theory for Dynamic Campaign Planning." Fort Leavenworth, Kans.: School of Advanced Military Studies, U.S. Army Command and General Staff College, 1988.
Stauffer, Robert W. "Comparison of Metabolic Responses of Men and Women in Acute Load Bearing Situations." West Point, N.Y.: Department of Physical Education, 1988.

GERMAN DOCUMENTS

Dossiers on the following German general officers are in the Captured German Documents Section, National Archives, Washington, D.C.: Gerhard Franz, Ernst Häckel, Josef Paul Krieger, Alfred Philippi, Wilhelm Richter, Otto Schiel, Helmut Thumm, Kurt Freiherr von der Mühlen, Wend von Wietersheim, and August Wellm.
The following daily operations journals are available in hard copy at the Bundesmilitärgeschichtliches Forschungsamt (Federal Military Historical Research Bureau), Freiburg im Breisgau, Germany, and on microfilm at the National Archives, Washington, D.C.:
Heeresgruppe G (Führungsabteilung). Kriegstagebücher, 2, 3, 3b, and *4.* September 1944 to January 1945.

MANUSCRIPT COLLECTIONS

The following papers are available in the Captured German Documents Section in the National Archives, Washington, D.C.:

Blumentritt, Günther. "Ausbildungsmethoden und Manöver im Deutschen Heer." MS. P-200, USAREUR Series. 1954.

———. "Specially Planned Work: Delaying Action Battle and Delaying Action Resistance." MS. B-704, USAREUR Series. 1947.

Botsch, Walter. "Nineteenth Army. Combat Operations of Nineteenth Army in the Forward Defense Zone of the Vosges, in the Vosges Mountains, and the Alsace Bridgehead." MS. B-263, USAREUR Series. 1950.

Brenner, Karl. "The 6th SS-Mountain Division 'Nord' and Its Part in Operation 'Nordwind,' Northern Alsace, 1 January to 25 January 1945." MS. B-476, USAREUR Series. 1947.

Britzelmayr, Karl. "19th Volksgrenadier Division during the Period 1 September 1944 to 27 April 1945." MS. B-527, USAREUR Series. 1946.

Bruhn, Johannes. "Engagements of the 553d Volksgrenadier Division in November 1944 on the Vosges Front." MS. B-379, USAREUR Series. 1947.

Emmerich, Albert. "First Army (20 December 1944–10 February 1945)." MS. B-786, USAREUR Series. 1947.

Feuchtinger, Edgar. "Report of Operations of the 21st Panzer Division Against American Troops in France and Germany, December 1949." MS. A-871, USAREUR Series. 1949.

Franz, Gerhard. "The 256 VGD from mid-Nov 44 to 8 Apr 45." MS. B-089, USAREUR Series. 1946.

Groppe, A. D. "Events, as Experienced by an Old Soldier During the NAZI Period 1933–1945." MS. B-397, USAREUR Series. 1945.

Häckel, Ernst. "The 16th Infantry Division, Part II: The Campaign in the Rhineland." MS. B-452, USAREUR Series. 1947.

Höhne, Gustav. "The Attack in the Vosges 1 Jan 1945 to 13 Jan 1945." MS. B-077, USAREUR Series. 1946.

———. "Report on the Reconnaissance and Construction of the Vosges Positions, 8 August to 15 October 1944." MS. B-043, USAREUR Series. 1950.

Hold, Kurt. "The Winter Battles in the Vosges." MS. B-767, USAREUR Series. 1948.

Kögel, Bernhard. "Offensive Operations of the 256th Volksgrenadier Division in Northern Alsace, during January 1945 (Operation 'Nordwind')." MS. B-537, USAREUR Series. 1947.

Krieger, Josef Paul. "Fighting of the 708th 'VolksGrenadier-Division' in November 1944 at the Vosges Front." MS. B-451, USAREUR Series. 1947.

Linke, Ernst. "Participation by the 257th Volksgrenadier Division in the Offensive Operation 'Nordwind'." MS. B-520, USAREUR Series. 1947.

Mellenthin, Friedrich-Wilhelm von. "Army Group G (8–16 November 1944)." MS. A-000, USAREUR Series. 1947.

———. "Army Group G (20 September to 8 November 1944)." MS. A-999, USAREUR Series. 1946.

———. "FFI Operations, Southern France and Lorraine." MS. B-018, USAREUR Series. 1946.

———. "Army Group G (16 November to 3 December 1944)." MS. B-078, USAREUR Series. 1946.

Mühlen, Freiherr Kurt von der. "Report Concerning the Participation of the 559th Volksgrenadier Division in Operation 'Nordwind'." MS. B-429, USAREUR Series. 1947.

Petersen, Erich. "IV Luftwaffe Feld Korps/XC Infantry Corps 18 September 1944 to 23 March 1945." MS. B-117 and MS. B-071, USAREUR Series. 1946.

Philippi, Alfred. "Attack by 361 Volksgrenadier Division in Northern Alsace." MS. B-428, USAREUR Series. 1947.

———. "361st Volksgrenadier Division (31 August–16 December 1944)." MS. B-626, USAREUR Series. 1947.

Reinhardt, Hellmuth. "Commentary to Supplementary Study on Volksgrenadier Divisions and Volkssturm." MS. P-065B, USAREUR Series. 1950.

———. "Training and Employment of NCO's [sic] and Privates in the German Army." MS. P-012, USAREUR Series. 1947.

Reschke, Kurt. "Defensive Combat of LXXXIX Inf Corps in the Lower Alsace and in the Westwall from 6 to 31 December 1944." MS. C-003, USAREUR Series. 1948.

———. "The LXXXIX Inf. Corps in the Operation 'Nordwind' from 31 December 1944 to 13 January 1945." MS. B-765, USAREUR Series. 1948.

Scherf, Dr. "Medical Commentary on Special Organizations Such as

Stomach Battalions and Stomach Divisions." MS. B-275, USAREUR Series. 1946.

Schuster, Kurt. "Commitment of the LIV A.K. from 1 to 16 November 1944." MS. B-482, USAREUR Series. 1947.

———. "The LXIV Corps from August to November 1944." MS. A-885, USAREUR Series. 1946.

Simon, Max. "Report on the Rhineland and Southern Germany Campaign." MS. B-487, USAREUR Series. 1947.

Stumpff, Horst. "106th Panzer Brigade." MS. B-251, USAREUR Series. 1946.

Täglichsbeck, Hans. "LXIV Corps Defensive Construction (16 September 1944 to 25 February 1945)." MS. B-504, USAREUR Series. 1947.

Thumm, Helmut. "Operation in the Central Vosges, 16 Nov–31 Dec 44." MS. B-468, USAREUR Series. 1947.

———. "Report on the Commitment of LXIV Corps in Alsace During the Period 28 September 1944 to 28 January 1945." MS. B-050, USAREUR Series. 1946.

Wiese, Friedrich. "19th Army in the Belfort Gap, in the Vosges, and in Alsace from the middle of September until 18 December 1944." MS. B-781, USAREUR Series. 1948.

Wilutzsky, Horst. "The Offensive of Army Group G in Northern Alsace in January 1945." MS. B-095, USAREUR Series. 1947.

INTERVIEWS

Ritgen, Helmut. Taped interview in *The Great Crusade*. Grenada Television International, 1985.

Upchurch, John J. Interview by the author, September 1986.

U.S. ARMY OPERATIONS AND INTELLIGENCE REPORTS

National Archives, Suitland Reference Branch, Suitland, Md. All boxes listed below are part of Record Group 407, Entry 427.

VI Corps
G2 Reports (Sep 44–Jan 45), Boxes 3637–3638, 3696–3698, 3702–3703.
G3 Reports (Sep 44–Jan 45), Boxes 3742–3743, 3792, 3980.
XV Corps

G2 Reports (Oct 44–Jan 45), Boxes 4733–4734.
G3 Reports (Oct 44–Jan 45), Boxes 4782–4783.
3d Infantry Division
    G2 Reports (Oct–Dec 44), Boxes 6147–6148.
    G3 Reports (Oct–Dec 44), Boxes 6161–6162.
36th Infantry Division
    G3 Reports (Oct 44–Jan 45), Boxes 9847–9848.
45th Infantry Division
    G2 Reports (Oct 44–Jan 45), Boxes 10896–10897.
    G3 Reports (Oct 44–Jan 45), Box 10945.
70th Infantry Division
    G2 Reports (Dec 44–Jan 45), Box 11329.
79th Infantry Division
    G2 Reports (Oct 44–Jan 45), Box 11849.
    G3 Reports (Oct 44–Jan 45), Boxes 11856–11857.
100th Infantry Division
    G3 Reports (Nov 44–Jan 45), Box 14238.
103d Infantry Division
    G2 Reports (Nov 44–Jan 45), Boxes 14543–14544.
    G3 Reports (Nov 44–Jan 45), Box 14547.
12th Armored Division
    G2 Reports (Dec 44–Jan 45), Box 16130.
    G3 Reports (Dec 44–Jan 45), Box 16149.
14th Armored Division
    G2 Reports (Nov 44–Jan 45), Box 16287.
    G3 Reports (Nov 44–Jan 45), Box 16296.
106th Cavalry Group
    G2 Reports (Dec 44–Jan 45), Box 18048.
    G3 Reports (Dec 44–Jan 45), Box 18048.
Seventh Army
    G2 Reports (Sep 44–Jan 45), Boxes 2585–2589.
    G3 Reports (Sep 44–Jan 45), Boxes 2636–2637.
The following reports are also found in Record Group 407, Entry 427:
    3d Infantry Division G2 Periodic Report 79, 3 November 1944, 7.
        Box 6147.
    3d Infantry Division G2 Periodic Report 80, 4 November 1944, 6.
        Box 6147.
    VI Corps Field Order 7, 7 November 1944, 1–3. Box 3980.

VI Corps G2 Periodic Report 70, 24 October 1944. Box 3698.

VI Corps G2 Periodic Reports, 15–19 October 1944. Boxes 3696–3697.

Inclosure 2 to VI Corps G2 Periodic Report 89, 12 November 1944, 1. Box 3702.

VI Corps G2 Periodic Report 90, 13 November 1944, 1. Box 3703.

VI Corps G3 Periodic Report 105, 28 November 1944, 1. Box 4848 (included in XV Corps records).

VI Corps Operations Memorandum 47, 29 September 1944. Box 3792.

Seventh Army G2 Periodic Report, 9 November 1944, 1. Box 3207 (included in VI Corps records).

Seventh Army G2 Interrogation Report 80, 15 October 1944, 1. Box 3696 (included in VI Corps records).

Seventh Army G2 Periodic Report: Interrogation Report 166, 9 November 1944, 1–2. Box 3702 (included in VI Corps records).

Seventh Army G2 Estimate of the Enemy Situation 6, 29 December 1944, 1. Box 4761 (included in VI Corps records).

XV Corps Operating Instructions 77, 28 December 1944. Box 4783.

36th Infantry Division Operations Instructions, 12 October 1944, 1–2. Box 9848.

36th Infantry Division G3 Periodic Report, 15 October 1944, 2. Box 9847.

36th Infantry Division Training Memorandum 19, 15 October 1944. Box 9847.

45th Infantry Division G2 Periodic Report 81, 4 November 1944, 5. Box 3701.

Annex C to 45th Infantry Division G2 Periodic Report 64, 18 October 1944, 4. Box 3697.

Annex 1 to 100th Infantry Division G2 Periodic Report 3, 12 November 1944. Box 3702.

U.S. ARMY COMPANY MORNING REPORTS

National Archives and Records Administration Annex, St. Louis, Mo.
  3d Infantry Division
    7th Infantry Regiment
      October, Item 10439, Reel 13.90.
      November, Item 21469, Reel 6.280.
      December, Item 9081, Reel 1.373.

15th Infantry Regiment
October, Item 10497, Reel 13.93.
November, Item 21479, Reel 6.281.
December, Item 9091, Reel 1.373.
30th Infantry Regiment
October, Item 10624, Reel 13.97.
November, Item 21486, Reel 6.281.

36th Infantry Division
141st Infantry Regiment
October, Item 11244, Reel 16.173.
November, Item 25930, Reel 8.267.
January, Item 17410, Reel 20.207.
142d Infantry Regiment
October, Item 11252, Reel 16.173.
November, Item 21532, Reel 6.284.
January, Item 17411, Reel 20.207.
143d Infantry Regiment
October, Item 11253, Reel 20.141.
November, Item 21525, Reel 6.283.
January, Item 17413, Reel 20.207.

44th Infantry Division
71st Infantry Regiment
November, Item 14663, Reel 9.259.
December, Item 10217, Reel 5.294.
January, Item 10824, Reel 16.342.
114th Infantry Regiment
November, Item 14677, Reel 9.259.
December, Item 10237, Reel 5.295.
January, Item 10845, Reel 16.343.
324th Infantry Regiment
November, Item 14700, Reel 9.261.
December, Item 10274, Reel 5.298.
January, Item 10884, Reel 16.345.

45th Infantry Division
157th Infantry Regiment

October, Item 11279, Reel 16.174.
December, Item 06430, Reel 5.262.
January, Item 17434, Reel 20.208.

179th Infantry Regiment
October, Item 25352, Reel 20.150.
November, Item 21533, Reel 6.284.
December, Item 06434, Reel 5.262.
January, Item 17435, Reel 20.208.

180th Infantry Regiment
October, Item 11323, Reel 16.176.
November, Item 21535, Reel 6.284.
December, Item 06435, Reel 5.262.
January, Item 17436, Reel 20.208.

63d Infantry Division
253d Infantry Regiment
January, Item 17461, Reel 20.209.
254th Infantry Regiment
January, Item 17462, Reel 20.209.
255th Infantry Regiment
January, Item 17464, Reel 20.210.

70th Infantry Division
274th Infantry Regiment
January, Item 11786, Reel 16.372.
275th Infantry Regiment
January, Item 11787, Reel 16.372.
276th Infantry Regiment
January, Item 26046, Reel 20.245.

79th Infantry Division
313th Infantry Regiment
November, Item 14697, Reel 9.260.
314th Infantry Regiment
November, Item 14698, Reel 9.260.
315th Infantry Regiment
November, Item 14699, Reel 9.261.

100th Infantry Division
  397th Infantry Regiment
    November, Item 21554, Reel 6.286.
    December, Item 06493, Reel 5.266.
    January, Item 17492, Reel 20.210.
  398th Infantry Regiment
    November, Item 21555, Reel 6.286.
    December, Item 6513, Reel 5.267.
    January, Item 17493, Reel 20.211.
  399th Infantry Regiment
    November, Item 21560, Reel 6.286.
    December, Item 6570, Reel 4.300.
    January, Item 17494, Reel 20.211.

103d Infantry Division
  409th Infantry Regiment
    November, Item 14711, Reel 6.244.
    December, Item 10283, Reel 5.299.
  410th Infantry Regiment
    November, Item 14712, Reel 6.244.
    December, Item 10284, Reel 5.299.
  411th Infantry Regiment
    November, Item 14713, Reel 6.244.
    December, Item 10287, Reel 5.299.
  442d Infantry Regiment (Separate)
    October, Item 11859, Reel 16.196.

12th Armored Division
  17th Armored Infantry Battalion
    December, Item 10184, Reel 1.413.
  56th Armored Infantry Battalion
    December, Item 10207, Reel 5.294.
  66th Armored Infantry Battalion
    December, Item 10212, Reel 5.294.

14th Armored Division
  19th Armored Infantry Battalion
    December, Item 10185, Reel 1.413.
    January, Item 10792, Reel 16.340.

62d Armored Infantry Battalion
November, Item 14661, Reel 9.258.
December, Item 10208, Reel 5.294.
January, Item 10815, Reel 16.341.

FIELD MANUALS

FM 100-5, Field Service Regulations. Washington, D.C.: U.S. Government Printing Office, 1941.
FM 100-5, Operations. Washington, D.C.: U.S. Government Printing Office, 1944.
FM 100-15, Field Service Regulations for Larger Units. Washington, D.C.: U.S. Government Printing Office, 1942.
FM 101-5, Staff Organization and Operations. Washington, D.C.: U.S. Government Printing Office, 1941.

GERMAN ARMY UNIT HISTORIES

17th SS Panzer Grenadier Division

Günther, Helmut. *Das Auge der Division: Die Aufklärungsabteilung der SS-Panzer-Grenadier-Division "Götz von Berlichingen."* Preussisch Oldendorf: Verlag K. W. Schütz KG, 1985.

106th Panzer Brigade

Bruns, Friedrich, ed. *Die Panzerbrigade 106 Feldherrnhalle: Eine Dokumentation über den Einsatz im Westen vom Juli 1944– Mai 1945.* Celle, France: Traditionsverband der Panzerbrigade 106 und Panzerbattalion 293 der Bundeswehr, 1988.

U.S. ARMY UNIT HISTORIES

Seventh Army

Seventh Army. *G-2 History: 7th Army Operations in Europe.* Headquarters, Seventh Army, 1944.
White, Nathan William. *From Fedala to Berchtesgaden: A History of the Seventh United States Infantry in World War II.* Brockton, Mass.: Keystone Print, 1947.

3d Infantry Division
Taggart, Donald, ed. *The History of the Third Infantry Division in World War II.* Washington, D.C.: Infantry Journal, 1947.

36th Infantry Division
The Fighting 36th. Nashville: Battery, 1979.
The Story of the 36th Infantry Division. Paris: Desfosses-Néogravure, 1945.

44th Infantry Division
Bishop, David, et al. *"Mission Accomplished": The Combat History of the 44th Infantry Division.* Atlanta: Albert Love, 1946.
Hasson, Joseph S. *With the 114th in the ETO: A Combat History.* Baton Rouge: Army and Navy, 1946.

45th Infantry Division
Bishop, Leo V., et al., eds. *The Fighting Forty-Fifth.* Baton Rouge: Army and Navy, 1946.
History of the 157th Infantry Regiment (Rifle) (4 June 43 to 8 May 45). Baton Rouge: Army and Navy, 1946.
Munsell, Warren P., Jr. *The Story of a Regiment: A History of the 179th Regimental Combat Team.* San Angelo, Tex.: Newsfoto, 1946.
Ready in Peace or War: A Brief History of the 180th Regiment. Munich: F. Bruckmann, 1945.

79th Infantry Division
The Cross of Lorraine: A Combat History of the 79th Infantry Division. Baton Rouge: Army and Navy, 1946.

100th Infantry Division
Bass, Michael A. *The Story of the Century.* New York: Century Association, 1946.
Boston, Bernard, ed. *History of the 398th Infantry Regiment in World War II.* Washington, D.C.: Infantry Journal, 1947.
Finkelstein, Samuel, ed. *The Regiment of the Century: The Story of the 397th Infantry Regiment.* Stuttgart: Union Drückerei, 1945.
Gurley, Frank, ed. *399th in Action with the 100th Infantry Division.* Stuttgart: Stuttgarter Vereinsbuchdrückerei, 1945.

103d Infantry Division
Mueller, Ralph, and Jerry Turk. *Report After Action: The Story of the 103d Infantry Division.* Innsbrück: Wagnersche Universitäts-Buchdrückerei, 1945.

442d Regimental Combat Team
Shirey, Orville C. *Americans: The Story of the 442d Combat Team.* Washington, D.C.: Infantry Journal, 1946.
Tanaka, Chester. *Go For Broke.* Richmond, Calif.: Go For Broke, Inc., 1982.

12th Armored Division
Costlow, Owsley, ed. "Combat Highlights of the United States Twelfth Armored Division in the European Theater of Operations, 1 December 1944 to 30 May 1945." Privately printed, 1954.
A History of the United States Twelfth Armored Division. Baton Rouge: Army and Navy, 1947.

14th Armored Division
Carter, Joseph. *The History of the 14th Armored Division.* Atlanta: Albert Love, 1946.

106th Cavalry Group
Howard, Thomas J., et al. *The 106th Cavalry Group in Europe 1944–1945.* Augsburg: Himmer, 1945.

781st Tank Battalion
Up from Marseilles: History of the 781st Tank Battalion. Nashville: Benson, 1945.

INDEX

Achen, 182–83, 204, 256
Aeduans, 14
Allarmont, 113
Allen, Maj. Gen. Roderick, 156,
  172, 194
Alpern, William, 133
Althorn, 210
Ancerviller, 112
Ariovistus, 14
Armies, German: *First,* 6, 68, 70,
  76, 80, 84, 86, 97, 104–05,
  110–11, 114, 124, 136, 139,
  141–42, 145, 147, 150, 155,
  163, 166, 169, 174, 181–82,
  186, 189, 193, 195–96, 200,
  202–05, 210, 223, 225, 228;
  Fifth Panzer, 166; *Sixth SS
  Panzer,* 166; *Seventh,* 166;
  Nineteenth, 11, 67–69, 76–79,
  81, 84–86, 88, 96, 104–06,
  111–14, 123–24, 135, 139, 146,
  150, 181–82, 224, 228
Armies, Free French: First, 69–70,
  76, 97, 104, 135–136, 141, 146
Armies, U.S.: First, 74, 76, 166;
  Third, 69–70, 74–75, 77, 81,
  87, 106, 140–41, 144, 146, 155,
  174; Seventh, 67, 69–70, 75–
  77, 84, 87–88, 101, 111, 116,
  119, 125, 136–37, 139–41, 146,
  156, 167, 172, 174, 176, 180,
  195, 203, 205, 211, 224, 231
Army Ground Forces, AGF, 178–
  79
Army Groups, German: *A,* 215;

B, 141, 163, 166, 181, 195, 212;
  C (in 1940 campaign), 256;
  Center, 215; *G,* 6, 7, 10–12, 69–
  70, 104–06, 114–15, 123–25,
  137, 139, 141, 181–82, 186,
  189, 195, 203–05, 208–12,
  215–16, 220, 223, 225, 227–
  28, 240; *Oberrhein,* 182, 210;
  South, 215
Army Groups, U.S.: 6th, 68–69,
  211; 12th, 11, 172
Army Specialized Training Program (ASTP), 63–64, 109, 133
Avricourt, 111

Baccarat, 70, 85, 113–14, 120, 131
Badonviller, 70, 107, 114
Baerenthal, 183, 202, 207, 209
Balck, General der Panzertrup-
  pen Hermann, 5, 68, 77, 85–
  87, 106, 114–15, 123, 139–40,
  181, 227–28
Bannstein, 183, 202
Barr, 134
Bas Rupt, 114
Battalions, Armored Field Artil-
  lery, U.S.: 69th, 253; 93d, 253;
  500th, 177
Battalions, Armored Infantry,
  U.S.: 17th, 257; 19th, 202; 56th,
  257; 62d, 177, 181, 202, 207;
  66th, 257
Battalions, miscellaneous, U.S.:
  10th Armored Engineer, 253;
  83d Chemical Mortar, 177;